WHY
PEOPLE
MATTER

WHY
PEOPLE
MATTER

A CHRISTIAN ENGAGEMENT
with RIVAL VIEWS
of HUMAN SIGNIFICANCE

Edited by
JOHN F. KILNER

B

Baker Academic

a division of Baker Publishing Group
Grand Rapids, Michigan

© 2017 by Russell DiSilvestro, John F. Kilner, David P. Gushee, Amy Laura Hall, Gilbert C. Meilaender, Scott B. Rae, and Patrick T. Smith

Published by Baker Academic
a division of Baker Publishing Group
P.O. Box 6287, Grand Rapids, MI 49516-6287
www.bakeracademic.com

Printed in the United States of America

Library of Congress Cataloging-in-Publication Data
Names: Kilner, John Frederic, editor.
Title: Why people matter : a Christian engagement with rival views of human significance / edited by John F. Kilner.
Description: Grand Rapids, MI : Baker Academic, a division of Baker Publishing, 2017 | Includes bibliographical references and index.
Identifiers: LCCN 2016019616 | ISBN 9780801049408 (pbk.)
Subjects: LCSH: Dignity—Religious aspects—Christianity. | Dignity.
Classification: LCC BT702 .W49 2017 | DDC 233—dc23
LC record available at https://lccn.loc.gov/2016019616

Unless otherwise indicated, Scripture quotations are from the New Revised Standard Version of the Bible, copyright © 1989, by the Division of Christian Education of the National Council of the Churches of Christ in the United States of America. Used by permission. All rights reserved.

Scripture quotations labeled NASB are from the New American Standard Bible®, copyright © 1960, 1962, 1963, 1968, 1971, 1972, 1973, 1975, 1977, 1995 by the Lockman Foundation. Used by permission.

Scripture quotations labeled RSV are from the Revised Standard Version of the Bible, copyright 1952 [2nd edition, 1971] by the Division of Christian Education of the National Council of the Churches of Christ in the United States of America. Used by permission. All rights reserved.

17 18 19 20 21 22 23   7 6 5 4 3 2 1

Contents

Contributors   vii

Preface   ix

Introduction

1. Why This Book Matters   3
   The Need for Common Ground in Debates Today
   JOHN F. KILNER

Part 1   Grounding Significance in Humanity

2. Persons Are Not Interchangeable   17
   Utilitarianism and Human Significance
   GILBERT C. MEILAENDER

3. His Eye Is on the Sparrow   39
   Collectivism and Human Significance
   AMY LAURA HALL

4. My Life Is Not My Own   65
   Individualism and Human Significance
   RUSSELL DISILVESTRO

Part 2   Grounding Significance in Science

5. More Than Meets the Eye   89
   Naturalism and Human Significance
   SCOTT B. RAE

6. The Privilege of Being Human   109
   Transhumanism and Human Significance
   PATRICK T. SMITH

Part 3   Grounding Significance in God

7. Special Connection and Intended Reflection   135
   Creation in God's Image and Human Significance
   JOHN F. KILNER

8. Nothing Human Is Merely Human   161
   Various Biblical Bases for Human Significance
   DAVID P. GUSHEE

   Conclusion

9. Why a Christian Outlook Matters   189
   Comparing Grounds for Human Significance
   JOHN F. KILNER

   Subject Index   215
   Scripture Index   221

Contributors

Russell DiSilvestro, PhD, is associate professor of philosophy and director of the Center for Practical and Professional Ethics at California State University, Sacramento. His latest book is *Human Capacities and Moral Status*.

David P. Gushee, PhD, is distinguished university professor of Christian ethics and director of the Center for Theology and Public Life at Mercer University. He is the author or editor of twenty books, including *The Sacredness of Human Life*.

Amy Laura Hall, PhD, is associate professor of Christian ethics at Duke University, with research funded by the Lilly and Pew Foundations among others. Her latest book is *Conceiving Parenthood: American Protestantism and the Spirit of Reproduction*.

John F. Kilner, PhD, is Forman Chair of Ethics and Theology at Trinity Evangelical Divinity School and director of bioethics degree programs at Trinity International University. He is the author or editor of over twenty books, including *Dignity and Destiny: Humanity in the Image of God*.

Gilbert C. Meilaender, PhD, is senior research professor at Valparaiso University, a Ramsey Fellow at the Notre Dame Center for Ethics and Culture, and a member of the US President's Council on Bioethics. He has authored over ten books, including *Neither Beast nor God: The Dignity of the Human Person*.

Scott B. Rae, PhD, is professor of Christian ethics and dean of faculty at Talbot School of Theology, Biola University. He has authored over ten books in ethics, including *Body and Soul: Human Nature and the Crisis in Ethics*.

Patrick T. Smith, PhD, is associate professor of philosophical theology and ethics at Gordon-Conwell Theological Seminary and lecturer in bioethics at Harvard Medical School, Harvard University. He is active in global education, especially in Africa and the West Indies.

Preface

The need for a book such as this is substantial. Books long available on such topics as "worldview" compare biblical-Christian outlooks with other outlooks on a wide range of topics. However, such projects have not included sufficiently in-depth treatment of the widely and deeply held conviction that "people matter." As noted in the introduction, how people view and handle many of the most important contemporary issues flows directly from this conviction and from the outlook that shapes the way that people build upon it.

Over time conversations among various contributors to this present volume fostered an unshakable sense that this book needed to be written, and the authors signed on one by one. Work on this book began in earnest when this outstanding team of authors gathered for a weekend at Trinity International University in Deerfield, Illinois. Each participant had been invited to make a presentation on one particular way of looking at the world, based on their respective expertise. After each presentation the team engaged in an energetic discussion of what needed to be included in a chapter addressing that way of thinking.

Armed with many insights, each author then began developing the first draft of their chapter. Next, all such drafts received at least two detailed critiques from fellow authors and the following exceptional critiquers who joined the project specifically to help make the book the best it could be:

Charles C. Camosy (Fordham University)

J. Kameron Carter (Duke University)

Millard J. Erickson (retired, Southwestern Baptist Theological Seminary)

Fabrice Jotterand (Regis University and University of Basel)

C. Ben Mitchell (Union University)

J. P. Moreland (Biola University)

Authors were now in a position to produce revised versions, which I as the book editor and Bob Hosack and David Cramer, editors at Baker Academic, refined and edited in dialogue with the authors.

Trinity International University, an anonymous foundation, my colleague John Dunlop, and my family provided the time and means necessary for me to do the research, writing, and editing of this book. Special thanks go to Trinity president David Dockery; deans Tite Tienou, Graham Cole, Tom Cornman, and Don Hedges; and my departmental colleagues for their support and encouragement. At various stages along the way, several graduate students—Rebecca Blevins, Austin Freeman, Madison Pierce, and Janie Valentine—provided invaluable assistance. For the numerous people above who contributed to this project in so many ways—as well as the anonymous foundation that contributed the necessary funding—I am profoundly grateful.

You have the result of this collaborative undertaking before you now. It draws on decades of study that the authors have invested in the particular ways of looking at the world that they discuss here. And it benefits from the range of perspectives represented by the contributors, who are younger and older, female and male, black and white.

People matter. So much hinges on recognizing and living this conviction. But for such recognition and action to take place and to be sustainable, such a conviction must be supported rather than undermined by people's ways of thinking and looking at the world. The present work commends a vitally needed way to shore up this conviction—a credible and consistent way to explain why people matter.

John F. Kilner

Deerfield, Illinois

Introduction

1

Why This Book Matters

The Need for Common Ground in Debates Today

John F. Kilner

Do people matter? Most people think so. But *why* do they matter? And why does it matter why they matter? In other words, why does this book matter?

The reason this book matters has to do with the huge importance of many ethical debates today, together with the seeming impossibility of resolving those disputes. People on opposing sides of the issues often seem to be living in different worlds, concerned about very different things. However, a closer look at their arguments reveals that there is substantial common ground after all. Opposing "sides" in so many disagreements argue that people matter—that how people are viewed and treated is crucially important. Sometimes the appeal is to human dignity; sometimes to human autonomy; sometimes to the importance of respect for dignity, autonomy, or some other human attribute. But the common theme is that people matter and ought to be treated accordingly.

If there is a common conviction generally at work on all sides of various debates, then there is hope for finding a way forward—a way of resolving disputes. It is worth taking time here in the introduction to provide some illustrations of debates in which both sides make their argument on the basis of human significance—on the basis that people matter. After that we can consider other evidence that human significance is central to the big issues of the day. We will then be in a position to ask: Since so many people appeal to the conviction that people matter, why is there so much disagreement over contemporary ethical issues? As we will see, the problem is not the conviction *that* people matter; rather it is the reason *why* people matter. But first we need to demonstrate the widespread support for the idea that people do in fact matter.

Opponents Agree That People Matter

Consider the following debates in which opposing sides argue their position on the basis that people matter. Examples abound in the realm of bioethics and in many other areas of contemporary life. Regarding bioethical disputes, many debates arise concerning end-of-life issues. When physician-assisted suicide/death was first legalized in the United States, the Oregon law that legalized it was called the "Death with Dignity Act."[1] The idea was that people matter—that they have (or ought to have) dignity—and therefore they ought to have the legal option of physician-assisted suicide/death. At the same time, opponents argued against legalizing the practice precisely on the grounds that its legalization would violate human dignity—both that of the patients and that of other vulnerable people.[2] Appeals to human dignity by both sides also take place in the broader euthanasia debate, where the question is whether it is right to go beyond legalizing assisted suicide/death to allowing some people to end the lives of others.[3]

Mutual concern for human significance appears in debates over beginning-of-life issues such as abortion as well. In US court decisions such as *Planned Parenthood of Southeastern Pennsylvania v. Casey*[4] and *Stenberg v. Carhart*,[5] appeals to human dignity appear in both the majority opinion and the dissenting opinion. In the United States, autonomy is invoked even more frequently than dignity. However, whether one is appealing to dignity or autonomy, the core concept—championed on all sides of the debate—is that the people involved

---

1. Oregon Revised Statutes 127.800–995.

2. John F. Kilner, Arlene B. Miller, and Edmund D. Pellegrino, eds., *Dignity and Dying: A Christian Appraisal* (Grand Rapids: Eerdmans, 1996).

3. Dónal P. O'Mathúna, "Human Dignity and the Ethics of Human Enhancement," *Trans-Humanities* 6, no. 1 (2013): 102–3; Daniel P. Sulmasy, "Human Dignity and Human Worth," in *Perspectives on Human Dignity*, ed. Jeff Malpas and Norelle Lickiss (Dordrecht: Springer, 2007), 17.

4. 505 U.S. 833 (1992). See the majority opinion at 851 and the dissent at 983.

5. 530 U.S. 914 (2000). See the majority opinion at 920 and the dissent at 962.

in abortion should be respected.[6] Similarly, reproductive cloning is rejected by the World Health Organization as "contrary to human dignity."[7] Yet others who support the practice recognize the importance of demonstrating that conceiving children through this means is fully consistent with human dignity.[8]

Protecting people because they matter is a widespread concern in many other debates in health care as well. Consider the matter of organ donation and presumed consent. Many people oppose the idea that we can presume that dead people have given their consent for donating their bodily organs to others in the absence of any indication to the contrary. A key argument for this position states that acting on this presumption is a violation of human dignity.[9] However, others are quick to maintain that the chances of such violation are "nearly nil" and that instead respect for human autonomy warrants the presumption of consent.[10] Appeals to the importance of respecting people feature prominently in debates over the rationing of health care resources as well. Some advocate forms of rationing by maintaining that such rationing best respects the dignity of all, while others oppose such rationing precisely on the grounds that it fails to respect human dignity.[11]

Not only more traditional health care debates but also debates over emerging biotechnologies illustrate the way that people on opposing sides appeal to the idea that people matter. Consider, for example, debates over the development of embryonic stem cell treatments. In response to claims that the dignity of disabled and dying patients requires pursuing restorative stem cell treatments that involve the destruction of human embryos, some claim that producing humans in embryonic form and destroying them for the benefit of others is an affront to human dignity.[12] Meanwhile, in the debate over radically enhancing humans through biotechnology to the point that they become "posthuman,"

6. Marc Chase McAllister, "Human Dignity and Individual Liberty in Germany and the United States as Examined through Each Country's Leading Abortion Cases," *Tulsa Journal of Comparative and International Law* 11, no. 2 (2003): 491–520; Francis Fukuyama, *The End of History and the Last Man* (New York: Free Press, 1992), 176.

7. World Health Organization, "Ethical, Scientific and Social Implications of Cloning in Human Health," Resolution WHA51.10, Fifty-First World Health Assembly, May 16, 1998.

8. Dieter Birnbacher, "Human Cloning and Human Dignity," *Ethics, Law and Moral Philosophy of Reproductive Biomedicine* 1, no. 1 (2005): 50–55.

9. "Proposed Federal Statutes: Minority Report," *Iowa Journal of Corporation Law* 18 (Spring 1993): 603.

10. Carl Cohen, "The Case for Presumed Consent to Transplant Human Organs after Death," *Transplantation Proceedings* 24, no. 5 (1992): 2169–70.

11. See the debate over Paul T. Menzel's rationing proposals (found in his book *Strong Medicine* [New York: Oxford University Press, 1990]) in Ron Hamel, "Cost and Choice: The Ethics of Rationing Health Care," *Christian Century*, May 1, 1991, 488–90.

12. John F. Kilner, "Human Dignity," *Encyclopedia of Bioethics*, 4th ed. (Farmington Hills, MI: Macmillan, 2014), 1557. On competing views of human dignity (intrinsic value) and human

the dignity of the entire human race is front and center. Advocates of such enhancements recognize the need to explain how radical human enhancement is an affirmation of human dignity.[13] Opponents emphasize the same concern for dignity, even though they affirm a different bioethical position: that radical enhancement rendering persons no longer recognizably human is a violation of human dignity.[14]

Examples of debates where opposing sides appeal to the widespread conviction that people matter, then, abound in the realm of bioethics. Examples are just as abundant, though, in other areas of contemporary life. Consider debates over how to address the problem of poverty. Some argue that governments should give impoverished people money and other resources out of respect for their dignity as humans, while others insist that such handouts are demeaning and thus undermine dignity.[15] Both sides in debates over affirmative action similarly agree that a high regard for all people is an important lens through which to evaluate an issue. One side argues on this basis for favoring members of a disadvantaged group whom discrimination has harmed in the past.[16] The other side argues on the same basis against such favoritism.[17] Where the use of drones is up for debate, there is agreement that a high regard for all people entails a regard for the safety of all. On such grounds some people discourage drone use,[18] while others commend such use precisely because of its safety.[19]

Debates over the infliction of punishment on people reflect the same core concern about human significance. A common reason for always opposing torture is a commitment to treating all people, even criminals, in a humane way. However, some argue that such respect for people can motivate one to support torture or "enhanced interrogation" techniques under at least one condition: when they might enable a more humane outcome for people who could be harmed unless a criminal divulges certain information.[20] The death

---

embryos, see Patrick Lee, "The Pro-Life Argument from Substantial Identity: A Defence," *Bioethics* 18, no. 3 (2004): 249–63.

13. Nick Bostrom, "In Defense of Human Dignity," *Bioethics* 19, no. 3 (2005): 202–14.

14. O'Mathúna, "Human Dignity," 99–119; Fabrice Jotterand, "Human Dignity and Transhumanism: Do Anthro-Technological Devices Have Moral Status?," *American Journal of Bioethics* 10, no. 7 (2010): 45–52.

15. Fukuyama, *End of History*, 176.

16. Prue Burns and Jan Schapper, "The Ethical Case for Affirmative Action," *Journal of Business Ethics* 83, no. 3 (2008): 369–79.

17. Shlomi Segall, "What's So Bad about Discrimination?," *Utilitas: A Journal of Utilitarian Studies* 24, no. 1 (2012): 82–100.

18. Aaron M. Johnson and Sidney Axinn, "The Morality of Autonomous Robots," *Journal of Military Ethics* 12, no. 2 (2013): 129–41.

19. Daniel Byman, "Why Drones Work," *Foreign Affairs* 92, no. 4 (2013): 32–43.

20. William O'Donohue et al., "The Ethics of Enhanced Interrogations and Torture: A Reappraisal of the Argument," *Ethics & Behavior* 24, no. 2 (2014): 109–25.

penalty has stimulated similarly animated debate in which human dignity has played an important role. Conflicting opinions of US Supreme Court justices in the cases of *Furman v. Georgia* and *Roper v. Simmons* illustrate this well.[21] In his concurring opinion in the *Furman* case, Justice William Brennan locates the problem with capital punishment in its violation of human dignity; in the *Roper* case, Justice Anthony Kennedy argues that the death penalty can be carried out in a way that respects human dignity.[22]

Endless further examples could be offered of debates where the conviction that "people matter" plays an important role on both sides, including debates over same-sex marriage, hate speech, genetic engineering, sex reassignment surgery, prostitution, decriminalization of drugs, shooting down hijacked aircrafts, protection against self-incrimination, life imprisonment, the use of lie detectors, and hunger strikes.[23] The frequent appeal to human significance by people on both sides of the same issue suggests how widely shared is the conviction that people matter.

Widespread Affirmations That People Matter

Another way to establish the widespread recognition of human significance is to observe how commonly people appeal to the importance of such notions as human autonomy (along with broader understandings of freedom) and human dignity. Willard Gaylin and Bruce Jennings, among many others, marvel at autonomy's "extraordinary moral power and appeal."[24] While they emphasize how "ubiquitous" this concept is in the West ("Americans live, breathe and dream autonomy"),[25] others note in the East (e.g., China) the huge influence of a more family-oriented form of autonomy—considered there to be particularly respectful and supportive of people.[26] Meanwhile, in

21. Furman v. Georgia, 408 U.S. 238 (1972); Roper v. Simmons, 543 U.S. 551 (2005).

22. For elaboration, see Helen J. Knowles, "A Dialogue on Death Penalty Dignity," *Criminology & Criminal Justice* 11, no. 2 (2011): 115–28.

23. Luis Roberto Barroso, "Here, There, and Everywhere: Human Dignity in Contemporary Law and in the Transnational Discourse," *Boston College International & Comparative Law Review* 35, no. 2 (2012): 332.

24. Willard Gaylin and Bruce Jennings, *The Perversion of Autonomy: The Proper Uses of Coercion and Constraints in a Liberal Society*, rev. ed. (Washington, DC: Georgetown University Press, 2003), 33. See also numerous essays in James S. Taylor, ed., *Personal Autonomy: New Essays on Personal Autonomy and Its Role in Contemporary Moral Philosophy* (Cambridge: Cambridge University Press, 2005).

25. Gaylin and Jennings, *Perversion of Autonomy*, 47–48.

26. Yanguang Wang, "The Principle of Autonomy, and Decision-Making Differences between American and Chinese Cultures," *Eubios Journal of Asian and International Bioethics* 25 (March 2015): 42–45.

the rapidly growing field of bioethics, many acknowledge that "autonomy trumps all."[27] As Charles Foster observes in his analysis of a wide array of bioethics-related legal decisions that appeal to autonomy, "the great god autonomy" is "the governing principle."[28] It has become so influential that it has achieved "ideological status."[29]

Among many other concepts that similarly underscore the widespread affirmation that people matter, a prime example is the idea of human dignity. Its importance is signaled by the many significant international documents and national constitutions in which it plays a central role. The following uses convey a sense of the widespread reliance on this concept.

The United Nations has produced some of the best-known international affirmations of the dignity of all humans. With a founding charter that celebrates the "inherent dignity" of "all members of the human family," the United Nations issued a Universal Declaration of Human Rights in 1948 whose preamble contains similar wording. Its first article echoes this language: "All human beings" are born "equal in dignity." In 1966 this document plus two other documents—the International Covenant on Economic, Social, and Cultural Rights and the International Covenant on Civil and Political Rights—became known as the International Bill of Rights. All three documents maintain that various human rights have their grounding in the dignity of all humans.[30] In 2005 this outlook shaped another international document developed by the United Nations Educational, Scientific, and Cultural Organization (UNESCO): the Universal Declaration on Bioethics and Human Rights. That declaration affirms the central importance of human dignity at least a dozen times, insisting that it is a universal moral principle (articles 3 and 28).[31]

Various European international documents have been equally forthright regarding the essential place of human dignity in guiding how people ought to act. For example, the Council of Europe's 1997 Convention on Human Rights and Biomedicine was designed to "protect the dignity" of "all human beings."[32] Two years later the European Commission issued its Basic Principles in Bioethics and Biolaw 1995–1998. Noting the increasingly widespread

27. Mary Diana Dreger, "Autonomy Trumps All," *National Catholic Bioethics Quarterly* 12, no. 4 (2012): 653–73.
28. Charles Foster, *Choosing Life, Choosing Death: The Tyranny of Autonomy in Medical Ethics and Law* (Portland, OR: Hart, 2009), 3.
29. Alistair Wardrope, "Autonomy as Ideology: Towards an Autonomy Worthy of Respect," *The New Bioethics* 21, no. 1 (2015): 57.
30. Kilner, "Human Dignity," 1558.
31. Jotterand, "Human Dignity," 46.
32. Kilner, "Human Dignity," 1558.

recognition of human dignity, this document concludes that dignity "has been universalized as a quality of the person as such. It now refers to both the intrinsic value of the individual and the intersubjective value of every human being in its encounter with the other." Accordingly, it is not surprising to find the European Court of Human Rights often appealing to human dignity as a basis for its decisions—for example, in *Goodwin v. United Kingdom*.[33]

This reliance on human dignity is by no means confined to European courts and organizations. The Inter-American Court on Human Rights has also shown a propensity to cite human dignity as a basis for its decisions, as in *Boyce v. Barbados*.[34] Major regional documents have likewise acknowledged the importance of human dignity.[35] According to the American Declaration of the Rights and Duties of Man issued by the Organization of American States, all people "are born free and equal, in dignity and in rights." The African Charter on Human and Peoples' Rights by the Organization of African Unity calls dignity an "essential objective for the achievement of the legitimate aspirations of the African peoples." Meanwhile, the Arab Charter on Human Rights by the League of Arab States acknowledges both a "belief in human dignity" and a "right to a life of dignity." Other examples abound.[36]

Many national constitutions affirm support for human dignity as well. The concept has appeared in over forty constitutions since the beginning of the twentieth century.[37] That includes countries as diverse as Germany, Japan, Brazil, Israel, and South Africa.[38] According to Article 6 of the German Constitution (Basic Law), for instance, "The dignity of humanity shall be inviolable. To respect and protect it shall be the duty of all state authority." South Africa's Constitution likewise states: "Everyone has inherent dignity and the right to have their dignity respected and protected. . . . The dignity of humanity shall be inviolable." Even China's basic law acknowledges that "the

33. Barroso, "Here, There," 342. See Goodwin v. United Kingdom, App. No. 28957/95, 35 Eur. H.R. Rep. 447, 476–77 (2002).

34. Barroso, "Here, There," 342. See Boyce v. Barbados, Preliminary Objection, Merits, Reparations and Costs, Judgment (Inter-Am. Ct. H.R. Nov. 20, 2007).

35. Sources for the following examples of regional documents are noted in Ryan F. Haigh, "South Africa's Criminalization of 'Hurtful' Comments: When the Protection of Human Dignity and Equality Transforms into the Destruction of Freedom of Expression," *Washington University Global Studies Law Review* 5, no. 1 (2006): 189–90.

36. E.g., the International Convention on the Elimination of All Forms of Racial Discrimination; the International Covenant on Economic, Social and Cultural Rights; the International Covenant on Civil and Political Rights; and the International Convention on the Elimination of All Forms of Discrimination against Women. For citations see Barroso, "Here, There," 441.

37. Jotterand, "Human Dignity," 46.

38. Barroso, "Here, There," 337.

personal dignity of citizens of the People's Republic of China is inviolable."[39] Similarly, the Supreme Court of Canada and the Israeli Supreme Court have affirmed human dignity to be a constitutionally grounded fundamental value.[40]

In light of such widespread international support for the importance of human dignity, similar support for this concept in the United States is not surprising. The US Supreme Court has employed this term in its deliberations over the meaning of the First, Fourth, Fifth, Sixth, Eighth, and Fourteenth Amendments to the Constitution.[41] The concept played a central role in the deliberations of the US President's Council on Bioethics, which devoted a major study and report to this topic.[42] Both Presidents George W. Bush and Barack Obama have invoked it. To the United Nations, President Bush insisted: "We have no intention of imposing our culture, but America will always stand firm for the non-negotiable demands of human dignity." In his acceptance speech for the Nobel Peace Prize, President Obama maintained: "Only a just peace based upon the inherent rights and dignity of every individual can truly be lasting."[43] The dignity of every human is as compelling an idea in the private realm as in public. Business leaders such as Jack Welch readily commend taking it seriously.[44] And cultural observers such as Francis Fukuyama note that the conviction that people matter "is innate to or characteristic of all human beings, whether they are great and proud conquerors or humble greengrocers."[45]

Why It Matters That People Matter

In light of the above discussion, it is no wonder that one detailed study has concluded: "Dignity unifies us as a species, transcending class and cultural divides."[46] Whether "dignity" per se or respect for some other indicator of significance such as "autonomy" is in view, the challenge here "is to take full

39. Detailed citations for these three examples are in Haigh, "South Africa's Criminalization," 190–91.
40. Barroso, "Here, There," 340.
41. Kilner, "Human Dignity," 1557. See also the survey of this court's connecting of human dignity and basic rights in Maxine D. Goodman, "Human Dignity in Supreme Court Constitutional Jurisprudence," *Nebraska Law Review* 84 (2006): 740–84.
42. US President's Council on Bioethics, *Human Dignity and Bioethics* (Washington, DC, 2008).
43. For details of the Presidents' speeches, see Mark P. Lagon and Anthony C. Arend, eds., *Human Dignity and the Future of Global Institutions* (Washington, DC: Georgetown University Press, 2014), 20–21.
44. Jack and Suzy Welch, "The Difference Dignity Makes," *Businessweek*, June 22, 2009, 76.
45. Fukuyama, *End of History*, 168.
46. Rhonda Gay Hartman, "The Face of Dignity: Principled Oversight of Biomedical Innovation," *Santa Clara Law Review* 47 (2007): 62.

advantage of the great potential for consensus across countries, regions, cultures, and faiths" regarding the conviction that people matter.[47] Whereas it often seems futile to engage in debates over particular contemporary issues, discussions at a deeper level may well turn out to be more fruitful. People with opposite positions on issues share the core conviction that people matter—that they should be treated with respect rather than abused. If people have that much in common, then the opportunity for fruitful discussion is great.

In light of the self-centeredness of human nature, people often feel particularly strongly that they themselves should not be abused—that they matter. This feeling creates a vested interest in the question of why people matter. Because they know that people (at least themselves) matter, they need to be able to explain why. Minimally, it is an issue of self-preservation. Moreover, how they explain why people matter will determine the particular course they take from what they know to be true—the conviction that people matter—to the positions they develop on various contemporary issues. How they explain human significance is governed by their basic life outlook or way of thinking.

The problem today is that many people have a life outlook that is incapable of supporting their conviction that people matter. Although they have never stopped to think about it, their outlook undermines their conviction. Many people have not consciously adopted a particular way of thinking in this sense—their life outlook has simply been imbibed from the surrounding culture. Only when they see that their outlook is in conflict with a core conviction that they hold dear are they likely to give conscious thought to which life outlook they should adopt. Only when people's way of thinking changes is there a substantial prospect for changes in their views on issues that their former way of thinking has shaped.

What are these influential ways of thinking—these life outlooks? This book will begin by considering five of them. For the sake of having one-word terms by which to refer to them, this book will use the terms *utilitarianism*, *collectivism*, *individualism*, *naturalism*, and *transhumanism*. But readers should not let these *isms* intimidate them. Each stands for a way of thinking about or approaching the world—a life outlook—that one will recognize in the daily news, in one's next-door neighbor, and perhaps even in oneself. The *ism* in each term indicates that the outlook identifies one particular thing as having supreme importance over everything else. That thing may have to do with the importance of society, the individual person, or science.

The first three outlooks ground human significance in humanity itself, whether in society as a whole or in the individual. Grounding significance

47. Lagon and Arend, *Human Dignity*, 17.

in society commonly takes one of two forms: utilitarianism or collectivism. Utilitarianism is the outlook in which maximizing utility (benefit) reigns supreme. The benefit of everyone needs to be taken into account. What is right is whatever produces the greatest good for the greatest number of people. When one hears the common refrain "The end justifies the means" in a social setting, utilitarianism is at work. It evaluates each thing that people do in terms of its consequences. Each action is a means to achieve some end; and if the end is beneficial enough, then the means are justified.

A somewhat different version of this focus on the "good of the whole" is collectivism. Utilitarianism includes in the right-wrong calculus the consequences for each individual affected by any decision under consideration. Collectivism, on the other hand, does not really see individuals but only the groups, or collectives, that constitute what matters about their identity. A person is a member of an ethnic group, an age demographic, and so on—not unique in any meaningful sense. Much marketing fosters and thrives on such an outlook. All that needs to be known about people and considered in decisionmaking is a function of their group identities. This way of thinking about people sorts, orders, understands, directs, or even seeks to control groups of people. It can also shape one's own identity, which may happen when people come to see themselves only as a small piece in a much larger machine, as in the military. When people insist that their organization and not they as individuals did something wrong—something that they manifestly did do—collectivism has dominated their thinking.

Those who recognize the shortcomings of a more communal or social perspective may do so because they think that the individual should be prioritized over the collective. The third *ism*, individualism, is the life outlook in which people each have their own values and preferences, and those determine what is right for them. There are no objective truths or standards binding on all. Personal choice is the prevailing standard. In the common refrain "It's my life and I can do what I want," individualism has gained the upper hand. This outlook does not simply affirm that each individual is important; it insists that the perspectives and wishes of the individual trump all other considerations where that individual is concerned.

For other people, their way of looking at the world is not so much shaped by a preoccupation with society or individuals as it is by the dictates of science. This commonly happens in one of two ways. One way is by relying on naturalism. According to this outlook, all that exists is the material world—that which can be scientifically, empirically measured and verified. No ultimate reality exists beyond the physical world. "What you see is what you get" and "Seeing is believing" are everyday expressions of this outlook. According to this outlook, there is no God, nor are there immaterial human components such as self-awareness that cannot ultimately be reduced to physical or material substances. Humans and all of life on earth are the result of the blind, random forces of evolution. There is no design or intelligence behind the world's past or future.

Another life outlook shaped by science is transhumanism. According to this view, biotechnology can enable people not just to improve themselves as humans but to become better than human—to become "posthuman." One or more capacities of posthumans would so exceed those of present humans as to render them something beyond merely human. For example, the length of their healthy life could so substantially increase that even the possibility of living forever could become realistic. Human intellectual, physical, and emotional capacities could increase far beyond anything yet seen in the human race. Uploading one's consciousness into a computer or robot is just one of the many transhumanist scenarios increasingly appearing in novels and movies.

Each such popular *ism*—utilitarianism, collectivism, individualism, naturalism, and transhumanism—has a certain appeal and many followers. However, each is fatally flawed. Each contradicts something that people widely acknowledge is vitally important: the conviction that people matter. In parts 1 and 2, our authors comment on these outlooks and their flaws in detail: Gilbert Meilaender on utilitarianism (chap. 2); Amy Laura Hall on collectivism (chap. 3); Russell DiSilvestro on individualism (chap. 4); Scott Rae on naturalism (chap. 5); and Patrick Smith on transhumanism (chap. 6). As these insightful discussions indicate, each of the outlooks considered is complex and requires careful examination in order to understand both its allure and its ultimate insufficiency. Parts 1 and 2 thus powerfully demonstrate the need for a better life outlook, one that can adequately explain why people matter.

One excellent alternative to these *isms* is biblical Christianity, as discussed in part 3. Central to the contrast is the way that a Christian outlook roots human significance in God rather than in humanity or science. As I explain in chapter 7, one way that a Christian outlook does so is by affirming that people are created in the image of God. Being in the image of God means that people have a special connection with God and that God, particularly as embodied in Jesus Christ, is the standard for who people are to be. There is nothing about particular individuals, groups, or their scientific tools that gives humans significance; rather, significance comes from the infinitely significant God. God has a special connection with humans and intends for them to be a genuine reflection of him. God is why people matter—people as individuals and humanity as a whole. This recognition has had a tremendously liberating impact in the world to date with inspiring potential for the future.

Because people are so specially connected with God, anything done to a person is also done to God. As David Gushee describes in chapter 8, that outlook informs teachings throughout the Bible in which the great significance of people is prominent. In support of human significance, four aspects of the Old Testament stand out: its creation theology, its depiction of God's compassionate care for humans, its covenantal and legal materials, and its prophetic vision of a just wholeness (*shalom*) for Israel and all creation in the promised eschatological future. In the New Testament, three primary elements also lend substantial support to the idea that people matter: the nature of Christ's ministry, key events in Christ's life (the incarnation, cross, resurrection, ascension), and the ethos and moral vision of the early church. Gushee develops all seven of these areas to illustrate the resounding affirmation of human significance that flows from the God of Scripture.

The concluding chapter of this book endeavors to weave together the insights from the three preceding parts. After summarizing the most important reasons why the five *isms* are unable to support the widespread conviction that people matter, it affirms how a biblical-Christian outlook provides a strong basis for human significance at many of the very points where the outlook of various *isms* is weak. The book thus concludes by commending a biblically grounded Christian outlook as providing the best basis for affirming human significance—not grounded in humanity or science but in God and God's design for humans.

PART 1

Grounding Significance in Humanity

Persons Are Not Interchangeable

Utilitarianism and Human Significance

GILBERT C. MEILAENDER

The principle of utility, at least as it is commonly used in ethical theorizing, is framed in terms of aggregate goods—promoting the greatest good for the greatest number of people. By contrast, the dignity bestowed on persons because of their relation to God is inherently individualizing (which, as I will note later, should not be equated with individualism, as we often understand it). This dignity bestows on each person a singular and unrepeatable identity. As the late Ralph McInerny, a discerning Christian philosopher, once wrote,

> The point of a proper name is that it [is] not common to many, and yet many people do bear identical names. . . . But even when two persons have the same proper name it does not become a common noun, like "man." All the John Smiths that have been, are, and will be have nothing in common but the name; it does not name something common to them all. There is an inescapable nominalism here. God calls us all by our proper name, and He is unlikely to confuse one John Smith with another.[1]

This contrast—between the aggregating nature of utility and the individualizing nature of dignity—lies at the heart of some of the questions that most trouble us when we think about how we ought to live.

---

1. Ralph McInerny, *I Alone Have Escaped to Tell You: My Life and Pastimes* (Notre Dame, IN: University of Notre Dame Press, 2006), 162.

Sidgwick and the Dualism of Practical Reason

One need not be, like McInerny, a Christian philosopher in order to sense the problem. For example, Henry Sidgwick, though little known today outside professional philosophy circles, was one of the most influential British moral philosophers in the last half of the nineteenth century. His book *The Methods of Ethics*, which he labored over for years and which went through seven (always carefully revised) editions, is still today one of the classic texts in the tradition of utilitarian thought.[2]

Perhaps strangely, however, although the *Methods* attends to most of the issues that have been important for utilitarian ethics, it is actually dominated by a somewhat different problem—what Sidgwick called "the dualism of practical reason." Utilitarians think that when we act we are aiming to produce happiness. For Sidgwick, happiness was reducible to pleasure, but some utilitarians have held that there are other ways of determining the greatest good for human life. At any rate, Sidgwick thought that we should aim to produce the greatest aggregate happiness possible. But, of course, someone else might take a different view, believing that I should aim at my *individual* happiness rather than the aggregate *general* happiness. Hence, Sidgwick recognized two forms of hedonism, which he called egoistic and universalistic hedonism. The universal form of hedonism was utilitarianism, the theory to which Sidgwick was committed. But he acknowledged that it might not be irrational for a person to pursue his own happiness rather than the general happiness.

Practical reason seems, then, to speak with two voices. On the one hand, Sidgwick argues at length that it is reasonable for us to seek the happiness of the larger whole ("the universe of sentient beings") to which we belong. On the other hand, it is also reasonable for us to act in whatever way is most conducive to our own happiness. These two voices cannot be reconciled, or so Sidgwick thought. Utilitarian though he was, and believing as he did that it is our obligation to pursue the greatest happiness for the greatest number, he nevertheless held that ethical egoism was not an irrational position to hold. Why he should have thought this, given his utilitarian commitments, is, as his biographer puts it, "one of the most important and puzzling problems arising out of over a century of commentary on the *Methods*."[3]

Sidgwick was the son of a clergyman, but as a young man he had experienced a crisis of faith. He remained wistfully eager to believe but unable to do so—to the degree that John Maynard Keynes is supposed to have said of

2. Henry Sidgwick, *The Methods of Ethics*, 7th ed. (Indianapolis: Hackett, 1981).
3. Bart Schultz, *Henry Sidgwick, Eye of the Universe: An Intellectual Biography* (New York: Cambridge University Press, 2004), 215.

him, "He never did anything but wonder whether Christianity was true and prove it wasn't and hope that it was."[4] It may well, I suspect, have been the lingering vestiges of Christian belief that made it so difficult for Sidgwick simply to dismiss the claims of the self and subordinate them to the general happiness. An important passage in the *Methods* emphasizes the distinctive significance of individual persons: "It would be contrary to Common Sense to deny that the distinction between any one individual and any other is real and fundamental, and that consequently 'I' am concerned with the quality of my existence as an individual in a sense, fundamentally important, in which I am not concerned with the quality of the existence of other individuals."[5] Were persons simply parts of a single whole, this dualism would vanish. But it was impossible for Sidgwick to think of persons that way so long as the remnants of Christian belief continued to shape his thinking.

Thus, writes his biographer, for Sidgwick moral reasoning contains "a potentially explosive contradiction, waiting to emerge, once the religious worldview fades. Put differently, Sidgwick questions, in a way that other secular utilitarians did not, the degree to which the utilitarian evolution of morality may in fact, perhaps paradoxically, have depended on the evolution of Christianity."[6] The problem, at least in Sidgwick's mind, was a simple one, and it consumed much of his intellectual energy throughout his life: If the world could no longer be believed to be one in which God would ultimately honor the distinctive dignity of each individual, what possible reason could there be for not simply pursuing one's own good here and now?[7]

Sidgwick spent many of his adult years investigating the claims of parapsychology. In 1882 he became the founder and first president of the Society for Psychical Research, in which he engaged with others in "an endeavor to reenchant the universe."[8] The sober philosopher found himself consulting mediums at séances. He engaged in careful study of telepathy (that is, transferring information from one person to another in some way other than through any of our normal sensory channels). He had a deep interest in reports of ghosts and haunted houses.

Why was he so committed to this research? Because he needed evidence of an afterlife if the universe were to be re-enchanted. For if the universe lacked moral order, if utilitarian virtue that aimed at the aggregate good of all sentient

4. Ibid., 4.
5. Sidgwick, *Methods of Ethics*, 498.
6. Schultz, *Sidgwick*, 247.
7. Sidgwick was by no means the first thinker to be troubled by this question. As Amy Laura Hall discusses in her essay on collectivism in this volume, the fact that people who rigorously act in accord with what duty requires often receive no reward for doing so forced Kant to reintroduce God into his account of human freedom.
8. Schultz, *Sidgwick*, 276.

beings were to go unrewarded, no one could say that it was irrational for individual persons to promote as best they could their own individual good. That was Sidgwick's problem: he was committed to a utilitarian theory that seemed to lose the distinctiveness of individuals in its search for an aggregate good. That distinctiveness might once have been defended in Christian terms, and those terms held just enough sway over Sidgwick that he could not discount the fundamental moral significance of each individual person, even though he no longer pictured the world in Christian terms. The only remaining defenders of individual distinctiveness were those who asserted that one's own good rather than an aggregate good ought to be a person's aim. Given his vestigial commitment to individual distinctiveness, Sidgwick could not claim that their egoistic view was contrary to reason. Yet given his commitment to utilitarianism, Sidgwick also regarded pursuit of the general good as reasonable and right. Hence the dualism of practical reason.

Christianity and Individual Distinctiveness

For Christians the defense of individual distinctiveness over against aggregate utility will necessarily take a different shape. Sidgwick's problem was that he could find no answer for those who asserted the reasonableness of seeking to maximize one's own individual good. Therefore, although committed to utilitarianism, he could find no way to rebut the claims of egoism, leaving him with a practical reason that could go in either of these directions. But Christians, who know that their life is "hid with Christ in God" (Col. 3:3), are eternally secure and should be freed from the temptation to suppose that they need to seek their own happiness. Hence, for Christians, utilitarianism will be problematic for different reasons, especially two that may be expressed as questions: (1) Do we wrong others in any way if we regard them simply as parts of a larger whole whose aggregate good we seek? (2) Do we wrong ourselves in any way if we think of ourselves simply as agents in service of promoting a general good? As a way to express the wrongs we might do to others or ourselves if we think solely in terms of promoting aggregate utility, the language of dignity has increasingly been used; after briefly characterizing our human nature, I will return to these questions about utility and dignity.

For Christians to explore these topics requires that we think about what we might call the strange two-sidedness of our creaturely nature.[9] In *The Magician's*

9. To be sure, not only Christians see this two-sidedness. One can find a somewhat similar viewpoint developed in purely philosophical terms in Thomas Nagel, *The View from Nowhere* (New York: Oxford University Press, 1986).

Nephew, sixth in the Chronicles of Narnia series, C. S. Lewis imaginatively depicts this. The great lion Aslan creates the land of Narnia and its inhabitants. In the course of doing so, he sets apart some animals as talking beasts, the primary inhabitants of Narnia. "He was going to and fro among the animals. And every now and then he would go up to two of them (always two at a time) and touch their noses with his." These animals "instantly left their own kinds and followed him," while the others wandered away. Then Aslan breathes on the chosen ones, and in the "deepest, wildest voice" the children had ever heard says: "Narnia, Narnia, Narnia, awake. Love. Think. Speak. . . . Be talking beasts." That these are *talking* beasts points to something more. "Creatures," says Aslan, "I give you yourselves."[10] They are no longer simply instinctive creatures. They can be other than they are, distancing themselves from themselves; for that is what it means that they are given themselves.

Lewis here imaginatively depicts a distinctive feature of human life, as Christians have understood it. Christians have learned to think of humans as complex creatures, located in time and place but simultaneously able to transcend that location at least in thought. "Man's involvement in finiteness and his transcendence over it" is, Reinhold Niebuhr suggests, "the basic paradox of human existence."[11]

A simple, if unlikely, illustration is one I have used to explicate what Niebuhr characterizes as a paradox.[12] If I fall from the top of a fifty-story building, the law of gravity takes over, just as it does if we drop a rock from that building; for we are finite beings, located in space and time and subject to natural necessity. Nevertheless, we are also free and able, at least to some extent, to transcend the limits of nature and history. Therefore, as I fall from that building, there are truths about my experience that could not be captured by any explanation in terms of mass and velocity. Something different happens in my fall than in the rock's fall, for *this* falling object is also a subject characterized by self-awareness. I can know myself as a falling object, which means that I can to some degree "distance" myself from that object. Hence, I both am and am not that falling object. I cannot simply be equated with it. I am that object and am freed from it, freed by my capacity to transcend it.

Similarly, I am the person constituted by the story of my life, a story marked in important ways by membership in various communities. I cannot simply be someone else with a different history, nor can I simply be a generic human. Yet

10. C. S. Lewis, *The Magician's Nephew* (New York: Macmillan, 1955), chaps. 9–10 passim.
11. Reinhold Niebuhr, *The Nature and Destiny of Man*, vol. 1, *Human Nature* (New York: Scribner, 1964), 175.
12. Cf. Gilbert Meilaender, *Bioethics: A Primer for Christians*, 3rd ed. (Grand Rapids: Eerdmans, 2013), 4.

I can also, at least to some extent, be any human being in the sense that I can step into another's story, see the world as it looks from his or her standpoint, and thus be free from the limits of my own history.

We can no doubt imagine a being who is pure spirit—an angel, say, or the god of the philosophers. We can also imagine a being who is entirely limited to the body—whose *anima*, whose life principle, has no capacity to transcend the limits of nature and history.

When we think of a human being, however, we have to think of one who is neither pure self-transcending spirit nor simply finite body—but somehow the union of both. Quite often Christians have expressed this by saying that the human person is a union of body and soul. True as that may be, when we try to articulate its meaning, we often think of such a person as a composite of two things that are in principle separable, that are temporarily glued together in this life, that will be separated in such a way that the person lives on after the body has died, and that will (by God's grace) one day have these two parts reunited in the resurrection.

That picture is likely to lead us astray when thinking of human dignity; for it necessarily invites us to think in dualistic ways and tempts us to reduce the "real" person in the end to either just body or just soul. Thus Sidgwick was unable to unify his sense of human beings as bodies, who are obligated to the well-being of others, and human beings as free, self-transcending spirits.

A somewhat different image than the simple body-soul distinction comes closer to the truth.[13] Think first of a rider mounted on his horse—two things temporarily joined but readily separated. But now suppose that instead of a mounted rider we imagine a centaur. In the centaur there is real union rather than a dualism that temporarily unites two essentially separate beings. With a centaur we cannot shoot the horse out from under and have the rider survive unscathed. Nor can we imagine the living horse apart from the rider, as if it were just an animal. The image of the centaur is that of a real union, an image of the union of free spirit and finite body that is the human person.

To honor the peculiar dignity of human persons—who are embodied creatures made from the dust of the ground but also self-transcending creatures made for union with God—we must let our actions be shaped by both aspects of our being. Because persons transcend their communities, their good is not just part of an aggregate good. We may not use them or treat them merely as parts of a whole or as means to the general well-being of their communities. At the same time, we are not solely free spirits; we are finite and limited beings

13. I borrow this image from C. S. Lewis, who used it in a somewhat different context. See C. S. Lewis, *Miracles* (New York: Macmillan, 1947), 166.

whose actions should recognize and acknowledge our own limits. We can briefly explore each of these constraints on any of our attempts to foster social utility.

Undermining Individual Dignity

As an example of how we might undermine the dignity of persons in an attempt to produce socially useful results, consider the justice or injustice of punishment, an issue with which any community, large or small, must deal. The notion that justice requires punishment of wrongdoers is a retributive and retrospective notion that Sidgwick criticized as "resentment universalised."[14] It is retrospective because it is backward-looking, seeking to respond to a wrong that has been done. Of such a view, that "justice requires pain to be inflicted on a man who has done wrong, even if no benefit result either to him or to others from the pain," Sidgwick, ever the consistent utilitarian, wrote: "Personally, I am so far from holding this view that I have an instinctive and strong moral aversion to it."[15]

The alternative is forward-looking, prospective punishment. This would mean distributing penalties in whatever way would be most useful for achieving the desired result of preventing future wrongdoing. But backward-looking retributive punishment seems to more adequately respect the dignity of the wrongdoer—holding him accountable for his actions and not regarding him simply as a pawn to be manipulated in the overall effort to achieve a desired social result. Every child whose teacher has punished the entire class in an effort to uncover an unknown wrongdoer intuitively realizes this. Retrospective punishment recognizes that each person, whatever his or her social location, indefinitely transcends that location and is not merely part of a larger social whole. It recognizes, we might even say, that in the most important sense each person is larger, of more ultimate significance, than any community he or she inhabits. That is the real point of our language about the dignity of human persons.

How deeply corrupting and destructive of human dignity a forward-looking deterrent approach to punishment is becomes clear when we realize that, as C. S. Lewis put it, for this approach "it is not absolutely necessary that the man we punish should even have committed the crime."[16] What counts for this approach is utility, the most effective method for preventing future misdeeds. Judgments of guilt or innocence are clearly secondary. "The punishment of a man actually

14. Sidgwick, *Methods of Ethics*, 281.
15. Ibid.
16. C. S. Lewis, "The Humanitarian Theory of Punishment," in *God in the Dock: Essays on Theology and Ethics* (Grand Rapids: Eerdmans, 1970), 291.

guilty whom the public think innocent will not have the desired effect; the punishment of a man actually innocent will, provided the public think him guilty."[17]

The danger that personal dignity may be undermined by the search for aggregate social utility is also near at hand when we deal with issues in bioethics.
For example, the enormous social (and medical) pressure to offer the "gift of
life" to the sick and dying through organ donation and transplantation has
invited (or tempted) us to treat human organs as a public resource that could
be routinely "harvested" from the newly dead, to contemplate treating organs
as commodities that could be bought or sold, and to try to expand the number
of available organs by redefining death in special cases (e.g., by simply stipu-
lating that anencephalic newborns are dead and hence available as sources for
organs, even when they continue to show evidence of brain stem activity).[18]

Even more significant, perhaps, have been recurring abuses in human experimentation, one of the issues that first caused the fledgling field of bioethics to
become a matter for public concern.[19] In 1966 Dr. Henry Beecher of Harvard
Medical School published in the *New England Journal of Medicine* an article
with the modest title, "Ethics and Clinical Research."[20] The article's title may
have been low-key, but its contents were not. Beecher identified twenty-two
instances of human experimentation that raised troubling questions about
whether the dignity of the persons who were research subjects had really been
honored. In the years since, some cases—such as the Tuskegee syphilis study
or the human radiation experiments—have become well known as instances
in which the search for medically useful knowledge was allowed to override the
dignity of the persons who were research subjects. But other less well-known
research from which all of us profit, such as the development of vaccines or
new therapies, has sometimes used subjects (including even fetuses) who lack
the ability to consent to their participation.[21]

One of the now classic essays in bioethics, first published in 1969, is Hans
Jonas's "Philosophical Reflections on Experimenting with Human Subjects."[22] It

17. Ibid.

18. Albert R. Jonsen, "Ethical Issues in Organ Transplantation," in *Medical Ethics*, ed.
Robert M. Veatch (Boston: Jones and Bartlett, 1997), 229–52.

19. See, e.g., Albert R. Jonsen, *The Birth of Bioethics* (New York: Oxford University Press,
1998), 125–65.

20. Henry K. Beecher, "Ethics and Clinical Research," *New England Journal of Medicine*
274 (1966): 1254–360.

21. Those wishing to pursue details of some of these episodes in human subjects research
might begin with the appropriate chapters in Jonsen, *Birth of Bioethics*, and Ana Smith Iltis,
ed., *Research Ethics* (New York: Routledge, 2006).

22. Hans Jonas, "Philosophical Reflections on Experimenting with Human Subjects," in
Philosophical Essays: From Ancient Creed to Technological Man (Englewood Cliffs, NJ: Prentice-
Hall, 1974), 105–31.

articulates at the very outset of the development of bioethics a difference between the desirable and the imperative. Jonas notes that sometimes it is imperative that a society avoid disaster; hence, we conscript soldiers to fight. The fact that we do not (ordinarily) conscript experimental subjects indicates that, however much we value the improvements to life made possible by medical research, we do not think of ourselves as having an obligation to make such improvements. Research brings betterment of our lives; it does not save our society. Because this is true, far from using those who might be most readily available as handy research subjects, we should be most reluctant to use them. Instead, Jonas defends "the inflexible principle that utter helplessness demands utter protection."[23] If that is the right way to respect the dignity of those who are most vulnerable, we will have to ask ourselves whether it is right to build our medical progress upon the lives of those who do not or are unable to give consent.

The tension between producing good results and honoring the dignity of particular individuals also appears in the use of new reproductive technologies. Aimed at providing babies for those who are infertile, such techniques have often made use of sperm or ova provided by donors whose anonymity is protected. (Actually these people are most often vendors, not donors, but the language of donation is commonly used.) As a result, however, the children produced are likely to lack significant information about their identity. The following imaginary scenario suggests how problematic it can be to treat genetic identity as insignificant.[24]

Mary Smith and her husband, John, are expecting the birth of their first child in a few weeks. John has a business trip that will take him briefly out of the country, and Mary would like to accompany him. Her physician says that it should be fine for her to do so, since the trip is relatively brief, and they should be back well before her due date. As long as she feels physically able to travel, her physician sees no reason why Mary should not.

Two days after they arrive at the location of John's meeting, Mary goes into labor—ahead of schedule, to be sure, but not so prematurely as to threaten the child's life. And indeed, although Mary is in labor for the better part of a day, she gives birth to a baby who should survive and live a healthy life. Mary is exhausted, of course, so John stays at her bedside while she rests, and the baby is taken by the nursing staff.

A few hours later Mary feels stronger, and she and John ask to see their baby. "Certainly," says the nurse. "We'll bring you a baby right away."

23. Ibid., 126.
24. With small alterations, I have taken the idea for this scenario from an illustration offered by one of the interviewees in the documentary *Anonymous Father's Day* (2011), produced by the Center for Bioethics and Culture.

"Well no," Mary replies, "we don't want to see *a* baby; we want to see *our* baby."

"Oh," says the nurse, "that's not how we do things here. We make sure all the babies are doing well, and then we give you one of those babies. So it works out fine for everyone. Every family leaves with a baby whose future with them should be bright."

We know instinctively that something has gone wrong here. It is as if something important to an individual's identity could simply be ignored as we produce a well-ordered society in which everyone can flourish. But that is what anonymous gamete donation does. To be sure, we could retain a commitment to reproductive technology while prohibiting anonymity in gamete donation, but then donations might be considerably fewer, and many who desire to produce a child through this technology might be disappointed. We buy the happiness of others at some considerable cost to the dignity of the children produced.

These are only examples of the sorts of puzzles we face if we make aggregate utility rather than individual dignity our most fundamental moral aim. For just such reasons, at least from the time of John Stuart Mill, utilitarians have often formulated their position in terms not simply of the greatest aggregate happiness but of the greatest happiness for the greatest number—thereby attempting to incorporate an individualizing principle of distribution into their norm. This too easily obscures the question of whether "the good of the aggregate of all persons is *each* person's good."[25] These concepts are not easily combined, however, and anyone "whose attention really focuses on 'the greatest value altogether' takes no notice, or should take no notice, of the [from that perspective] quite incidental difference between *mine* and *thine*."[26]

Thus, in many ways we may forget that respect for the dignity of others should serve as a red light that keeps us from simply co-opting them into the service of socially useful projects, even very important ones. Each person, made for God, transcends the communities to which he or she belongs. No one's good is simply part of an aggregate good. That is one way in which honoring the dignity of persons will set limits to our pursuit of what is socially useful.

Undermining Limits on Human Agency

Self-transcendence is only one aspect of who we are. Because we are made to rest in God, we are not ourselves gods. As embodied humans we are also

25. Paul Ramsey, *Basic Christian Ethics* (New York: Scribner, 1950), 237.
26. Ibid.

located and limited. That simple fact, taken seriously, should keep us from inflating our responsibility for producing socially useful results, as if we could really see with the eye of the universe. It should form our sense of ourselves as moral agents who are obligated to seek socially useful ends but obligated also to respect certain limits in that search.

Why not take organs for transplant from patients who are in a persistent vegetative state and who are therefore no longer able to interact with us, pursue any projects of their own, or be conscious of their surroundings? Why not punish wrongdoers more harshly than seems fair, if doing so will prevent others from following their example? Why not use so-called "spare" embryos from in vitro fertilization procedures for research? (After all, since they are almost surely destined for destruction anyway, will not something be gained and nothing lost?) Why not target civilians in war if doing so will help accomplish our war aims or bring a speedier end to the conflict?

We could no doubt multiply examples, but there is no need. Engaging in such practices may violate the dignity of those whom we use to accomplish our (quite possibly good) purposes. That danger, discussed above, is the first way in which a focus on utility may undermine individual dignity. There is also a second issue: a willingness to engage in such activities may involve coming to think of ourselves in ways that obscure the truth that our freedom is limited by our relation to God. And apart from that relation, the dignity of the human person may be endangered.

Aldous Huxley's *Brave New World*, whatever its merits or demerits as a work of fiction, remains still today a powerful reminder of how, even when seeking to better human life, we may instead undermine the dignity of persons. Huxley imagines at one point the thoughts of Mustapha Mond, one of the World Controllers of a future world in which the power to reshape our humanity seems to have few limits.

"A New Theory of Biology," was the title of the paper which Mustapha Mond had just finished reading. He sat for some time, meditatively frowning, then picked up his pen and wrote across the title page: "The author's mathematical treatment of the conception of purpose is novel and highly ingenious, but heretical and, so far as the present social order is concerned, dangerous and potentially subversive. *Not to be published.*" He underlined the words. "The author will be kept under supervision. His transference to the Marine Biological Station at St. Helena may become necessary." A pity, he thought, as he signed his name. It was a masterly piece of work. But once you began admitting explanations in terms of purpose—well, you didn't know what the result might be. It was the sort of idea that might easily decondition the more unsettled minds among the higher castes—make them lose their faith in happiness as the

Sovereign Good and take to believing, instead, that the goal was somewhere beyond, somewhere outside the present human sphere; that the purpose of life was not the maintenance of well-being, but some intensification and refining of consciousness, some enlargement of knowledge.[27]

Are humans really fit to exercise the kind of power Mond does? There may often be circumstances in life when our search for the socially useful invites us to do evil. And if we give in to that temptation, we might say that "*things* will be better, what *happens* will be better. . . . But I will have done something worse."[28] To give in at such moments is to lose the sense of ourselves as limited moral agents. It is as if we tried to view our action from the outside and thought of it as a choice made by someone else—a choice about what is best on the whole from the point of view of the universe. It is as if I were asked to "decide directly among states of the world, as if I were taking a multiple choice test."[29] But in losing the limits on our agency, we lose something essential to the peculiar dignity of a human being.

John Finnis once wrote of the "secret, often unconscious legalism" that pervades utilitarian (and, more broadly, consequentialist) moral reasoning with "its assumption that there is a uniquely correct moral answer (or specifiable set of correct moral answers) to all genuine moral problems."[30] In part this means that an obligation to maximize good results demands too much of us—moralizing the whole of life by seeing every decision as an occasion in which we are obligated to seek whatever is best overall. Alternatively, instead of saying that it asks too much, we might say that it asks the wrong thing of us. It invites us to think of love apart from trust, to imagine that the destiny of the world lies not in God's hand but in ours.

An obligation to love separated from the freedom to trust in God's providential care makes life a heavy burden indeed, for then we constantly bear the godlike responsibility of providing for the general well-being in our every action. If maximizing utility is our most fundamental duty, we must be stern moralists in every moment. Each action must be weighed and calculated to determine whether it really fosters the greatest good. To play with one's child, talk with one's spouse, read a book, write a friend, work in a garden, devote long hours to a work of art—all such possibilities will need justification from the perspective of Sidgwick's "eye of the universe." The dignity of much

---

27. Aldous Huxley, *Brave New World* (New York: Bantam, 1968), 119–20.
28. Nagel, *View from Nowhere*, 180.
29. Ibid., 183.
30. John Finnis, *Fundamentals of Ethics* (Washington, DC: Georgetown University Press, 1982), 93.

ordinary human activity is undermined when drawn under the umbrella of obligation.

Sidgwick understood the difficulty. Recognizing that utilitarianism was sometimes criticized as rather vulgar (because of its focus on pleasure), he argued that one might more plausibly charge it with setting too high a standard and requiring too much, thereby diminishing personal autonomy.[31] While recognizing the same problem, Christians might respond a bit differently. Limits on our obligation to seek what is best on the whole cannot finally be grounded in a supposed claim to independence or autonomy. Instead, those limits have their ground in our created nature's finite and limited character. To imagine ourselves as having the responsibility to adopt a more universal standpoint would be to want to be like God, to lose the dignity characteristic of the human person, and to fail in trust.

When we forget this, the results for moral thinking can be very strange. Sidgwick considers in some detail a practical perplexity that confronts utilitarians. Their theory enjoins us always to act in such a way as to seek the greatest happiness overall. But many pleasures—which presumably contribute to a good outcome—can be experienced only if we do not aim at them. Hence, surprising as it may seem, Sidgwick recommends that most of us, most of the time, ought not try to live each moment as if we were utilitarians seeking the greatest good overall. Put most generally, the problem is that to aim in all of one's action at producing the greatest overall happiness would almost surely make life worse; it would be far from a happy way to live.

To deal with this problem utilitarians are almost forced to suggest that things will be better if people do not at every moment aim to produce the greatest happiness—if, that is, they do not always act as if they believed utilitarian theory. We might note how this—adopting a moral theory that is hard actually to live—almost inevitably creates division and incoherence within the person. Our theory's justification for action cannot take flesh in the motives that move us. We are divided between the person who acts and the person who theorizes.

And we are divided also among ourselves, between those who can look with the eye of the universe and those for whom life is happier when lived less reflectively. Because those in the first group know that things will be better on the whole if those in the second group do not try to act as utilitarians, the theory begins to look highly manipulative. Perhaps the dignity of persons is better honored when with glad hearts we accept the limits of our finitude.

---

31. Sidgwick, *Methods of Ethics*, 87.

This acceptance of our limited responsibility is not a defense for self-concern and failure to care for those in need. Although finite, we are not limited entirely by our present location. Hence Einar Billing suggested that "the call [of God] constantly has to struggle against two adversaries: stereotyped workmanship and unresponsible idealism."[32] If the heart that trusts God's providential care does not seek unlimited responsibility for achieving what is best overall, neither may it be closed to the call for love and service in new ways.

We might remember the famous exchange in Dickens's *Christmas Carol* between Scrooge and two businessmen who are collecting for the poor. "Are there no prisons?" "And the union workhouses? Are they still in operation?" Scrooge's questions make clear that he is well satisfied with current provisions for the poor. The businessmen point out that, while prisons and workhouses continue to function, many people would rather die than go there.

> "If they would rather die," said Scrooge, "they had better do it, and decrease the surplus population. Besides—excuse me—I don't know that [they would rather die]."
>
> "But you might know it," observed the gentleman.
>
> "It's not my business," Scrooge returned. "It's enough for a man to understand his own business, and not to interfere with other people's. Mine occupies me constantly."[33]

Scrooge's vice is not that he fails to respond to this particular Christmas appeal; it is that he never responds to any need that calls him beyond the concerns of his business. Such decisions are almost always personal and particular. They cannot be willed universally from any impersonal standpoint that is nowhere in particular, for humans are always located. But in making such decisions, in attempting both to honor the limits of our vocation and in freedom partially to transcend them, we are never solely servants of the greatest aggregate good.

This outlook was nicely illustrated by the philosopher J. B. Schneewind in an article with the seemingly puzzling title, "The Divine Corporation and the History of Ethics."[34] Schneewind sketched a way of understanding an

32. Einar Billing, *Our Calling*, trans. Conrad Bergendorff (Philadelphia: Fortress, 1964), 17.
33. Charles Dickens, *Christmas Books* (London: Collins, 1954), 24.
34. J. B. Schneewind, "The Divine Corporation and the History of Ethics," in *Philosophy in History*, ed. Richard Rorty, J. B. Schneewind, and Quentin Skinner (New York: Cambridge University Press, 1984), 173–91. I draw here on my earlier summary of this article in my book *The Freedom of a Christian: Grace, Vocation, and the Meaning of Our Humanity* (Grand Rapids: Brazos, 2006), 129–30.

ethic—the traditional, received Christian ethic—in which our responsibility to achieve socially useful aggregate goods is always limited. To be sure, Schneewind did this in part for the sake of explaining how modern moral philosophy had developed by turning away from that received Christian ethic. But to understand his notion of the divine corporation is to comprehend something of the concept of personal dignity as I have been using it here.

We begin by imagining our world as a cooperative endeavor created, ordered, and governed by God. In it, as in any cooperative endeavor, participants play their respective roles, carry out the tasks assigned them, and in so doing join together to produce a good which none of them could have produced alone.[35] No one participant is responsible for achieving the good of the whole or the best overall good possible, yet the work of each is ordered toward that good. Sometimes individual agents will see more or less clearly how their tasks are related to the overall good. If they only fulfill their assigned task, then, and ignore altogether the general good, they would—and should—be subject to criticism. For in addition to carrying out one's individual task, each person needs to act creatively in ways that are not simply given in any role. That is part of what it means to be an agent who is not only finite but also free.

At other times, however, an individual may not be able to see the larger good his assigned duty serves. In such cases, he cannot really be criticized for ignoring the larger good while just "minding his own business," for he simply does not know that larger good.[36] We can imagine a world in which the overall good is very important but also very complex, far too complex for any individual agent always to be sure of how his work helps to produce it. And we can also imagine that the supervisor in charge of this supremely important but very complex project is able to foresee problems and deal with emergencies, is fair in his supervision, and is good—"too good ever to assign any duties that would be improper from any point of view."[37] Such a world, imagined as a cooperative endeavor with God as that uniquely qualified supervisor, is the Divine Corporation. The dignity of individual agents who work within that Divine Corporation is closely connected to the limits on what they should attempt to do. To try simply to be all freedom, to act without limits in order to produce the aggregate good they think best, would be to picture themselves as something other—and more godlike—than humans. It would be to suppose that they could fill the role of that uniquely qualified supervisor.

35. Schneewind, "Divine Corporation," 176.
36. Ibid., 177.
37. Ibid., 178.

We can supplement Schneewind's workplace metaphor with a helpful literary one drawn from C. S. Lewis. Think of individuals not as agents in the Divine Corporation but as characters in a play. They know the part that has been given them, and each must play it in his own way. But none of them is the dramatist or director, and none of them is responsible for working out the play's plot satisfactorily. Something like that is our situation in life. We are not the author but characters in the story—under authority. Thus, as Lewis put it,

> We do not know the play. We do not even know whether we are in Act I or Act V. We do not know who are the major and who the minor characters. The Author knows. . . . That it has a meaning we may be sure, but we cannot see it. When it is over, we may be told. We are led to expect that the Author will have something to say to each of us on the part that each of us has played. The playing it well is what matters infinitely.[38]

Whichever metaphor we prefer, it is clear that if God recedes as a governing, directing, authorial presence whose responsibility it is to see to the good of the whole or work out the plot of the play, it may seem that human responsibility correspondingly increases and intensifies. We may come to see ourselves as the agents whose responsibility it is to make things work out best on the whole. That is, it becomes our task to determine and achieve the greatest aggregate good, and utility displaces the dignity that characterizes limited human beings in our understanding of the moral life.

I have made this point in a manner that is intended to suggest a problem with utilitarian theory—namely, the way in which it invites us to lose a sense of limits. We will not see or appreciate the lure of utilitarianism, however, unless we also acknowledge what is appealing here. Imagine a world—Sidgwick's world—in which morally serious people have lost a sense of God's providential governance. In that world an earnest person such as Sidgwick can hardly avoid feeling the lure of utilitarianism. After all, in a world filled with suffering and terrors, we might easily suppose that those of us who remain morally serious must accept the burden of shaping the best consequences possible. Even standard Christian moral language of freedom from legalism and love for those in need might be conscripted in service of accepting that burden and thereby increase the appeal of utilitarian thinking. We are readily drawn to lose a sense of our moral limits.

This can happen on a very large scale through both governmental and nongovernmental agencies—in Washington, DC, and in Davos, Switzerland.

---

38. C. S. Lewis, *The World's Last Night and Other Essays* (New York: Harcourt Brace Jovanovich, 1960), 105–6.

Perhaps the illustrations that speak to most of us are closer to home, however. Fathers and mothers, at least in their best moments, know better; for parenthood is nothing if not a school in which we learn the limits of our ability to shape the future. John Ames, the 76-year-old preacher who is the narrator of Marilynne Robinson's *Gilead* and who is writing a long letter about life to his young son, recounts a sermon he had once preached on Abraham and his sons Isaac and Ishmael. Abraham had been prepared to sacrifice Isaac at the Lord's command; Ishmael he sent off into the wilderness with his mother Hagar. Ames reflects that "any father, particularly an old father, must finally give his child up to the wilderness and trust to the providence of God. . . . Great faith is required to give the child up, trusting God to honor the parents' love for him by assuring that there will indeed be angels in that wilderness."[39] When we reflect on the most significant bonds in our lives, we know that we are not and should not try to be simply agents in service of the general good. Dirty Harry speaks the truth: "A man's got to know his limitations."[40]

An Extended Illustration

One extended example may help to illustrate the way in which a commitment to personal dignity can keep us from making relief of suffering and production of happiness our sole, or even central, moral aim.

In February 2014 the Belgian Parliament acted to permit euthanasia for children experiencing "chronic and unbearable suffering," if those children were able to and did request euthanasia (and if parental consent was also given). This represents a somewhat more restrictive practice of pediatric euthanasia than that in the Netherlands, where infants with a "hopeless prognosis" may be euthanized even if the child is too young to request or assent to such action.

No doubt the lives of these children can hardly be happy ones. They are likely to have relatively short and pain-filled lives even under the best of circumstances and with the best medical care. What follows from that? What follows, if we honor their dignity as persons, is that it is our obligation to seek for these children a death that does not undermine their equal dignity but that cares for their lives and honors their time among us from first to last.

Faced with the sadness and suffering of such cases, and forced to confront the limits of our own expertise and ability to help, we are tempted to turn in either of two directions that may seem at first to be complete opposites but

---

39. Marilynne Robinson, *Gilead* (New York: Farrar, Straus and Giroux, 2004), 129.
40. The line "a man's got to know his limitations" is part of the wisdom of Clint Eastwood's character "Dirty" Harry Callahan in the movie *Magnum Force* (1973).

that in fact are closely related kin.[41] We are tempted *either* to struggle with all our power and technical skill against death, never giving up that fight until we have nothing left to do and must admit defeat, *or* we are tempted to decide to hasten death, solving the problem of suffering by eliminating the sufferer.

However different these two approaches may seem on the surface, each is a form of abandonment. Neither constitutes "care" for this child, and our obligation is precisely to care for the child, relieving suffering as best we can while honoring the child's dignity as our equal.

Deeply embedded in our moral tradition is the distinction between, on the one hand, allowing someone to die and, on the other hand, intentionally causing death. For chronically ill and suffering children who face life-threatening illness, appropriate care will sometimes mean ceasing to struggle against death. Medical treatments may rightly be withdrawn if they are either useless or excessively burdensome. Thus, honoring human dignity does not mean always prolonging life.

No one should be subjected to useless treatment, and no one need suffer any and all possibly life-saving or life-prolonging treatments, however burdensome they may be. That much can be clear even if we do not always know how best to evaluate the facts of a particular case. The questions we should ask ourselves are questions about what is medically indicated, what is medically best for a child: Will a treatment benefit the life this child has? Is a treatment excessively burdensome to the life of this child? These questions are a little different from others we may be tempted to ask ourselves: Is it a benefit to have this life? Is this life a burden?

That second set of questions would fail to honor the child's dignity as a person. Those questions invite us not just to allow a child to die but to embrace his death as a good at which we aim—that is, to take into our character a willingness to intentionally kill the innocent. That would be to think of ourselves not as fellow humans and fellow sufferers with this child but instead as people who are fit to exercise an ultimate authority over the life of another. We often speak of the need for compassion when we think about such troubling cases, but we do not always pay close attention to what the word actually means and what it asks of us: that we "suffer with" the one who needs our care, entering as best we can into his suffering, not distancing ourselves from him as if we were not equals in dignity.

The danger to equality arises from two angles, both that of the person for whom euthanasia is sought and that of the person who offers it. If I seek to give ultimate authority over my life to others, I become something less than

41. Paul Ramsey, *The Patient as Person* (New Haven: Yale University Press, 1970), 144–57.

their equal. I join what John Locke called the "inferior ranks of Creatures" and make my person an object to be possessed and controlled by others.[42] And the same is true when I give such authority over a child's life to others. Likewise, the person who carries out the euthanizing deed pulls rank and in effect exercises a more-than-human authority over the life of one who is in fact his moral and political equal. For us to try to exercise such authority is to pretend to be what we in truth are not—something other than beings of equal dignity. And that would be to lose one of the greatest achievements of our civilization's tradition, an affirmation of equal dignity laboriously gained at great cost over centuries.

To say this is not to say that we always know how best to care for such children. Here, if ever, we run up against our own inability even to know how to maximize human happiness and well-being. We know only that we must seek a choice that honors their life, not a choice aimed simply at eliminating that life—even in the name of the aggregate well-being of the child, the child's parents, and, perhaps, the larger society.

It is even possible—not guaranteed, but possible—that honoring the child's dignity in this way may over time maximize good results. For if we simply sweep such children off our doorstep every morning with euthanasia, medicine will never learn better ways to help them and others like them. A commitment to the dignity of individual persons must come first, but that commitment need not ignore the limited pursuit of greater aggregate good.

Individual Persons, Always in Relation

I have suggested at least two significant ways in which personal dignity is an inherently individualizing concept: it resists our inclination to think of the well-being of others chiefly in terms of aggregate social utility, and it resists our inclination to think of ourselves as if we were other than or more than limited, located agents, with a correspondingly limited responsibility for producing socially useful results through our actions. This is what it means to think of ourselves as those strange two-sided creatures who are simultaneously located and distanced from themselves. Distinctively individual, we are not simply parts of any aggregate social whole, and faithful action on our part is not primarily aimed at producing such an aggregate good.

This consideration, however, invites further, important questions: Is this emphasis on individual distinctiveness problematic? Is it individualistic in a

---

42. John Locke, *Two Treatises of Government* (New York: New American Library, 1965), 311.

way that should trouble Christians? Such questions might naturally occur to us, and it remains to consider this problem briefly. In order to think about the dignity of persons, we need to recall the distinctively Christian understanding of what it means to be a person. And although many today may have forgotten this, Christians formed their notion of a person by thinking about the triune character of the God they worshiped. A brief foray into the structure of trinitarian belief is therefore needed.

Noting that the language of three persons (of the one God) might seem to suggest three individual substances or three gods, Saint Augustine writes: "Since the Father is only called so because he has a Son, and the Son is only called so because he has a Father, these things are not said substance-wise, as neither is said with reference to itself but only with reference to the other. . . . Therefore, although being Father is different from being Son, there is no difference of substance, because they are not called these things substance-wise but relationship-wise."[43] Put a little more simply, the distinction between Father and Son is one of relation, not of substantial characteristics or qualities. Thus, because he will not distinguish the three persons by means of any qualities they individually possess, Augustine can say quite straightforwardly: "So, then, the Father is almighty, the Son is almighty, the Holy Spirit is almighty; yet there are not three almighties but one almighty."[44]

That short passage has a kind of verbal echo in the third of the great ecumenical creeds, commonly known as the Athanasian Creed though almost surely not written by Athanasius and produced a century or so later than Augustine. It articulates the equality of the three divine "persons" in a series of rhythmic assertions: "Uncreated is the Father; uncreated is the Son; uncreated is the Spirit." Father, Son, and Spirit are likewise said to be "infinite," "eternal," and "almighty." "And yet," as the Creed puts it, "there are not three eternal beings, but one who is eternal; as there are not three uncreated and unlimited beings, but one who is uncreated and unlimited."[45]

Thus, if we ascribe any quality or capacity to one of the three persons, we will need to ascribe it to each of the other two. We do not distinguish among the three persons by pointing to any qualities or capacities, and yet we must distinguish them. How? Only in terms of the relations that mark their shared history. "The Father was neither made nor created nor begotten; the Son was neither made nor created, but was alone begotten of the Father; the Spirit was neither made nor created, but is proceeding from the Father and the Son. . . .

43. Saint Augustine, *The Trinity*, trans. Edmund Hill (Brooklyn: New City, 1991), V.6 (192).
44. Ibid., V.10 (196).
45. Jaroslav Pelikan and Valerie Hotchkiss, eds., *Creeds and Confessions of Faith in the Christian Tradition* (New Haven: Yale University Press, 2003), 676.

And in this Trinity, no one is before or after, greater or less than the other; but all three persons are in themselves coeternal and coequal."[46]

What, then, does it mean to speak of a person? Put most simply, a person is a distinctive (and distinguishable) "someone," not a "something"—not a something marked by certain properties but a someone marked by a history in relation, a someone who is not interchangeable with any other but whose distinctiveness is a matter not of qualities but of relations.[47]

The first followers of Jesus were, of course, fully committed Jewish monotheists, but they quickly realized that they seemed to have found in Jesus more than just another fellow human being. After all, they prayed to Jesus and worshiped him. They spoke of him as having been sent by his Father, the God of Israel, and as having promised to send a Spirit who would continue his own presence in the world. So while they continued to believe in one God, they told a story in which that God was named three ways. Somehow they needed to distinguish the three without undermining their equality and without abandoning monotheism.

Trinitarian doctrine, slowly and gradually worked out over time, was the result. According to that doctrine, the three persons—Father, Son, Spirit—are *numerically* but not *qualitatively* distinct. That is, we cannot distinguish them from each other by pointing to any capacities they individually possess. Instead, they are distinguished only in terms of their relations to one another. Hence, the Son is not *different from* the Father or the Spirit but *other than* the Father and the Spirit.[48] The individual persons are never alone; they are always in relation, in community.

That this is a great mystery Christians would not deny. But the mystery is not just about the being of God but about what it means to be an individual person. Augustine affirms the mystery in a passage at which one cannot help but smile: "When you ask 'Three what?' human speech labors under a great dearth of words. So we say three persons, not in order to say that precisely, but in order not to be reduced to silence."[49] Each person is marked by what the philosopher John Crosby terms an "incommunicability" or an "unrepeatability." Those who knew and loved Socrates, Crosby writes, "will insist that there was in Socrates something absolutely unrepeatable, they will say that there was a mystery of the man and that Socrates was not a mere instance or specimen of this mystery but that he *was* this mystery, so that a second

46. Ibid., 676–77.
47. Robert Spaemann, *Persons: The Difference between 'Someone' and 'Something'* (New York: Oxford University Press, 2006), 11.
48. Ibid., 26.
49. Augustine, *The Trinity*, V.10 (196).

Socrates is strictly, absolutely impossible. When Socrates died, a hole was left in the world, such that no subsequent person could possibly fill it."[50]

In each of those unrepeatable persons we discern a dignity that we should attempt to honor. This is not a destructive individualism; it is the sober truth of who we are before God. Distinctive, singular, and unrepeatable as each of us is, none is ever an isolated individual, and individualism does not have the last word. For to be a person is to be a someone who exists always in relation; it is to be an individual who is never alone.

Further Reading

Huxley, Aldous. *Brave New World*. New York: Bantam Books, 1968.

Huxley's influential and frequently cited novel depicts a future in which the attainment of general happiness may seem to come at the expense of human dignity.

Meilaender, Gilbert. *Neither Beast nor God: The Dignity of the Human Person*. New York: Encounter Books, 2009.

Distinguishing within a theological perspective two concepts of dignity—human and personal dignity—the author explores their differences and their relationship.

Nagel, Thomas. *The View from Nowhere*. New York: Oxford University Press, 1986.

This is an important work by a philosopher who, while appreciating the appeal of and the need for attention to utilitarian considerations, argues that regarding action only from a utilitarian perspective cannot capture the meaning of human agency.

Ramsey, Paul. *Basic Christian Ethics*. New York: Scribner, 1950.

Ramsey's examination of the meaning of Christian love distinguishes it sharply from utilitarian attempts to maximize happiness.

Smart, J. J. C., and Bernard Williams. *Utilitarianism: For and Against*. New York: Cambridge University Press, 1973.

In brief compass two philosophers exchange arguments for and against utilitarian moral theory.

US President's Council on Bioethics. *Human Dignity and Bioethics*, 2008, https://bioethicsarchive.georgetown.edu/pcbe/reports/human_dignity.

This volume offers a number of strikingly different perspectives on the meaning and implications of human dignity.

---

50. John F. Crosby, *Personalist Papers* (Washington, DC: Catholic University of America Press, 2003), 11, emphasis in original.

His Eye Is on the Sparrow

Collectivism and Human Significance

A M Y   L A U R A   H A L L

Are not two sparrows sold for a penny? And not one of them will fall to the ground without your Father's will. But even the hairs of your head are all numbered.

—Matthew 10:29–30 (RSV)

I sing because I'm happy, I sing because I'm free, For His eye is on the sparrow, and I know He watches me.

—Civilla D. Martin, 1905

Each individual Christian is part of a larger body. We are part of the body of Christ. But we are not just part of the body. The body of Christ cannot itself be measured or parceled. Consider the Lord's Supper as a weekly reminder of this fact of Christian faith: Christians believe the body of Christ is indiscriminately there, on the table, across the world in ways that not even Google Maps can map. And each individual in the body of Christ cannot be authoritatively measured, parceled, or evaluated numerically. Being part of Jesus Christ means that each individual, as a whole, is whole in an incalculable

39

way. We are each, as little bitty parts of the body of Christ, unto our own, beloved beyond reckoning by God as individuals.

Here I further suggest, with centuries of Christians, that Jesus came in one single body with a name, history, and story for a reason. Jesus is not a symbol of some other truth that is beyond his particularity, whether that truth is political or spiritual or aesthetic. His individual body marks our individual bodies as known by God in ways that must shape how we seek to know one another not as symbols or instantiations of another reality but as real, as incarnate. Numbering people—and trying to know them by a category that can be counted, assessed, and sent by experts into the right pen—is a lie that Christians need to refuse. This chapter is one way to explain why the particularity of Jesus Christ matters for the particular matter that makes each person a unique person. You, I, and that woman next to us—each one of us is too inscrutable for a larger description and decisive evaluation by another human or another group of humans who seek to study us.

There is another way into this argument. I have borrowed the title for this chapter from a song that was sung at my grandmother's and great-grandmother's funerals, each held in Mineral Wells, Texas.[1] My great-grandmother's husband came home from World War I, "the war to end all wars," and like many veterans of that war he came home with wounds on his soul from which he never recovered. My grandmother's husband came home from World War II, specifically from the war in the Pacific. Historian John Dower has termed that theater of war to have been a "war without mercy,"[2] and my grandfather had sustained so many wounds from a sniper that he was never the same. Before the war he had played the mandolin regularly in a band with his four brothers. After the war his hands shook from trauma; he was not able to play the music that had given him joy.

My great-grandmother and my grandmother, then, might even be considered war widows. Each had three children, and both women watched changes as their hometown shifted from a regional health destination (Mineral Wells) to a military town with one of the largest infantry replacement training centers in the United States (Fort Wolters). My great-grandmother was known for her impeccable skills as a seamstress, and she took in alteration jobs to supplement her modest pension. My grandmother, her daughter, was known for her fried pies and downright profligate shopping sprees, almost always for her daughters and granddaughters. Neither woman was famous. Neither

---

1. Civilla D. Martin, "His Eye Is on the Sparrow" (1905).
2. John Dower, *War without Mercy: Race and Power in the Pacific War* (New York: Pantheon, 1987).

changed the world. But his eye is on the sparrow, and I know he watched them and watches them still. When Jesus Christ returns, he will restore every single hair to their beautiful heads and restore their healed husbands to their ready arms. If Jesus Christ was indeed raised from the dead, then my grandmothers' very particular, nuanced, singular lives were not in vain. They are not redeemed as part of any humanly created strategy for national progress or as part of a large sweep of all of human history. They will each individually be redeemed and raised by grace through Jesus Christ alone.

I here make a case for Christian attention to each individual human being against what I call collectivism. There is an importantly collective dimension to human existence. However, people are sometimes understood so dominantly in terms of some social category or structure that their individual significance is in danger of being lost. This way of thinking about people is a destructive *ism*—collectivism—that sorts, orders, understands, directs, or even seeks to control groups of people. The proper response is not to counter with another *ism*, individualism, since reducing all human significance to the individual ironically ends up undermining that very significance.[3] Rather, the concern here is to critique collectivism in a way that safeguards appropriate attention to the uniqueness of particular persons.

Of particular import is the faulty epistemology in the collectivism I address below. *Epistemology* is a word philosophers use for how people (usually philosophers) think about thinking. The problem with collectivism (as I am using the term) is that it involves a way of thinking about thinking that describes the best way of thinking as a view from above the fray of individual faces and affections and particular idiosyncrasies of lived lives with real people, as a real person. One form of this collectivism is social Darwinism, a way of applying ideas about the history and development of the earth to human beings, sometimes with an aim to direct those human beings toward a goal, sometimes with an aim simply to try to understand and predict how human beings will move about in the world politically, sexually, domestically, and so on.

The most immediately accessible version of collectivism for many readers is niche marketing in postindustrial capitalism. All you have to do to watch this form of thinking about thinking is turn on the television and view critically. Advertising and even entire channels on radio or television use predictive models to determine how to attract particular types of eyeballs or ears to their brand. Readers may best have experienced this tactic when they have been (accidentally or occasionally) subjected to messaging aimed

3. See Russell DiSilvestro's essay, "My Life Is Not My Own: Individualism and Human Significance," in the present volume.

at a very different demographic than their own. Some elderly adults who have been watching television in the United States since they were young have found themselves watching the Super Bowl in the last decade thinking during each advertisement, "Clearly I am not their target audience." The mechanisms of marketing to particular demographics in order to persuade and direct people about what to buy and what to care about make up a whole field of study.

Bob Pittman, the cocreator of MTV (Music Television), offers one of the bluntest declarations of this intentional form of study and control. In a 1982 *Washington Post* article on Pittman's creation, Christian Williams explains, "MTV's target audience is aged 14 to 34. It is a classic example of 'narrowcasting,' as opposed to 'broadcasting.' That is, MTV delivers an audience with specific demographics." Note that Williams explains here that MTV first creates a particular audience and then delivers an audience to advertisers. The social body that makes up people-who-watch-MTV was not there before. That social body of MTV-people was created by the carefully wrought construction of a plan to create a demographic that would be then useful for people eager to market and persuade a particular, newly created audience. Williams quotes Pittman as distinguishing between the old-fashioned term "demographic" and a new form of marketing Pittman called "psychographics." And then Williams quotes Pittman's blunt declaration of control: "At MTV, we don't shoot for the 14-year-olds—we own them." Noting that music itself has been used by many different cultures at different times for self-definition and for top-down control, Williams quotes Pittman again: "You tell me the music people like and I'll tell you their views on abortion, whether we should increase our military arms, what their sense of humor is like, what their favorite TV programs are, their response to political candidates, even their taste in jokes."[4]

Three decades later, if you do a simple internet search for the particularly provocative statement "we own them," you will find that many commentators are most troubled that it was the creator of MTV who spoke these words. Christian parents have indeed objected over the decades to the aim that Pittman took at teens in America. My point is more direct than that, however, and has nothing really to do with whether the music on MTV is debauched or inspired. Consider what it means that human beings are seeking through meticulous study of "psychographics" to "own" any group of people, whether the group to be "owned" is impressionable Midwestern teens in the 1990s or economically insecure, working-class white men in the 2010s.

4. Christian Williams, "Now, Music to Their Eyes: Bob Pittman's MTV Changes the Channel," *Washington Post*, September 16, 1982.

It is not the hip shaking or sagging jeans on a television station that troubles me here. It is the intentional study, creation, and manipulation of a group of people by another group of people. God created human beings out of nothing and saves each of us by Jesus Christ. Those who today perform predictive programming really do try to "play God" (a phrase that is overused by ethicists). And they try to make other merely human projects, whether idle ones or grand ones, that will claim our attention and even our worship.[5]

While this chapter could focus exclusively on the presumption of advertising, there are other forms of collectivism that are worth attention and criticism. Below I explain why forms of social Darwinism prevalent in common discourse about individuals and social groups beg for an account of holy individuality. Specifically, I note the work of social Darwinists E. O. Wilson and Jonathan Haidt, legal scholar and cultural critic Amy Chua, neurobiologists Joan Chiao and Katherine Blizinsky, and social psychologists Hazel Rose Markus and Shinobu Kitayama. I do not wish to argue that any one of these authors is nefarious. As far as I have been able to determine through research, none have so bluntly stated, as did Pittman, that they hope to "own" a particular group of people.

However, what they have written is contrary to the witness within Christianity that human beings matter in their specificity. They have forgotten, or perhaps have never quite known, why people matter. Some scholars try to find common ground between new forms of social science and Christianity; I do the opposite. I look for assumptions in social biological scholarship that require critical engagement and even refusal.

Next in this chapter I describe what is at stake when Christians take on ways of seeing the world that blur the lines between one particular child of God and another, making persons seem primarily part of something larger called a "people."

Finally, I explain how, by seeking a view from "above," mere mortals can shape an individual soul in such a way that he forgets himself. Wilson, Haidt, Chiao, and the others I discuss do wrong by their "human subjects" by climbing

---

5. One example of an MTV creation used also by various Christian rainmakers is the phenomenon known as "Bono." This phenomenon is also a human being and the lead singer of the rock band U2. But he was highlighted and used as an icon of politically left-leaning Christianity, to the point where even mainstream evangelicals were practicing a U2-themed "Eucharist" called U2charist. See their website: http://u2-charist.com/. Bono has gone on to become a spokesman for Louis Vuitton handbags, but before that he was used as an example of the miraculous possibility of Christianity mixed with politics by way of the supposed conversion of Senator Jesse Helms Jr. to the importance of funding for HIV/AIDS relief in sub-Saharan Africa. See J. W. Busby, "Bono Made Jesse Helms Cry: Jubilee 2000, Debt Relief, and Moral Action in International Politics," *International Studies Quarterly* 51 (June 2007): 247–75.

up a ladder to look down and count or dissect groups. I believe it is important
to note that this view from above can lead a human to lose himself.

To help convey this point, I use Errol Morris's documentary about Robert
McNamara, *The Fog of War*. In one scene McNamara tries to sort out why
it is that he thought his architectural plans for firebombing civilian popula-
tions in Japan (in that "war without mercy") were required of him.[6] As a
documentarian, Morris elicits from McNamara both vulnerability and dignity, even while encouraging in him a recognition of what his particular story
says about American ways of war. McNamara's story is about an individual
human and also about that one human's part of a story that caught him up
and perhaps carried him away.

His Coming Kingdom of Peace

Theologian Jürgen Moltmann writes:

> Between the God of evolution and the God of Christian faith there is contra-
> diction: the general "struggle for existence" knows only survivors and victims;
> but the God of the crucified Christ is the saviour of the victims and the judge
> of the survivors. Out of the victims in the history of nature and the victims of
> human history, God builds his coming kingdom of peace.[7]

If Jesus was raised from the dead in all his particular beauty and mortality, so do Christians witness to the truth of individual dignity in the face of
collectivism. This requires a reckoning with a form of collectivism wrought
from popularized notions of social Darwinism. I have in mind narrative forms
of thought that range from Francis Fukuyama's teleology of capitalism in
The End of History and the Last Man to Jonathan Haidt's recent reclama-
tion of the "hive hypothesis" for public policy.[8] In the realm of philosophy
and religion, it is important to consider critically not only Immanuel Kant's
version of Enlightenment individualism but also the abiding significance of

---

6. *The Fog of War: Eleven Lessons from the Life of Robert S. McNamara*, directed by
Errol Morris (Sony Pictures Classics, 2004), DVD. McNamara worked as the president of Ford
Motor Company after serving in World War II and before serving as the Secretary of Defense.
And he served as the president of the World Bank following his resignation from the cabinet
of L. B. Johnson.

7. Jürgen Moltmann, *Sun of Righteousness, Arise! God's Future for Humanity and the Earth*
(Minneapolis: Fortress, 2010), 223.

8. Jonathan Haidt, J. Patrick Seder, and Selin Kesebir, "Hive Psychology, Happiness, and
Public Policy," *Journal of Legal Studies* 37 (June 2008): 133–56. See also Francis Fukuyama,
The End of History and the Last Man (New York: Free Press, 1992).

his main conversation partner, G. W. F. Hegel (1770–1831). Hegel sought to solve the problem of individualism in his day with a collectivist, progressive account of human history, an account that inspired thinkers ranging from Karl Marx (1818–1883) to Charles Darwin (1809–1882).

Immanuel Kant (1724–1804) left in his work a question that troubled his successors. Either individual duty stands alone, and the individual must learn to stay true to his duty regardless of reward or consolation, or the individual is consoled by the probability, given the structures of human thought, that God and heaven are plausible. Philosophers in the eighteenth century eager to throw off the shackles of Christianity were hardly satisfied with the re-introduction of God into Kant's account of individual freedom. But many of those same philosophers were not content to leave their beloved Western Europe bereft of hope in a future wherein truth, goodness, and beauty all could eventually and materially cohere. This is where Hegel was so useful for his era and continues to be useful today for people who find belief in the absurdities of Christianity to be onerous, embarrassing, or inconvenient. Hegel wrote that human beings of a particular sort are able to stand above human history, observe it (and us), and push the future forward.

Hegel's legacy of human ambition is at least as problematic for determining why people matter today as the call to individual conscience that Kant left behind in the eighteenth century. Here I can do no better than to quote a Danish philosopher who studied both Kant and Hegel in Germany in the early nineteenth century and then returned home to write in his quaint, native tongue. In a section that he ultimately deleted from *Philosophical Fragments*, Søren Kierkegaard explains what is at stake in Hegel's way of thinking about thinking:

> Too bad that Hegel lacked time; but if one is to dispose of all of world history, how does one get time for the little test as to whether the absolute method, which explains everything, is also able to explain the life of a single human being. In ancient times, one would have smiled at a method that can explain all of world history absolutely but cannot explain a single person even mediocrely.[9]

Kierkegaard wrote indirectly, through a pseudonym, in many of his books, including *Philosophical Fragments*. He sought to prompt questions in each of his individual readers about how Hegelian assumptions had made their way into the sense of what makes "common sense" sensible in their day. More importantly, he sought to help each reader consider the ways that philosophically sophisticated

9. Supplement to *Philosophical Fragments*, section deleted from final copy. See Søren Kierke-gaard, *Philosophical Fragments*, trans. Howard V. Hong and Edna H. Hong (Princeton: Princeton University Press, 1985), 206.

forms of Christianity in Western Europe at the end of the nineteenth century had taken within their systems assumptions about human progress and the movement of history through advanced forms of human knowledge.

Kierkegaard's point in the little scrap about explaining individuals is that, for all of Hegel's expertise, he lacks the capacity to explain the nonsensical existence of this one, particular, singular human life. Kierkegaard is hinting for his readers that the existence of this one, single, individual human being is not to be explained at all but taken as an inexplicable, incalculable given. That knowledge, however, requires going backward in philosophical progress, from before Kant's deism, to consider again the gratuitous case of Jesus Christ and salvation through him.[10]

Christians during Kierkegaard's day who wanted to keep up with their peers in a German coffee shop had to show they knew and respected the mastery of Hegel. A marker today of cultural sophistication is a thinker's obeisance to the work of Charles Darwin, who was himself strongly influenced by the Hegelianism of European thought. The late Stephen Jay Gould (1941–2002) tried in various ways to correct and complicate the form of Darwinism that prevails in the popular, academic imagination in the late twentieth and now early twenty-first century.

As Gould notes, the way many people think of Darwinism is embedded in a notion of upward progress across the entire history of the world and, when applied to humans, is embedded in a notion that some human groups or individuals are more advanced at any particular point in time than other groups or individuals. When part of Western thought, this notion is often embedded in an account of how democratic capitalism will save the world. This is not the only possible reading of Darwinism, but it is the reading that is most useful for thinkers and writers hoping to promote any scheme for pushing human history onward and upward.

In his essay "Ladders and Cones: Constraining Evolution by Canonical Icons," Gould explains:

> The most serious and pervasive of all misconceptions about evolution equates the concept with some notion of progress, usually inherent and predictable, and leading to a human pinnacle. Yet neither evolutionary theory nor life's actual fossil record supports such an idea. Darwinian natural selection only produces adaptation to changing local environments, not any global scheme of progress. We can interpret local adaptation as "improvement" in a particular circumstance (the hairier elephant that becomes a woolly mammoth does better

---

10. For an illustration of Kierkegaard's indirect way of prompting each reader again to return to Jesus Christ, see the suggested reading at the end of this chapter.

in ice age climates), but a historical chain of sequential local adaptations does not accumulate to a story of continuous progress.[11]

Gould was not trying to correct specifically *Christian* Darwinism but simply to give all readers who consider themselves in allegiance with Darwin a perspective on the interpretive lenses they had balanced on their own noses, so to speak. He wanted to show how people using Darwin's thought had taken on a way of seeing the world that was not internal to Darwinism but was instead a way of interpreting the world through an interpretation of Darwinism.[12] Gould contended it was bad for scientists to be stuck seeing the detailed particularity of the earth through only this prism.

In the second half of the twentieth century, there was an ongoing debate between Jürgen Moltmann and Pierre Teilhard de Chardin on the compatibility of social Darwinism with Christianity that is a helpful supplement when read alongside Gould's essay. This debate addresses Christian Darwinism in particular, and it is an important corrective to different funding schemes to present a form of religiosity that is supposedly compatible with both traditional Christianity and "social biology."[13] Moltmann's *Nein!* to Teilhard's *Oui!* is a response that bears repeating, as social Darwinism reproduces itself today in different collectivist accounts of human and natural history.

Moltmann moves us forward from the nineteenth to the twentieth century, as mainstream Western theologians reckoned with the success of Darwinian Hegelianism. In his *Phenomenon of Man* (1955), Teilhard wrote an account of Christian eschatology that included natural selection and progressive evolution (from lower consciousness toward higher consciousness) in the story of God's salvation. Teilhard embedded the mechanisms popularly associated with Darwinism into an account of God's redemption of Israel and the nations.[14] German Reformed theologian Moltmann responded to this French Jesuit's synthesis repeatedly in his own account of Christian hope and the

11. Stephen Jay Gould, "Ladders and Cones: Constraining Evolution by Canonical Icons," in *Hidden Histories of Science*, ed. Robert B. Silvers (New York: New York Review of Books, 2003), 42–43.

12. For another, particularly Christian correction to social Darwinism, see Marilynne Robinson, *The Death of Adam* (New York: Houghton Mifflin, 1998). See especially the chapter "Darwinism," 28–75.

13. Here I mean to indicate some of the schemes and scholars funded by the Templeton Foundation or more recently the Gates Foundation, which present a purportedly Christian formulation of the world that is congenial to a Darwinist or social biological description of the human world.

14. Pierre Teilhard de Chardin, *The Phenomenon of Man*, trans. Bernard Wall (New York: Harper Perennial Modern Classics, 1959). It is worth noting that the foreword to the book was written by unrepentant eugenicist Julian Huxley.

future of the earth, refusing the confluence of this form of Darwinism and Christian eschatology:

> Evolution always means selection. Many living things are sacrificed in order that "the fittest"—which means the most effective and the most adaptable—may survive. In this way higher and increasingly complex life systems, which can react to changed environments, undoubtedly develop. But in the same process milliards of living things fall by the wayside and disappear into evolution's rubbish bin. Evolution is not merely a constructive affair on nature's part. It is a cruel one too. It is a kind of biological execution of the Last Judgment on the weak, the sick and the "unfit."[15]

Moltmann contends it is vital for Christians to testify explicitly against any worldview that presents human lives as "fertilizers" of a redeemed future.[16] As in the quotation at the start of this section, Moltmann witnesses against a story that solidifies a "struggle for existence" as the motor toward God's goodness, and he posits a fundamental "contradiction" in any form of Christian Darwinism that cannot be resolved. God "builds his coming kingdom of peace" with what Darwinism deems to be the flotsam and jetsam of the wave of progress: "out of the victims in the history of nature and the victims of human history" God makes a new world that does not cohere to what social Darwinism posits as the rules of scarcity, competition, and death.[17]

We may read Moltmann as refusing a system that would call Christians either to sacrifice themselves on the altar of divine progress or to fight for their place in a struggle toward a teleology of collective flourishing for the sake of future generations. Neither sacrifice nor victory is warranted to secure God's good future, because that job has been taken by Jesus Christ. As many Christians affirm weekly in the liturgy for the Lord's Supper, "Christ has died; Christ is risen; Christ will come again." God's "coming kingdom of peace" anchors hope in a different mode of thinking and living than the Darwinian socialist accounts of survival, sacrifice, and humanly wrought progress.[18]

15. Jürgen Moltmann, *The Way of Jesus Christ* (Minneapolis: Fortress, 1980), 294.
16. Ibid., 297.
17. Moltmann, *Sun of Righteousness*, 223.
18. One way to read Moltmann's warning against Teilhard is as a retrieval of the old "Nein" given to Hegel by Kierkegaard in 1843. See Søren Kierkegaard, *Fear and Trembling*, trans. Howard and Edna Hong (Princeton: Princeton University Press, 1983). I read forms of social Darwinism today in the United States to be both influenced by and to be influencing some forms of aspirational postmillennial Protestantism in the United States, from the Social Gospel movement during the Progressive Era (in the early twentieth century) to the supposedly neo-Calvinist movement "to change the world" led by James Davison Hunter of the University of Virginia. See James Davison Hunter, *To Change the World: The Irony, Tragedy, and Possibility*

One local example of how this debate about social Darwinism works within Christianity may help clarify the import of Moltmann's witness. Duke University is a school with an ambitious Methodist robber baron as its founder. The relationship between Duke University and the town of Durham, where most of the faculty and staff live, is complicated in many ways. One of those ways is the palpable Southern Christianity (both African-American and Anglo American) that endures in some areas.

The Duke administration sponsored a series on "Science, Religion, and Evolution" in 2006, and faculty across the university received a message from the university provost (our boss) specifically encouraging not only colleagues but also all staff to attend this important series.[19] By the estimation of many people on staff, it was an attempt to disabuse the locals of their backward ideas about religion and evolution. The series happened to fall the very same year that the "town" (Durham) and the "gown" (Duke) were embroiled in a human tragedy and convoluted media disaster known as the "Lacrosse Scandal." The story had divided Durham in ways that people were only beginning to sort, but one of the images that people used repeatedly about Duke, in conversation and in articles on the story, was "ivory tower."

Enter Daniel Dennett, philosopher and cognitive scientist, who came as part of the series to instruct the Duke community on "Darwin, Meaning, and Truth." The people gathering for his lecture made up a large group of scientists and nonscientists. I attended in part because I was concerned that staff members who were Christian or of other faiths were going to be depicted as ignorant and in need of correction. Toward the end of his lecture, Dennett showed a large slide of an indistinct item and asked the audience to guess what it was. People called out their best guesses: "A close-up of a tongue?" "A swarm of insects?" After a few more (incorrect) guesses, Dennett suggested we take a perspective from high above the earth and try again. After more incorrect guesses, Dennett explained that the image was a satellite photograph of "mammals gathered at the Ganges."

The image was a photo of people practicing the Hindu ritual of bathing in the Ganges. Dennett's lecture was in part on the evolution of religious practices, from "folk" religions to "sectarian" religions to religions that are open to Enlightenment principles and are explicitly tolerant of Western forms of science. In showing the satellite image of people practicing the Hindu ritual, he was

---

of *Christianity in the Late Modern World* (New York: Oxford University Press, 2010). For a classic from the earlier Social Gospel movement, see Walter Rauschenbusch, *Christianity and the Social Crisis in the 21st Century* (New York: HarperOne, 2008).

19. For more information about the series, see Robert J. Bliwise, "In Defense of Darwin," *Duke Magazine*, March–April 2006, dukemagazine.duke.edu/issues/030406/darwin-education1.html.

clearly proposing that we take a God's eye view, over and even against religious practices and the people who practice them. The only way to answer his question correctly was to see the individual people from a satellite perspective, blurred of their distinctive stories and particular faces. It was the worst sort of example of a detached, ivory tower perspective, and Dennett had embedded the superiority of exactly that way of seeing other human beings into his intellectual scheme.

Rituals of Allegiance to the Gods

I have kept in mind Dennett's perspective as I have thought about myrmecologist E. O. Wilson's work on humans as hive insects. But first, a pastoral reminder: God has God's eye on you, me, and the curious sparrow sitting here on my porch. And God has each of us in mind not so that we can be cast into the dross but so that we can be part of a heavenly banquet. Wilson's eyes are on insects (myrmecology being the study of ants), particularly hive insects that practice what is called eusociality.[20] Eusociality involves a set of humanly recorded behaviors that seem (to particular observers who use a particular language) to indicate (1) the perpetuation of newly hatched insects not directly genetically related to those tending them and (2) what scientists have termed "caste" systems of "governance." Wilson not only uses the words "caste" for nonhuman animals and "governance" for groups of bees and wasps, but he turns the terms back around to aver that termites, bees, ants, and wasps that exhibit non–genetically specific feeding systems, caste divisions, and hierarchical governance systems signal how functional human societies will conquer (over time) less eusocial groups of people.

In his candidly titled treatise *The Social Conquest of Earth* (2012), Wilson describes the social evolution toward such forms of human flourishing:

> Responsibility is divided among specialists, including soldiers, builders, clerks, and priests. With enough population and wealth, the public services of art, sciences, and education can be added—first for the benefit of the elite and then, trickling down, for the general public. The heads of state sit upon a throne, real or virtual. They ally themselves with the high priests, and clothe their authority with rituals of allegiance to the gods. The ascent to civilization, from egalitarian band and village to chiefdom to state, has occurred through cultural

20. In a review essay of Wilson's book *The Social Conquest of Earth*, science writer Natalie Angier offers a helpful, succinct definition of eusociality: "To qualify as eusocial, in Wilson's definition, animals must live in multigenerational communities, practice division of labor and behave altruistically, ready to sacrifice 'at least some of their personal interests to that of the group'" ("Cooperate or Die," *Smithsonian*, April 2012, 20).

evolution, not through changes in genes. It is a spring-loaded change, unfolding in a manner parallel to, but far grander than, the one propelling insect groups from aggregates to families, then to eusocial colonies with their castes and division of labor. . . . They may then continue to expand if they are able, ultimately blossoming into empires or fissioning into new, competing states. With larger size and farther reach comes greater complexity. And as with complexity of any physical or biological system, the society, in order to achieve stability and survive and not quickly crumble, must add hierarchical control.[21]

Wilson counts "hierarchical control" as a marker of "civilization itself" and "division of labor" as essential for "ascent" into societies that function as beautifully as the insect groups he has chosen as markers of excellence. "Allegiance to the gods" would presumably require, in such a society, reinforcing hierarchy and division of labor as part of liturgical (or, as he would put it, ritualistic) practice. Wilson makes it explicit that a civilized system that fails to reinforce the division of labor would experience dysfunction: "Hierarchies work better than unorganized assemblages. . . . Put another way, you cannot expect success if assembly-line workers vote at executive conferences or enlisted men plan military campaigns."[22]

The way that the sanctity of an individual human being is lost in such an account of human history may be apparent to some readers. As much as many of us appreciate the intricate beauty of ants or bees, to suggest human beings are at our best when we are like ants or bees seems to some people to be odd. To return to our opening passage and song, to compare me to a sparrow is to reverberate back and forth from bird to human being in a way that makes each one of us glisten with significance. While Jesus Christ often spoke in parable, this story is not the kind of story where the sparrow stands in for a human being, merely as a symbol. The point is that each feather is known and each hair is counted by God in a way that non-Christians might call "magical" and that Christians might describe as incalculable grace.

An extended section of another one of Wilson's popular books, *Consilience: The Unity of Knowledge*, displays how a human can become a matter of mere scientific interest. The passage requires repeating in order to convey Wilson's story of human beings in time. He asks readers to imagine a scenario that will clarify his particular way of seeing how people matter:

Five hundred miles southeast in Amazonian Peru lives Pablo Amaringo, mestizo shaman and artist. Drawing on the traditions of his Amerindian forebears . . . ,

21. E. O. Wilson, *The Social Conquest of Earth* (New York: Norton, 2012), 98.
22. Ibid., 99.

Amaringo conjures visions and depicts them in paintings. . . . Imagine that we
can speed or slow the time we spend with him, while expanding or shrinking the
space we see in and around his person. So we enter his house, we shake his hand,
and Amaringo shows us a painting. The actions consume seconds or minutes.
An obvious fact, so why mention it? The question makes more sense when put
in another form: Why did these familiar actions not consume millionths of
seconds, or months, instead? The answer is that human beings are constructed
of billions of cells that communicate across membranes by chemical surges
and electrical impulses. To see and speak with Amaringo entails a sequence
of these units covering seconds to minutes, not microseconds or months. We
think of that span of time as normal and somehow standard for the world in
which we live. It is not. Because it involves Amaringo and us, all of whom are
organic machines, it is only organismic time. . . . Imagine now that with the
best of our instruments (and his permission!) we can look into the brain of
Pablo Amaringo. . . . We are now in biochemical time. . . . Amaringo shrinks
in proportionate size and speed-walks jerkily out of the room, like an actor in
an early silent film. . . . Detached from other human beings and shorn of their
emotions, godlike at last, we witness the world in evolutionary time and space.[23]

The blurring of an actual individual like Pablo Amaringo into a symbol for a
group of people is problematic. He becomes, in Wilson's description, an example
of a person in an exotic area of the world perceived, without special descriptive
help, to be symbolically Edenic or prehistoric. So even though Pablo Amaringo
himself has emerged sufficiently out of the Peruvian boondocks to appear with
his art on Wikipedia, in Wilson's description he is still symbolic of an idea, not
an individual. This blurring of distinction involves a "godlike" form of vision
that, as Kara Slade and I have written elsewhere, is contrary to the gracious vision that is possible when human life is viewed liturgically. To view any person
as individually intricate and uniquely problematic is a gift of the Lord's Supper,
a gift possible as we perceive one another as of the same body that is a church.[24]

It is a symptom of Wilson's perception that he suggests not only that his
reader imagine recalibrating time so as to perceive this group of people in Peru
within the scope of evolution but also that his reader enter "into the brain" of
this person-as-symbol. As Wilson suggests that "a century of *their* time col-
lapses into a minute of *ours*," he has narrated himself and his readers into the
place of a skilled entomologist, viewing "them" as if they are beneath "us."

23. E. O. Wilson, *Consilience: The Unity of Knowledge* (New York: Vintage, 1999), 79–90.
I am indebted to Kara Slade for pointing out the importance of this passage for understanding
Wilson's impact on social biology and popular science today.
24. Kara Slade and Amy Laura Hall, "The Single Individual in Ordinary Time," *Studies in
Christian Ethics* 26 (February 2012): 66–82.

For Wilson, inasmuch as we are all moving toward a goal wrought by the great entomologist in the sky, creatures that are human are still somehow quasi-related. For our purposes in this chapter, I would add to the argument Kara Slade and I made elsewhere. In his account of the church as body in, for example, 1 Corinthians 12, Paul makes it clear that any arm that forgets to listen to a hand, ear, or foot is going about church all wrong. Christians should respond to Wilson that we long ago refused to see people in the way that he suggests people should be seen. Even though Christian caste systems survive in some way through honorifics of various sorts (on British Airways tickets or during academic processions), at our core we are to know that each of us receives the same gratuitous portion of the body of Christ at the Lord's Supper, and each ingests that body into our very particularly quirky, beset, blessed, and confused bodies.

In sum, Wilson's thought experiment fails on three counts. He suggests readers imagine themselves, first, outside of mortal time and space and, second, entering into another human being's brain. And finally, as a fancy, scientifically dressed-up version of the pop song lyrics by Julie Gold, he suggests readers can best understand another human being "from a distance," from a godlike vantage point. Whether Bette Midler or E. O. Wilson sings it, a story with a god who sees from a distance is about a different god than the God revealed in the flesh in Jesus Christ.[25]

Another social scientific theorist who has made himself indispensable is Jonathan Haidt. Haidt's TED talks are very popular; his books are best sellers; and his smiling image has reliably been the first result of a Google internet search on his last name. In other words, Haidt is not merely a public intellectual. He is now a celebrity, dispensing wisdom about human beings, morality, and happiness itself.

Haidt's opinion piece in the *New York Times* after the execution of Osama bin Laden, "Why We Celebrate a Killing," crystalizes well the idea that he and Wilson share about how human beings best function as a collective. The problem with the essay is the way Haidt describes the supposed wisdom of the crowd who surrounds and celebrates an execution as friends. He describes human love as a kind of cohesion of one group against another and human joy as the force reverberating within a group when it perceives itself to be more like a hive than like a gathering of individuals.

Here is an excerpt from Haidt's account of morality:

> Humans, far more than other primates, were shaped by natural selection acting at two different levels simultaneously. There's the lower level at which individuals

25. Julie Gold, "From a Distance," 1985.

compete relentlessly with other individuals within their own groups. This competition rewards selfishness. But there's also a higher level at which groups
compete with other groups. This competition favors groups that can best come
together and act as one. Only a few species have found a way to do this. Bees,
ants and termites are the best examples. Their brains and bodies are specialized
for working as a team to accomplish nearly miraculous feats of cooperation like
hive construction and group defense. . . . We have all the old selfish programming
of other primates, but we also have a more recent overlay that makes us able to
become, briefly, *hive creatures like bees*. . . . This two-layer psychology is the
key to understanding religion, warfare, team sports and last week's celebra-
tions. . . . America achieved its goal—bravely and decisively—after 10 painful
years. People who love their country sought out one another to share collective
effervescence. They stepped out of their petty and partisan selves and became,
briefly, just Americans rejoicing together.[26]

When read alongside Wilson's account of how people matter and how people
who think about thinking are best able to see rightly, this account of "love"
stands out. Wilson depicts tribal religion as functional inasmuch as religion
binds people together to accept and reinforce the systems that define them.
Haidt here explains that "10 painful years" are redeemed through what some
sociologists might describe as love. I contend that Christian readers should
be able to discern his essay as agitation propaganda. In other words, Haidt
describes humans at their best in a way that solidifies the celebration of a
nation-state and the aims of the nation-state.

     If a Christian writer suggested that even the crucifixion of Jesus was cause
for "joy," theologians would rightly ask whether the death of Jesus is so
quickly swept into the realm of "rejoicing" (much less the death of Osama
bin Laden). Christians who practice the liturgy of Lent do not use the word
"Alleluia" during those forty days. "Rejoicing" is rightly reserved for the season
of Eastertide, when Christians rejoice that death has been overcome, through
the resurrection of Jesus. Joy is reserved for the resurrection of the one and
only one who can redeem Peter, Saul, me, you, and my grandmothers, all of
us waiting for the time when Jesus returns. Haidt's description of religiosity
turns people into ants and bin Laden into a source of ritualistic joy. I suggest
his work is at best pagan, describing and prescribing rituals to other gods.

     In language borrowed from Scottish philosopher David Hume (1711–1776),
both Haidt and Wilson take what might be an "is" and turn it into an "ought."[27]

     26. Jonathan Haidt, "Why We Celebrate a Killing," *New York Times*, May 7, 2011, http://
www.nytimes.com/2011/05/08/opinion/08haidt.html, emphasis added. A similar analysis of
Haidt may be found in Slade and Hall, "Single Individual."
     27. David Hume, *A Treatise of Human Nature* (Garden City, NY: Doubleday, 1961).

It may be that groups of people sometimes resemble hive creatures. (There have been many scientists who have disagreed with Wilson and outright dismissed Haidt on that point alone.) But to turn that apparent observation into a virtue is to forget something as basic to Christians as the distinction between what we currently see around us and what we hope to see. Or, to put this in epistemological terms, both Haidt and Wilson cannot begin to speak to how Christians are called to see one another when together at the Lord's Supper. Neither can they begin to describe how Christians are to pray for and with people far away from the publishers who make Wilson and Haidt currently famous in US book-buying markets. This is a form of collectivism that Christians have countered and should continue to counter.

Hardwired to Connect—or Not?

The Institute on American Values published the book *Hardwired to Connect* in 2003 with proof that human beings need to create "Authoritative Communities" for the sake of our young. I have capitalized the A and the C in the term because the concept has become a way of thinking about parenting and childhood. (Theories about the best form of family and the best ways to form the optimal family have shifted often over time.) "Authoritative Communities" has become a term to describe the solution for families beset by everything from niche marketing by people like MTV founder Bob Pittman, to a currently increasing workday for men and women in the economic classes ranging from professional to working, to images of what any family is supposed to be like according to sources such as *Good Housekeeping* and *Better Homes and Gardens*.[28]

A popularized account of an Authoritative Community is the 2011 best seller by Amy Chua, *Battle Hymn of the Tiger Mother*.[29] The book describes for mothers in the United States why students in China continue to receive higher scores in state standardized tests for math, science, and musical precision than students in the United States. Chua does not talk about how the Chinese feudal system was tragically hierarchical and brutal. She does not discuss the way that a newly Maoist China divided families from one another

28. Commission on Children at Risk, *Hardwired to Connect: The New Scientific Case for Authoritative Communities* (New York: Institute for American Values, 2003). See also Kathleen Kovner Kline, ed., *Authoritative Communities: The Scientific Case for Nurturing the Whole Child* (Heidelberg, Germany: Springer, 2008).

29. Amy Chua, *Battle Hymn of the Tiger Mother* (New York: Penguin, 2011). See also Amy Chua and Jed Rubenfeld, *The Triple Package: How Three Unlikely Traits Explain the Rise and Fall of Cultural Groups in America* (New York: Penguin, 2014); and Peter D. Kiernan, *Becoming China's Bitch: And Nine More Catastrophes We Must Avoid Right Now* (Nashville: Turner, 2012).

and continues to dictate how many births families from different regions are allowed by law to have without punishment. She does not describe the way that the tyrannical Chinese government tests preschool children for aptitude in different forms of learning and then, as logistically and geographically possible, channels children into the rubbish or the specialized bin.

Chua's book plays on fears among mothers who worry that, in spite of their paying attention to every kind of optimal diet and optimal toilet training plan, and in spite of their taking off years of employment to follow these plans, their own children are going to be less secure financially than they or their parents were.

One year later Peter Kiernan was on the talk show circuit explaining his own best-selling book, *Becoming China's Bitch*. Taken together, the two books reach parents in the United States and explain why Chinese ways of raising children and disciplining workers are beating out mushy, nonauthoritative, liberal parenting and egalitarian management styles. Amy Chua and her husband, Jed Rubenfeld, published a sequel to *Tiger Mother* in 2014, *The Triple Package: How Three Unlikely Traits Explain the Rise and Fall of Cultural Groups in America*, describing why certain immigrant groups in the United States seem culturally conditioned to beat out competitors.

These books assume a functionalist account of human affection. I first learned the term "functionalist" when I was an undergraduate taking classes in sociology. I heard people I loved and a faith I loved described as either functional or dysfunctional, and Christianity was often on the dysfunctional side. But then, as I became a part of the faculty at Duke, I heard really smart people trying to make a case that "religion" is "functional" by some marker or another. I was and am still clear that families, friendship, and faith are not functional or dysfunctional by any reliable measure. As I suggested in the introduction to this chapter, Jesus did not prioritize human beings according to their functionality. But Amy Chua and Jed Rubenfeld have done so in their popular books. "Communities" that foster obedience and success are good inasmuch as they foster obedience and success.

The logic of their work is both circular and insular, defining as good those systems that reinforce the definition of good with which they are working and including as good those systems that see other people as competitors rather than neighbors or even friends. These studies, books, and warnings currently abound. There are many highlighted voices on TED talks and on the shelves of the few remaining brick and mortar bookstores about fear of losing in an economically competitive and brutally violent time. These best-selling gurus of parenting and economics use a logic of scarcity and competition that renders human beings very much like groups of insects vying to stake out territory for our eggs.

The scriptural passages that most come to my mind as students bring me books like *Becoming China's Bitch* are those in which Jesus warns his disciples against trying to discern the signs of the end times. Does the charge to keep your wick burning mean you need to sort the price of oil first? And what if the servant next to you misunderstands the master's charge and buries his talents? How do you prioritize searching for the lost coin if you do not know how much a coin is actually worth in relation to a Chinese yuan? These parables from the New Testament have been so wrongly interpreted over the last two centuries in the United States that it is hard to remember that Jesus mocked the Roman Empire by telling complicated puzzles to create a thirst for the good news. If God's eye is on the sparrow, then the logic of how much the sparrow is worth in the global economy seems very clearly not the point. God's eye is on the sparrow.

There is another, even more problematic wing to this body of literature on authority and personhood. The authors do not write best-selling books. Instead they receive funding for their studies, which may in turn encourage funding for future best-selling books. In numerous publications, Hazel Rose Markus and Shinobu Kitayama contrast "Western" ways of perceiving "the self" with "Asian" ways of perceiving people. Markus and Kitayama write articles with charts and graphs rather than with Chua's form of mommy-blog narrative. I am not doing disservice to their narrative style by explaining their work in a less rhetorically subtle form.

According to Markus and Kitayama, there are groups of people who believe in a "construal of the self as independent" and people who believe in a "construal of the self as interdependent." They write that "these construals can influence, and in many cases determine, the very nature of individual experience, including cognition, emotion, and motivation." They open one essay with this: "In America, 'the squeaky wheel gets the grease.' In Japan, 'the nail that stands out gets pounded down.'" These are the kind of "anecdotes" that Markus and Kitayama seek to document and explain using social psychological research for abiding differences between Asians and Western Europeans. Acknowledging that "the self" is a "delicate category" to try to investigate, the authors make such generalizations. According to Markus and Kitayama, in the West "there is a faith in the inherent separateness of distinct persons," whereas in the East responsiveness to others is a matter of "strategically" gauging one's options "to express or assert the internal attributes of the self."[30]

Quoting research from as far back as 1946, the authors contend that "in Chinese culture, for instance, there is an emphasis on synthesizing the constituent

---

30. Hazel Rose Markus and Shinobu Kitayama, "Culture and the Self: Implications for Cognition, Emotion, and Motivation," *Psychological Review* 98 (1991): 224–53.

parts of any problem or situation into an integrated or harmonious whole" and that "persons are only parts that when separated from the larger social whole cannot be fully understood." Markus and Kitayama quote other studies that contrast Western with non-Western peoples, for example, describing the "importance of simpatico among Hispanics" and noting that "Thais place a premium on self-effacement, humility, deference and on trying not to disturb others." Groups within "American culture" who test as more non-Western are deemed part of "subcultures" like "the Quakers."[31]

This extended, well-funded, and ostensibly scholarly effort to contrast Asian and Western ways of seeing the world reminds me very much of the literature I have read from Germany during the Third Reich. During Hitler's rise to power, a whole apparatus of science and popular writings encouraged humans to see one another not only as of a different sort but of a different kind of human. A marker of the difference in species was the way that a group of people thought about and reckoned people in relation to money.

The ways that people are divided into categories is so crude in the literature today about Western and non-Western people that I lately have wondered about the academic standards in the social sciences. In one extended passage on the contrasting etiquette of making a sandwich for a friend from another culture, Joan Y. Chiao and Katherine Blizinsky inadvertently display precisely the problem with all of these generalizations about "Asian" and "Western" people. They try to explain other people's ideas of themselves using generalizations that collapse distinctions between particular individuals in a group. To promote the idea that there is a quantity called "Asian" and an "Asian" way of being a self in the world is to make a research sandwich out of someone else's reality.

And here is the kicker: Chiao and Blizinsky are using what they call "neuroscience" to show that "collectivistic cultural values" are actually written into the "gene coevolution of human brain and behavior," so that Asian peoples are, due to an interaction of genetics and cultural adaptation, more naturally suited to "collectivistic cultures." To borrow a phrase from the Institute on American Values, Asians are depicted as quite concretely "hard-wired to connect." They write, "Our findings illustrate that gene frequency plays a unique role in explaining global variation in the adoption of cultural norms and is fundamental to any comprehensive understanding of culture." Certain genetically similar people are adapted so that they are interested in "maintaining social harmony."[32]

I contend that the kind of social science going on in such research is not to be used but refused by Christians hoping to begin the arduous work of forming

31. Ibid.
32. Joan Y. Chiao and Katherine D. Blizinsky, "Culture-Gene Coevolution of Individualism-Collectivism and the Serotonin Transporter Gene," *Proceedings of the Royal Society, Biological Sciences* 277 (2010): 529–37.

friendships across cultural divides in the name of Jesus Christ. I contend that this is precisely the sort of mishmash of cultural hegemony, hubris, and plain stupidity that had missionaries from the West paving literal highways across the continent of Asia. Under this social scientific, neurobiological framework, Maoism is a hereditary trait rather than a grand, brutal, and geopolitical lie.

Any discourse that puts itself above other human beings is most likely off-kilter, overly optimistic, and lacking in eschatological humility. Again, this is a form of collectivism. If God's eye is on the sparrow, then who are humans to try to determine how to see other human beings, as if we were scientists dissecting sparrows or mapping an ant hill? To bring this section full circle, it seems a very bad way to raise a child to encourage her to learn the skills to survive in a struggle of ant against ant or queen bee against queen bee. This cannot be how God intends Christians to think about one another as we look at our children, ourselves, our neighbors, and the people who appear on the television morning show to talk about standardized testing and our inadequate showing as this or that demographic in the latest tallying of excellence or failure.

The Inner Ring

In addition to being a Christian ethicist, I am a Methodist minister who has inadvertently specialized in hearing the stories of people who are two generations older than I am. I was called to the ministry while serving shut-ins on the membership list for two Methodist churches in Texas and Connecticut. If you go to visit people who cannot easily move about and who have a Christian heritage, and if you convey genuine care for them, they will tell you stories. It did not hurt that I brought to my ministry many stories from my grandfather and his beloved wife, my grandmother, about the ways that war functions in the United States.

Robert Strange McNamara was high above my grandfather in the chain of official command. He legitimized the war in Asia that followed long after World War II, and during World War II itself was the strategist responsible for the plan to firebomb Japanese cities. The strategy kept Allied military casualties low and killed 100,000 people in Tokyo in one night and an estimated 350,000 civilians in one year. When asked specifically by Errol Morris in *The Fog of War* about the rationale for firebombing Japanese cities, McNamara says something that has remained with me since I first watched the film in 2003: "Well, I was part of a mechanism that in a sense recommended it." He understands himself to have been part of a *mechanism*. Later in the film,

McNamara surmises that both he and General Curtis LeMay would have been tried as war criminals had the Allied forces not won the war. He says this without cynicism but with a sense of what might be called moral realism.

Using C. S. Lewis's essay "The Inner Ring," I here explain how a sense of an inner circle—a form of collectivism—may have been just the poison to control and dehumanize a whiz kid like McNamara. McNamara was "part of a mechanism" that encouraged men to believe themselves in a category above mutual accountability. I want to give words for a hope in individual salvation through Jesus Christ that is not only crucial for my otherwise anonymous late grandmothers and late grandfather but also for a notorious architect of war like McNamara. God's eye is on the sparrow, even on the sparrow who mistakes himself for a hawk.

Lewis originally wrote his essay as an address from a "middle age moralist" to a group of students at King's College, London, in 1944.[33] Lewis was part of the famed Inklings, a literary circle so beloved by Western Christians that the pub in Oxford, England, where they went to talk serves now as a mecca of Christian friendship. His essay has turns of phrase as he describes a mutually deluding process of exclusion and encirclement:

> There are no formal admissions or expulsions. People think they are in it after they have in fact been pushed out of it, or before they have been allowed in: this provides great amusement for those who are really inside. It has no fixed name. The only certain rule is that the insiders and outsiders call it by different names. And you will be drawn in, if you are drawn in, not by desire for gain or ease, but simply because at that moment, when the cup was so near your lips, you cannot bear to be thrust back again into the cold outer world. It would be so terrible to see the other man's face—that genial, confidential, delightfully sophisticated face—turn suddenly cold and contemptuous, to know that you had been tried for the Inner Ring and rejected. And then, if you are drawn in, next week it will be something a little further from the rules, and next year something further still, but all in the jolliest, friendliest spirit. It may end in a crash, a scandal, and penal servitude; it may end in millions, a peerage and giving the prizes at your old school. But you will be a scoundrel. Of all the passions, the passion for the Inner Ring is most skillful in making a man who is not yet a very bad man do very bad things.[34]

McNamara was also part of a kind of inner circle called the Whiz Kids. In *The Fog of War*, filmmaker Errol Morris overlays images of intelligence-testing

33. C. S. Lewis, "The Inner Ring," in *The Weight of Glory: And Other Addresses* (New York: Macmillan, 1949), 141–57. (Also available online: http://www.lewissociety.org/innerring.php.)
34. Ibid., 154.

scan sheets running through a large computer with the audio of McNamara's recollections. McNamara recounts with amusement being chosen as an elite statistician during World War II, remembering that he and his colleagues were deemed the "best and the brightest" of their generation. After the war, a group of them went on to reestablish the faltering Ford Motor Company.

From teaching *The Fog of War* for a decade, I have come to appreciate how Morris was able simultaneously to narrate particulars of geopolitics during World War II and the Cold War, while eliciting from McNamara glimmers of his singular conscience. Historians have noted that McNamara flat out lies at certain points in the film, but the viewer cannot discern with any certainty whether McNamara is lying to himself or to the camera. Memory is a tricky business, and confession is a trickier task. What strikes me most each time I watch and teach the film is the question of McNamara's capacity to confess. When faced with the direct question of his responsibility for targeting civilians through firebombing in Japan, McNamara notes that he was part of a "mechanism." He names outright the way that a human being can be individually distinct as a person but also part of a larger regime that renders him a tool.

This is the form of collectivism that should trouble people—Christians in particular—throughout our lives. How do any of us become part of a mechanism that recommends killing civilians? How do any of us become part of a mechanism that describes our own children as combatants in an economic war or a conventional or unconventional war? How does a mother raise her child to resist a story about a state of perpetual conflict? How does the assumption of scarcity and competition shape our perceptions of baptism or the Lord's Supper?

I want to ask with Lewis how inner circles of individuals are encouraged to see one another as set apart for something through their quantifiable gifts in such a way that they are paradoxically rendered machinery for the future of a larger, national or international economic or cultural project. Morris depicts this starkly with the imagery of the intelligence tests rolling through the computer but also later in a visual where numbers fall through the sky like bombs onto maps showing cities where human beings were incinerated using the statistical analysis of war. McNamara seems to believe that he and others with him were guilty of crimes of war. He also suggests that this guilt is blurred by their participation in a larger project, beyond their individual accountability.

In closing, I return to the hymn with which we started. I thank God that it is not my responsibility to reckon with McNamara's guilt or innocence. It might have been the responsibility of a judge at the United Nations, should he and General LeMay actually have been held accountable for the firebombing of Japan. But their and my final reckoning involves a logic that is incalculable and qualitatively different than human computation. It is a world of knowing and not knowing that Christians practice each week through the means of grace at worship and each year through the repetition of Advent to Ordinary Time to Lent to Ordinary Time to Advent. Lewis's address to the young men in 1944 depends on the possibility of their recognition that something is awry when human beings believe themselves set apart, individually distinct through their human traits to be responsible for pushing human history forward up the hill toward the kingdom. Lewis's appeal depends on a residual conscience existing in the midst of his particular hearers.

McNamara's own narrative breaks apart at points. Students often note that he sheds tears at moments in his story that seem almost nonsensical given the scope of what he has seen and what he has wrought in his lifetime. Rather different is Morris's more recent endeavor, an interview with Donald Rumsfeld.[35] Nevertheless, for all such set-apart men, trained to see themselves as gifted for the sake of national security, it may someday come as good news that the hairs on their head have been counted, and counted with a calculus that will make no sense at all in the world they have known. As Lewis explains, "The true road lies in quite another direction."[36]

Unscientific Postscript

I am writing this chapter on collectivism for a book on why people matter during the adventurous season of Advent. Advent is corporate and individual, meaning it is about the salvation of a chosen people and the salvation of you and me as each uniquely chosen and precious children of God. I have been thinking in new ways about what the individual part of Advent means.

While I was teaching at Central Men's Prison in Raleigh two years ago, one of the men said to the group that he hopes he still has himself intact when he is finally out. In other words, he hopes he still has a self left after so many years in a place that can suck the life right out of each man, whether inmate or guard. God gave me a vision there in that room that has stayed with me since. The Old Testament prophet Ezekiel saw a vision of dry bones being knit back together, sinew by sinew (Ezek. 37). Ezekiel knew this was about God's people Israel being knit back together as a people after horrible desolation by their enemies. When the student in prison spoke his words to the group,

35. *The Unknown Known*, directed by Errol Morris (Anchor Bay, 2014), DVD.
36. Lewis, "Inner Ring," 157.

I had a vision of each of us there, waiting for God to eventually knit back together our individual lives and individual souls. If God could bring those dry bones Ezekiel saw back to life, then maybe God can bring a dismembered self back to life today. I believe it is possible for the man still in prison, for my grandmother, for my grandfather, for Robert McNamara, for E. O. Wilson and Jonathan Haidt, for all the scholars writing about patterns of ethnicity, for Amy Chua, and for me.

Further Reading

Kierkegaard, Søren. *Works of Love*. New York: HarperCollins, 2009.
> Written as a response to the collectivist thinking of Hegel, this profound examination of the nature and importance of love has spoken for generations to other forms of collectivist thinking as well.

Lewis, C. S. "The Inner Ring." In *The Weight of Glory: And Other Addresses*, 141–57. New York: Macmillan, 1949. Available online at http://www.lewissociety.org/innerring.php.
> In this essay Lewis explores the delusional and corrupting idea that there is some sort of inner circle that one must be a part of in order for one's efforts in life to amount to anything.

Moltmann, Jürgen. *Sun of Righteousness, Arise! God's Future for Humanity and the Earth*. Minneapolis: Fortress, 2010.
> Moltmann explains that out of the victims in natural and human history, God makes a new world that does not cohere to what social Darwinism posits as the rules of scarcity, competition, and death.

Robinson, Marilynne. *The Death of Adam*. New York: Houghton Mifflin, 1998.
> This is a particularly Christian correction to social Darwinism—especially its chapter that bears the title "Darwinism."

Slade, Kara, and Amy Laura Hall. "The Single Individual in Ordinary Time." *Studies in Christian Ethics* 26 (February 2012): 66–82.
> The blurring of distinction between particular individuals and symbolic types of people, note Slade and Hall, involves a godlike form of vision that is contrary to the gracious vision that sees each person as individually intricate and uniquely problematic.

My Life Is Not My Own

Individualism and Human Significance

RUSSELL DiSILVESTRO

I think we finally have to say that Jesus' enduring relevance is based on his historically proven ability to speak to, to heal and empower the individual human condition.

—Dallas Willard

If individuals live only seventy years, then a state, or a nation, or a civilisation, which may last for a thousand years, is more important than an individual. But if Christianity is true, then the individual is not only more important but incomparably more important, for he is everlasting and the life of a state or a civilisation, compared with his, is only a moment.

—C. S. Lewis

At the heart of liberty is the right to define one's own concept of existence, of meaning, of the universe, and of the mystery of human life.

—Anthony Kennedy

There are many ways to value human individuals, as the above epigraphs illustrate. But there is a difference between valuing human individuals and reducing everything of value to them. The latter is what constitutes individualism. The *ism* here signifies that only that thing ultimately matters. And that reduction is precisely where the problems with individualism begin. This chapter focuses on individualism and especially its attempt to account for the widely shared intuition that people matter, that human life is significant. The individualism in view here is a postmodern autonomy approach, according to which people determine what they think is right (for them) by considering their own values and preferences in the absence of any objective truths or binding standards. Applied to the widely shared intuition that people matter, such individualism is the attempt to find human significance in a world where the self's own perspectives, values, and desires are the focus of existence.

This individualistic outlook is so widespread that it is familiar to most people. There is no need to credit (or blame) any particular thinkers or academic movements for its influence,[1] as such individualism is a current of thought that reflects a perennial human tendency dating back millennia: "In those days there was no king in Israel; everyone did what was right in his own eyes" (Judg. 21:25 NASB). Yet this way of viewing things has become especially influential in our postmodern era. It functions as a default philosophy of life for many people in contemporary Western democracies like the United States. One can find it in popular magazines, newspapers, and websites; in court opinions, university policies, and even church pulpits; in family, friends, and even oneself. Indeed, each of us can observe it whenever we prioritize our own self-interest.

In the remainder of this chapter, I begin with a careful description of the individualistic approach to life and an explanation of its appeal to so many people. I then explore some of individualism's weaknesses, both those that are recognizable without relying on distinctively Christian knowledge and those best seen from the vantage point of such knowledge. Finally, I discuss individualism's valid insights that a mature Christian approach should affirm. Along the way, we shall be sensitive to the difference between the proper significance of the individual—part of any adequate biblical outlook on human persons, as the epigraphs from Willard and Lewis illustrate—and the narrowness of individual*ism*. In the latter, the importance of the social or communal and ironically even the values of other individuals get underappreciated or lost entirely.

1. For a seminal discussion of where the influence might come from, see Robert Bellah, Richard Madsen, William M. Sullivan, Ann Swidler, and Steven M. Tipton, *Habits of the Heart: Individualism and Commitment in American Life* (Berkeley: University of California Press, 1985; updated with a new introduction, 1996).

People Matter—Because They Say So?

Consider first how individualism—the postmodern autonomy approach—accounts for the widely shared intuition that "people matter" or that "human life is significant." While individualism can be described more broadly as an approach to different branches of moral philosophy such as the theory of obligation ("what is my duty?") and the theory of value ("what is truly good?"), here we will explore how individualism accounts for the intuition that people matter in two more specific areas: (1) the moral status of human persons and (2) the meaning of human life.

The concept of moral status has been analyzed in recent work by Mary Anne Warren[2] and Elizabeth Harman,[3] but the basic idea is familiar because most of us are strongly predisposed to think that we have moral status. If something has moral status, that is a strong and standing reason not to harm or wrong it but to give it respect, justice, or benefit when we can.[4]

The concept of the meaning of life is nicely illustrated by the opening words of the Westminster Shorter Catechism:

Q. What is the chief end of man?

A. Man's chief end is to glorify God, and to enjoy him forever.[5]

The intuition that people have a "chief end" of some sort is connected to several influential approaches to the meaning of life, as philosopher Thaddeus Metz notices:

Many major historical figures in philosophy have provided an answer to the question of what, if anything, makes life meaningful, although they typically have not put it in these terms. Consider, for instance, Aristotle on the human function, Aquinas on the beatific vision, and Kant on the highest good. While

---

2. Mary Anne Warren, *Moral Status: Obligations to Persons and Other Living Things* (Oxford: Clarendon, 1997), 3: "If an entity has moral status, then we may not treat it in just any way we please; we are morally obliged to give weight in our deliberations to its needs, interests, or well-being."

3. Elizabeth Harman, "The Potentiality Problem," *Philosophical Studies* 114 (2003): 174. She offers the following illustration: "There are reasons not to harm both Alice and her car; but only Alice has moral status. Harms to Alice provide reasons against action simply in virtue of being harms to her. But harms to Alice's car provide reasons against action only in virtue of being harms to Alice."

4. This idea is adapted from Russell DiSilvestro, *Human Capacities and Moral Status* (Dordrecht, Netherlands: Springer, 2010), 12.

5. See Joel R. Beeke and Sinclair B. Ferguson, eds., *Reformed Confessions Harmonized* (Grand Rapids: Baker, 1999), 3; also online at http://www.creeds.net/Westminster/shorter _catechism.html.

these concepts have some bearing on happiness and morality, they are straight-forwardly construed as accounts of which *final ends* a person ought to realize in order to have a life that matters.[6]

The concept of the meaning of life, as the catechism and these philosophers agree, can be understood as the claim that an individual has a point, purpose, or "end" to life.

As stated above, individualism is essentially the postmodern autonomy approach according to which people determine what they think is right (for them) by considering their own values and preferences in the absence of any objective truths or binding standards. According to individualism, the perspectives, values, and desires of individual persons determine what is meaningful, significant, valuable, good, and right for those individual persons—whether it is a small part of life (like yesterday's breakfast) or the whole of it (one's entire life or very existence).

Concerning moral status, individualism turns out to be a kind of relativism. One's life has the moral status that one personally gives it—regardless of what one's culture or any group one belongs to says. Concerning the meaning of life, individualism turns out to be the sort of view that Metz classifies as subjectivism. The way individualism asks and answers questions about the meaning of life, in contrast to the Westminster Shorter Catechism, is nicely illustrated in a short scene from the 1991 movie *City Slickers*, a comedy in which Mitch and two friends agree to process their midlife crises by taking a two-week cattle drive with a tough old trail boss named Curly:

> CURLY. Do you know what the secret of life is? (*Holds up one finger.*) This.
> MITCH. Your finger?
> CURLY. One thing. Just one thing. You stick to that and the rest don't [matter].
> MITCH. But, what is the "one thing"?
> CURLY. (*Smiles.*) That's what *you* have to find out.[7]

The message is straightforward: the meaning or "secret" of human life is different for each individual, and it can only be discovered by each individual. Metz notes that in philosophy "some of the most widely read texts" that purport to be about the meaning of life are "subjectivist" approaches, including "Jean-Paul Sartre's . . . existentialist account of meaning being constituted

---

6. Thaddeus Metz, "The Meaning of Life," in *Stanford Encyclopedia of Philosophy*, last revision June 3, 2013, http://plato.stanford.edu/entries/life-meaning/, emphasis added.

7. Lowell Ganz and Babaloo Mandel, *City Slickers*, directed by Ron Underwood (Castle Rock Entertainment, 1991), DVD; see http://www.imdb.com/title/tt0101587/quotes.

by whatever one chooses" and "Richard Taylor's . . . discussion of Sisyphus being able to acquire meaning in his life merely by having his strongest desires satisfied."[8] The common denominator of subjectivist views, Metz claims, is that "there are no invariant standards of meaning because meaning is relative to the subject, i.e., depends on an individual's pro-attitudes such as desires, ends, and choices. Roughly, something is meaningful for a person if she believes it to be or seeks it out."[9]

Regarding both moral status and meaning in life, then, individualism accents the autonomy of the individual. It emphasizes the self-rule or self-government of each human person: life's meaning and moral status is not what others—country, family, neighbors, God—say it is but what the individual says it is. And individualism is postmodern because it contrasts with earlier modern approaches in the history of Western culture. Thinkers like René Descartes, John Locke, and the authors of the American Declaration of Independence were optimistic that human reason or experience could discover the contents of morality and the meaning of human life by grounding them in what is objectively true—natural properties or supernatural realities: "We hold these truths to be self-evident, that all men are created equal, that they are endowed by their Creator with certain inalienable rights, that among these are life, liberty, and the pursuit of happiness." But the individualism in focus here avoids the modern project—sometimes consciously, sometimes not—and takes instead what might seem like the shortcut of grounding meaning and moral status in each person's individual perspective.[10]

The Appeal of Individualism

It is revealing to consider individualism's appeal in relation to the outlooks discussed in other chapters of this book: utilitarianism, collectivism, naturalism, and transhumanism. While such comparisons in this section must be selective and schematic, we shall consider them before exploring further reasons why individualism may appeal to many.

Utilitarianism and individualism might seem to be natural allies (especially if utilitarianism's "greatest good for the greatest number" is understood in terms of the subjective values and preferences of individuals), but individualism

8. Metz, "Meaning of Life."
9. Ibid.
10. A recent discussion of how modern thinkers like Locke and Kant approached "why people matter" compared to how postmodern thinkers like Nietzsche approached it is found in David P. Gushee, *The Sacredness of Human Life: Why an Ancient Biblical Vision Is Key to the World's Future* (Grand Rapids: Eerdmans, 2013), chaps. 7–8.

may appeal to some by giving the individual presidential veto power when confronted with the demands of the moral legislature. If the moral law (on the utilitarian picture) makes demands to an agent—"Do more!" or "Sacrifice up to and including your very life!"—the individualist can always uphold her individuality against the assertions of the greater good. Individualism allows one to value her own life and the lives of her associates without regard to how they contribute to some impersonal aggregate goodness.

Against collectivism, individualism asserts the moral priority of the agent. While it is fine for one to enter into various collectives (marriage, family, church, state, and so on), what determines the relative investment appropriate to each is one's own preferences and values. So any move that would automatically trump the smaller groups (e.g., family) for the benefit of the larger (e.g., nation) is blocked, as is any move that would automatically trump the individual herself for the benefit of a group of any size.

The appeal of individualism over naturalism can be seen in a thought experiment. As John Lennon requested, imagine that there is no heaven—or in other words, that naturalism is true—and that objective values might therefore be nothing more than a prescientific illusion. In such a scenario, would you then conclude that none of your values gave your life any purpose, point, or value? Or would you rather seek to treasure the values—family, friends, work, health, Beatles music—that still remain? If you choose the latter, then you understand the appeal of individualism: it offers a subjective fallback position for a naturalist who is disturbed by the (supposed) lack of objective value in a world (supposedly) void of God. As the popularity of Jean-Paul Sartre's existentialism suggests, the individual-and-her-values approach may be the most appealing option in a world without God.[11]

Finally, individualism might seem to accommodate the common human desire to overcome many normal human limitations, which drives the transhumanist outlook. After all, who has not wished at one time to be able to sleep less, jump higher, think faster, or love God and neighbor more faithfully? But individualism also provides a rebuke to those elements of transhumanism that can appear to support leaving behind all human desires themselves. According to individualism, if you personally desire or value something that does not fit into the transhumanist project, that is the transhumanist's problem, not yours.

Beyond these comparative appeals of individualism over other outlooks, there are at least six additional explanations for why individualism is so

11. Jean-Paul Sartre, *Existentialism Is a Humanism*, trans. P. Mairet (London: Methuen & Co., 1948). For a recent survey of what naturalists can best argue for here, see Erik J. Wielenberg, *Value and Virtue in a Godless Universe* (Cambridge: Cambridge University Press, 2005).

appealing to so many people. First, if we honestly reflect on what makes our own life meaningful, many of us think about things we desire, prefer, or value. I think about my family, friends, job, church, and sense of calling or vocation. I think about love of God and neighbor. It is somewhat natural to think that my subjective states toward these objects—desiring, preferring, or valuing them—is what makes my life meaningful, enjoyable, or significant.

An illustration makes the second point. Imagine an older family man who brings his wife and adult son with him to receive a diagnosis from his oncologist. The news is disheartening. The oncologist diagnoses the man with a certain type of cancer and presents him with three options: treatment A, treatment B, or watch and wait. Immediately his wife begins lobbying hard for treatment A: it offers the best likelihood of survival. His son interrupts with a hard sell for treatment B: it is less invasive, and the reported quality-of-life for those who undergo it is better despite a shorter projected life expectancy. The oncologist jumps in with his own strong recommendation to watch and wait: it is the most commonly recommended and accepted of the three options. Eventually the man raises his hand and asks: "Excuse me, but is there any room in this discussion for asking what the patient prefers?"

Such a situation might elicit the reaction: of course there is room for what the patient prefers—indeed, it may even be the most important, decisive factor that trumps all else. After all, the patient's own life is at stake here. And who but the patient is in a position to know what his life is worth to him? He is in the best—and perhaps only—position to rank the different possible outcomes (e.g., shorter life with higher quality or longer life with lower quality) according to his own perspective, values, and desires. It has not always been this way. A more paternalistic, beneficence-focused ethic was dominant for a long time in medicine. But many people believe that the shift toward greater respect for the patient's own values has been on balance a morally good one. Even outside the medical context, many believe that no one but the one living a given life is in sufficient proximity to know what it is really like to live that life—nor knows what matters most for that life.

A third point builds on this: some of individualism's appeal comes from its apparent affinity with a kind of political protection of the individual. Consider these lines from a famous 1978 court case in which a judge refused to order a man to donate bone marrow to his cousin:

> Our society, contrary to many others, has as its first principle, the respect for the individual, and that society and government exist to protect the individual from being invaded and hurt by another. . . . For our law to compel the defendant to submit to an intrusion of his body would change the very concept and

principle upon which our society is founded. To do so would defeat the sanctity
of the individual, and would impose a rule which would know no limits, and
one could not imagine where the line would be drawn.[12]

The individualist might ask here: What else besides individualism resonates
with (and indeed reinforces) this political prioritization of the individual?
Individualism loudly and confidently proclaims an adaptation of the Texas
slogan: "Don't mess with individuals!"

Relatedly, individualism may appear to be the best or only hope for securing
autonomy for individuals that adequately parallels the autonomy of states
or other types of collectives. Consider philosopher Sarah Buss's statements
regarding the parallel between political and personal autonomy:

> When people living in some region of the world declare that their group has
> the right to live autonomously, they are saying that they ought to be allowed
> to govern themselves. In making this claim, they are, in essence, rejecting the
> political and legal authority of those not in their group. . . . When an individual
> makes a similar declaration about some sphere of her own life, she, too, is
> denying that anyone else has the authority to control her activity within this
> sphere; she is saying that any exercise of power over this activity is illegitimate
> unless she authorizes it herself.[13]

It is not difficult to see how such individualism might fit well with political
or economic systems committed to letting individuals make free choices as
citizens or consumers. A basic philosophy of individual self-governance is both
a cause and an effect of more liberal institutions. Individualism reflects the
fact that individual desires, values, and preferences often differ from person
to person. Even a single individual's preferences can change over time, and
individualism allows for these changes as well.

Fourth, individualism is able to counter several unsatisfactory approaches
with which it is sometimes confused. For example, individualism is not necessarily attached to ethical egoism (doing whatever advances one's self-interest)
or ethical hedonism (doing whatever feels good). An individual may have
desires (e.g., to be healthy), preferences (e.g., to be courageous rather than
cowardly), and values (e.g., being faithful to one's spouse) that require giving
up what looks self-interested or what feels good in both the immediate moment
and over the course of one's life. What is important for individualism is that

12. McFall v. Shimp, 10 Pa. D. & C. 3d 90 (1978).
13. Sarah Buss, "Personal Autonomy," in *Stanford Encyclopedia of Philosophy*, last revision
June 10, 2013, http://plato.stanford.edu/entries/personal-autonomy.

the significance of one's life is in some way grounded in one's own complex psychological states—desires, preferences, values. Individualism is compatible with egoism and hedonism, but it is also compatible with their opposites.

Fifth, consider the appeal of a wrinkle within individualism for those who deny all objective truth: if all people share the same value, then there is a "truth" or standard that is binding on all persons. But it would not be an objective truth or standard; it would still be subjective. It would be right for me because it fits my values, and right for you because it fits your values. Its fit with both of our sets of values would not increase its rightness for either of us but would merely be a happy coincidence.

Sixth, individualism is a form of moral relativism that easily avoids a glaring drawback of cultural/group relativism. According to cultural/group relativism, right and wrong are whatever some group (or its majority portion) says they are. If what is right for me is relative to whatever culture/group I am a part of (as with the slogan "When in Rome, do as the Romans do"), then the norms of the relevant culture determine what is right for me to do, no matter what my own individual values may say. If I am horrified by slavery and think it is morally repugnant, cultural relativism does not notice or care. If the relevant culture says that owning and beating another human being as a slave is morally permissible (or even obligatory), then it is morally permissible (or obligatory) for me. Individualism firmly challenges this obligation. Its focus on and indeed prioritization of the individual prohibits the culture or group from trumping personal values.

In sum, just as American democracy is sometimes described as a government of, by, and for the people, so also individualism seeks to be a theory of, by, and for human individuals. But can individualism accomplish this in a satisfactory way? There are many reasons to think not.

Non-Christian Critiques of Individualism

While I have attempted to identify the most appealing features of individualism above, the truth is that its weaknesses are far greater and more numerous. This section will consider weaknesses that depend on no specifically Christian assumptions; the next will examine overtly Christian critiques.

As noted above, in individualism the importance of the social or communal (and ironically the values of other individuals) gets underappreciated or lost entirely. To explain why this is so, we will first explore some weaknesses of individualism in relation to other outlooks discussed in this book before moving on to some distinctive internal weaknesses.

Utilitarianism often appears at its strongest when it emphasizes impartiality (e.g., that each person is to count for one, and none are to count for more than one) and beneficence (e.g., that we have duties to aid others, prevent some harms, and promote some goods). But individualism will not accept either impartiality or beneficence as binding on an individual agent unless and until that individual agent authorizes or values such things herself. This seems to utilitarians (and many others) to get things precisely backward. That you owe others a certain regard seems to be the basis for thinking you ought to care for and value them—not the other way around.

Collectivism too urges duties toward the group(s) one is part of—whether we want them or not. Your duties to care for your aged parents, help your brother load up his moving van, support your troops, and donate to your church are duties that appear to exist prior to you wanting them. More generally, if I value my life dramatically more (or less) than everyone else in my own group does, is there reason for categorically letting my view of my life's value override theirs? If everyone thinks my life is worth living, but I think otherwise (perhaps after reading a particularly depressing existentialist), is there compelling reason to believe that they are all wrong and I am the authority? The danger of self-delusion is rampant here.

Naturalism sometimes makes individualism look exceedingly weak. As philosophers like Albert Camus and Thomas Nagel have (differently) argued,[14] a cosmos without God can look like a very bleak place. What Nagel calls the "external" perspective of a vast and uncaring cosmos can seem to overwhelm or trump the "internal" perspective of a small and relatively infinitesimal individual human, no matter how much she cares about her life. Naturalism sometimes maintains its posture of prioritizing the objective facts of the natural sciences; therefore any view, like individualism, that ranks subjective preferences more highly is suspect from the start.

Transhumanism is perhaps most convincing when it makes conventional preferences appear to be contingent features of our stage in history. For example, the fact that I only want to live to a given age may simply be a quirk of when I live. In the first century, I might think living to forty years is good enough and anything much more might appear unnatural; in the twenty-first century, I might think the same thing about living to one hundred. However, there may not be good reason simply to take these preferences as authoritative. Individualism seems to take these and countless other preferences as authoritative and is thus deficient from a transhumanist perspective.

14. Albert Camus, *The Myth of Sisyphus*, trans. J. O'Brian (London: H. Hamilton, 1955); Thomas Nagel, *The View from Nowhere* (New York: Oxford University Press, 1986).

Beyond these comparative weaknesses, there are numerous independent reasons why individualism cannot account well for the intuition that people matter. Perhaps the most decisive objection concerns the practical difficulties of applying individualism to large groups of diverse individuals. However, it may be more instructive to begin with the problems that this approach faces when there is just one human individual to consider and then work toward cases involving more than one individual.

Imagine situations with just one human individual on the scene—Adam or whoever takes his place in rival accounts of human origins. Even in this simple case, individualism seems implausible. If you were this lone individual, why should you think that your own thoughts are the causes rather than the effects of value in the world? When the two alternatives are clearly stated—your mind reflects, detects, and discovers values in the world, *or* your mind creates, constructs, and invents value in the world—it seems difficult to be confident of the second alternative, which is individualism. Individualism appears narcissistic compared to the first alternative. Likewise, even in this simple case, individualism seems impractical. In the very moment of a choice, individualism gives the individual no guidance other than "just choose" or perhaps (what might seem better) "just choose based on your values." But such guidance merely raises the question: What should you value (and how much should you value it)? All that individualism can advise is to "just value what you value"—extremely unhelpful advice. This counsel only becomes more suspect the moment you realize that your subjective values can fluctuate as often as the weather. Why should you choose for the future based on your subjective values today when it is possible (or even probable) that your subjective values in the future will be different?

A second and closely related critique is that in the process of rightly seeking to resist the domination or exclusion of the individual by forces greater than the individual, individualism risks making the individual and her worth stand at the mercy of forces lesser than she is—forces within herself. As C. S. Lewis notes, we may think we are our own person, standing on our own ideas, but internal and external subpersonal forces can explain much of that.[15] Lewis is especially alert to the inevitable way that moral subjectivism can lead to resentment and rudderlessness—irrespective of theological considerations. Humans have to make choices. When it dawns on them that even their own psychology is nothing more than the result of subrational factors (according to many accounts), they realize that their choices are at the mercy of whatever happens to be their strongest desires at the moment.[16]

15. Lewis, *Mere Christianity* (New York: Macmillan, 1947), 225.
16. C. S. Lewis, *The Abolition of Man* (New York: HarperCollins, 2015). See especially lecture 3, "The Abolition of Man."

Thaddeus Metz articulates how people who have no belief in anything supernatural typically resort to either subjectivism or objectivism when they think about the meaning of life. As we summarized above, subjectivism is basically individualism applied to the meaning of life. In contrast, objectivism says that meaning in life is a real thing that exists at least partly outside of any human person's mind, so that the standards for meaning in life do not vary from one person to another, even when the subjective opinions about meaning in life do so vary.[17]

Metz notices a historical shift here: while subjectivism dominated the first three quarters of the twentieth century because of its affinity with other then-influential philosophical movements, the final quarter of that century saw the rise of still other movements that have been used to support objectivism and dethrone subjectivism. Subjectivist arguments have often taken such forms as "meaning in life comes from *realizing* yourself" (e.g., by satisfying your deepest desires) or "meaning in life comes from *losing* yourself" (e.g., by becoming absorbed in an activity or experience). A common strategy for handling such arguments has been to confront these arguments with apparent counterexamples such as: What if "realizing yourself" means deliberately harming others? What if you can "lose yourself" in the activity of intentionally keeping count of the precise number of hairs on your head? These activities are not "realizing" oneself or "losing" oneself in a way that confers meaning—no matter how much one desires such activities or is consumed by them.[18] In short, since subjectivism is at the heart of individualism, the latter is only as strong as the former. Since subjectivism is recognized to have serious flaws, individualism is thereby shown to be seriously flawed as well.

Another critique extends these observations to moral status. Individualism says that the moral status of a human life is no more and no less than whatever that human thinks it to be. This implies that there is no criticizing someone who thinks too highly—or too lowly—of himself and his life. In fact, this view suggests that if a person does not value her life at all, then her life does not have any value. Hence, the very feature of individualism praised in many quarters as a potential virtue—its sensitivity to the values of different individuals—is here exposed as a serious vice regarding the value of one's own life. To adapt an old adage: those who live by the individualist approach will die by the individualist approach.

The above arguments demonstrate that individualism is problematic when only one individual is in view, but the problems become even greater when other

17. Metz, "Meaning of Life."
18. Ibid.

people are involved. Several questions introduce our final line of critique: Does individualism typically help make a marriage stronger? Or even a romance, friendship, or day at the office? Does not the presence of another individual quickly bring one person's individualism to an abrupt and poetically just halt?

The individualist can seek to allay this concern by reminding us here that the strongest preferences for most individuals are for relationships of the standard types with other people. But this reply misses the point. Granted, individualism can produce harmonies. Nevertheless, it is just as possible, and just as permissible, for individualism to cause a dissonant stalemate—or worse. With mild matters, the problem is not as acute: if Adam wants a vegetarian dinner, and Eve is a fruititarian, individualism does not break the tie but leaves them to hash it out for themselves. But more serious matters are just over the horizon, even for thought experiments: if Abel values his own life, and Cain strongly desires Abel dead, individualism does not break *this* tie either. Cain asks, "Am I my brother's keeper?" (Gen. 4:9). Individualism answers: "Only if you want to be."

Herein lies one of the biggest ironies or paradoxes of individualism. A view that sets out to fortify the individual and her preferences ultimately puts every individual and her preferences at the mercy of every other individual and his preferences. Indeed, when an individualist ends up as an eye witness to gross injustice—even more so if she becomes the victim of such injustice—she is likely to jettison the moral relativism and subjectivism at the core of her view and replace it with some sort of absolutism or objectivism which assigns strict duties (e.g., not committing gross injustice) to each and every individual.

Christian Critiques of Individualism

Individualism has further weaknesses that can be recognized from the standpoint of distinctively Christian knowledge. Individualism is a version of what Christian philosopher Alvin Plantinga calls creative anti-realism: "the view that it is human behavior—in particular, human thought and language—that is somehow responsible for the fundamental structure of the world and for the fundamental kinds of entities there are."[19] It is a type of anti-realism because it seeks to "construct" the significance of human life from the values and preferences of the individual. In his famous talk "Advice to Christian

19. Alvin Plantinga, "Advice to Christian Philosophers," in *The Analytic Theist: An Alvin Plantinga Reader*, ed. James F. Sennett (Grand Rapids: Eerdmans, 1998), 313. This now famous essay was originally published in *Faith and Philosophy* 1 (1984): 253–71 and is also available online at http://www.faithandphilosophy.com/article_advice.php.

Philosophers," Plantinga describes why this way of viewing things is a non-starter for a believer in God:

> From a theistic point of view . . . universal creative anti-realism is at best a mere impertinence, a piece of laughable bravado. For God, of course, owes neither his existence nor his properties to us and our ways of thinking; the truth is just the reverse. And so far as the created universe is concerned, while it indeed owes its existence and character to activity on the part of a person, that person is certainly not a human person.[20]

We will return to Plantinga's words in the next section. But for now they suggest another Christian critique of individualism, namely, that it does not adequately appreciate how the meaning or significance of an individual life requires a broader context within which to situate it. From a Christian perspective, that context is God's kingdom, which is incalculably superior to the mere perspective and values of the individual herself. Christian philosopher Dallas Willard argues that meaning "is a 'going beyond,' a transcendence of whatever state we are in toward that which completes it."[21] He argues that this feature of life is reflected in language. For example, the word *water* can function as a noun or a verb, and we literally do not know what the word means until we see the word used in context. The same is true with other language units such as letters or sentences. Imagine you see the letter *I* printed on a page. Without context you would not know what it means or what it is referring to. But if you expand your vision to see that the letter *I* is part of the word *It*, that tells you something useful, although now you wonder about the meaning of *It*. Expand your vision again to see that the word *It* is followed by *was*. Continue expanding your vision until you get the clause of a sentence: *It was the best of times*. Expand further to get the whole sentence:

> It was the best of times, it was the worst of times, it was the age of wisdom, it was the age of foolishness, it was the epoch of belief, it was the epoch of incredulity, it was the season of Light, it was the season of Darkness, it was the spring of hope, it was the winter of despair, we had everything before us, we had nothing before us, we were all going direct to Heaven, we were all going direct the other way.

Now that is a meaningful mouthful! But even here, you will not adequately appreciate what this sentence means unless you know that it is the opening

20. Ibid.
21. Dallas Willard, *The Divine Conspiracy: Understanding How God Changes Lives* (New York: HarperCollins, 1998), 386–87.

line of Charles Dickens's *Tale of Two Cities*. And you will not fully appreciate what it means unless you read the book.

This linguistic lesson applies profoundly to human life, as Willard explains:

> Events in a human life are like that, and so is a human life as a whole, as well as human life itself. They resemble the opening words in an unfinished sentence, paragraph, chapter, or book. In a sense we can identify them and grasp them, but we cannot know what they mean and really are until we know what comes later. Thus we are always seeking the meaning of events we live through and of our lives themselves. . . . And it is always true that meaning is found, when it is found, in some larger context.[22]

Another critique of individualism from a Christian perspective is that it can easily become a form of idolatry in which the self or its parts become elevated far beyond what they deserve. G. K. Chesterton captures this well:

> Of all horrible religions the most horrible is the worship of the god within. . . . That Jones shall worship the god within him turns out ultimately to mean that Jones shall worship Jones. Let Jones worship the sun or moon, anything rather than the Inner Light; let Jones worship cats or crocodiles, if he can find any in his street, but not the god within. Christianity came into the world firstly in order to assert with violence that a man had not only to look inwards, but to look outwards, to behold with astonishment and enthusiasm a divine company and a divine captain. The only fun of being a Christian was that a man was not left alone with the Inner Light, but definitely recognised an outer light, fair as the sun, clear as the moon, terrible as an army with banners.[23]

Here Chesterton is keen to resist even religious movements that elevate looking inward at the expense of looking outward. This outlook reflects the biblical wisdom that "the heart is devious above all else" (Jer. 17:9) and the biblical admonition to "trust in the LORD with all your heart, and do not rely on your own insight" (Prov. 3:5).

In this connection it is worth recalling Sara Buss's quotation above, especially where she writes that when an individual makes a declaration of the right to autonomy "about some sphere of her own life," she "is denying that anyone else has the authority to control her activity within this sphere; she is saying that any exercise of power over this activity is illegitimate unless she authorizes it herself."[24] That outlook on authority may have some validity

---

22. Ibid., 387.
23. G. K. Chesterton, *Orthodoxy* (1908; repr., San Francisco: Ignatius, 1995), 81.
24. Buss, "Personal Autonomy."

in the human sphere, but it is a far cry from the famous line of Christian academic and statesman Abraham Kuyper: "No single piece of our mental world is to be hermetically sealed off from the rest, and there is not a square inch in the whole domain of our human existence over which Christ, who is Sovereign over *all*, does not cry: 'Mine!'"[25] To borrow the language of Buss, Christ has the "authority to control" any activity within any "sphere" of my own life. His "exercise of power" there is perfectly legitimate even if I do not "authorize it" myself. This is a rebuke of individualism.

A final critique of individualism from a Christian perspective is that human individuals themselves are by God's design deeply dependent both on one another and on God. Consider Lewis's explanation for why human individuals are not really separate from one another:

> They look separate because you see them walking about separately. But then, we are so made that we can see only the present moment. If we could see the past, then of course it would look different. For there was a time when every man was part of his mother, and (earlier still) part of his father as well: and when they were part of his grandparents. If you could see humanity spread out in time, as God sees it, it would not look like a lot of separate things dotted about. It would look like one single growing thing—rather like a very complicated tree. Every individual would appear connected with every other. And not only that. Individuals are not really separate from God any more than from one another. Every man, woman, and child all over the world is feeling and breathing at this moment only because God, so to speak, is "keeping him going."[26]

Lewis's words reflect the apostle Paul's language from his speech in Athens— "For in [God] we live and move and have our being" (Acts 17:28)—as well as Paul's words to the church in Colossae that Christ "is before all things, and in him all things hold together" (Col. 1:17). This metaphysical dependence of each human individual upon other human individuals and ultimately at each moment upon God makes even more implausible any outlook that grounds the significance of human life on the values and desires of an individual herself.

Christian Appreciation of the Individual

Although the exclusive focus on the individual inherent in individual*ism* is problematic in so many ways, there are at least six reasons why great appreciation

25. Abraham Kuyper, "Sphere Sovereignty," in *Abraham Kuyper: A Centennial Reader*, ed. James D. Bratt (Grand Rapids: Eerdmans, 1998), 488, emphasis in original.
26. Lewis, *Mere Christianity*, 180.

for the individual has a significant place in a mature Christian approach to the question of why people matter. Some of these have already been sketched above. However, since humanity is created in God's image, the valid insights of any philosophical approach can be seen as part of God's creation reflecting back some aspects of divine wisdom. As Scripture teaches, that reflection may be "in a mirror, dimly" (1 Cor. 13:12) or "plain" to see (Rom. 1:19).

A biblical view can happily affirm that individuals are indeed important. Concepts of individuality come in both weaker and stronger forms. Individualism inclines toward the stronger form, which problematically says that individuals exist in a way wholly separate from and independent of each other. However, the weaker form makes a more modest claim with which Christian theism can concur. That claim maintains simply that human individuals exist and that they are real. Although this claim might seem obvious, not all views of the world affirm it.[27]

A second point is more sophisticated, though it builds on the simple point just mentioned. The moves made by individualism when it is at its most valiant—when it is working its hardest to twist itself into a shape that can rebut the problem of fluctuating, aberrant desires—actually point us in the direction of God. Where atheistic individualism centered upon humans proves shallow, a Christian appreciation for individuality centered upon God runs deep.

Human persons have been created in God's image. While it is not wise or biblical to interpret this entirely in terms of how human individuals are like God now, the reality is that humanity has been designed by God to have a destiny of conforming to the beauty and wisdom of Christ, who *is* the image of God (Col. 1:15).[28] This recognition helps explain some of the appeal of both objectivism and subjectivism in a way that sheds light on the question of moral realism. One of objectivism's insights is that moral reality does not seem to depend on human minds. For example, humans could all come to highly value something like a piece of lint without it really being so valuable. Likewise, humans could all come to believe some moral proposition like "torturing the innocent for fun is morally right" without it really being true.

Nevertheless, one of subjectivism's sound insights is that moral reality does seem to depend on minds *of some sort* in a deep and ineliminable way. It is hard to believe that value and moral truth would exist in a possible world if we imagine that possible world to have *no minds at all*—no God, no humans, no intelligent angels or aliens. Even if such a possible world had galaxies,

27. Peter K. Unger, "I Do Not Exist," in *Perception and Identity*, ed. Graham F. Macdonald (Ithaca, NY: Cornell University Press, 1979).

28. For further discussion of this idea, see John F. Kilner, *Dignity and Destiny: Humanity in the Image of God* (Grand Rapids: Eerdmans, 2015).

stars, planets, water, and forms of unconscious complexity (like apples or Apple computers), it is still hard to believe that some states of that possible world would be more valuable than others. The question *More valuable to whom?* is necessarily unanswerable there, since there is no one there—not even God—to prefer one state of affairs to another.

Likewise, it is hard to believe that any moral proposition in such a world would be true. For example, consider the proposition "torturing the innocent for fun is morally right" along with the opposite proposition "torturing the innocent for fun is morally wrong." Both propositions would seem false, or at least meaningless, in such a mind-less world. This type of observation occasionally unites some Christians and atheists who otherwise disagree about much.[29]

The idea that human persons have been made in God's image helps explain these competing insights from objectivists and subjectivists. Moral reality may depend in a deep and ineliminable way on God's mind but not on human minds. The piece of lint may not really be so valuable, even though all humans highly value it, because God does not so value it; one proposition about torture is true and the other false because of how they map (or fail to map) onto God's mind.[30]

This recognition echoes Plantinga's remark about how all of created reality really does owe its existence and character to a person—just not to a human person. In terms of individualism, it may be that the preferences, desires, and values of an individual (or individuals[31]) help explain the meaning and moral status of human life—just not a human individual. Yet the fact that we have been made in God's image helps explain why we are sometimes tempted to think that moral reality depends in a deep and ineliminable way on our minds. A person who sees a friend's image (in a photograph, mirror, or computer screen) is sometimes tempted to think that the image of the friend has other properties of the friend—especially when the person does not realize that it

29. For an excellent presentation of several representative views in dialogue with each other, see Robert K. Garcia and Nathan L. King, eds., *Is Goodness without God Good Enough? A Debate on Faith, Secularism, and Ethics* (New York: Rowman & Littlefield, 2009), especially the closing statements by William Lane Craig and Paul Kurtz, 165–214.

30. Here I sidestep important debates among Christians about how best to articulate the relations between God's mind/will/character and the right and the good. For a helpful survey, see Phillip L. Quinn, "Theological Voluntarism," in *The Oxford Handbook of Ethical Theory*, ed. David Copp (Oxford: Oxford University Press, 2006), 63–90.

31. Here I attempt to gesture at the many important trinitarian contributions to a full discussion of individualism, both human and divine. It is not exactly one divine person but three that generate the moral realities of goodness and rightness. It seems that even God is not "individualistic" but communal to the core.

is just an image. Given that humans are made in God's image, it is understandable why some people might anchor their belief that people matter upon something as godlike as human individuals.[32]

A third way that individuals are important has to do with their moral importance to God. Individuals figure centrally, for instance, in all of the major divisions of morality sketched by Lewis: harmony between individuals, harmony within an individual, and the purpose of human life as a whole.[33] But the moral importance of individuals is not just a taxonomic tool; as the above epigraph by Willard suggests, it is a fundamental feature of our relation to God and his relation to people.[34] The past, present, and future glory of each believer matters greatly to God.[35]

A fourth way that Christians can recognize the importance of individuals is evident in so-called individualistic methodology, an idea popularized by famed sociologist Max Weber. According to Weber, "Social phenomena must be explained by showing how they result from individual actions, which in turn must be explained through reference to the intentional states that motivate the individual actors."[36] From a Christian perspective, such methodology seems unobjectionable and even attractive.[37] It does not commit one to the kind of subjective and anti-realist commitments of individualism critiqued above. Indeed, Weber himself was careful to note that "it is a tremendous misunderstanding to think that an 'individualistic' *method* should involve what is in any conceivable sense an individualistic system of *values.*"[38]

A fifth way that Christians can welcome an emphasis on individuals involves recognizing that individual differences between people really do matter. While

32. As John Kilner explains in his chapter "Special Connection and Intended Reflection: Creation in God's Image and Human Significance" in the present volume, the Bible presents both humanity as a whole and individual people as created in God's image. Accordingly, there are other influences at work that account for why some atheists take a turn toward the individual while others take a turn toward the communal.

33. Lewis, *Mere Christianity*, 72.

34. See also ibid., 168: "When Christ died, He died for you individually just as much as if you had been the only man in the world."

35. C. S. Lewis, "The Weight of Glory," in *The Weight of Glory: And Other Addresses* (New York: Macmillan, 1949).

36. Joseph Heath, "Methodological Individualism," in *Stanford Encyclopedia of Philosophy*, last revised January 21, 2015, http://plato.stanford.edu/entries/methodological-individualism.

37. C. S. Lewis seems to recognize this when he writes that "nothing but the courage and unselfishness of individuals is ever going to make any system work properly. . . . You cannot make men good by law: and without good men you cannot have a good society" (*Mere Christianity*, 73).

38. Max Weber, *Economy and Society*, ed. Guenther Roth and Claus Wittich (1922; repr., Berkeley: University of California Press, 1968), 18; quoted in Heath, "Methodological Individualism," emphasis in original.

the above epigraph by Lewis gives a reason for thinking individual persons are more important than collective things, Lewis elsewhere makes the distinct point I am focusing on here. He notes that individual persons are not meant to be mere duplicates—even everlasting, precious duplicates—of one another. Echoing Paul's thinking in 1 Corinthians 12, Lewis observes that just as the body of a human organism has many individual yet interdependent parts with different functions, so too the body of Christ has many individual yet interdependent members whose individuality shines forth best, not by being exactly alike, but by mutually building up the other members in service to the whole.[39]

My sixth and final point builds directly on the fifth. While the Reformation is sometimes faulted for pushing the church and world in the direction of the type of individualism critiqued above—especially through its emphasis on the priesthood of all believers—a more sympathetic narrative is that Luther and other Reformers were reclaiming biblical knowledge essential to a mature Christian appreciation of the importance of the individual.[40] As Peter admonishes Christian individuals,

> Like living stones, let yourselves be built into a spiritual house, to be a holy priesthood, to offer spiritual sacrifices acceptable to God through Jesus Christ. . . . You are a chosen race, a royal priesthood, a holy nation, God's own people, in order that you may proclaim the mighty acts of him who called you out of darkness into his marvelous light. (1 Pet. 2:5, 9)

By reaffirming this biblical insight (see also Exod. 19:6; Isa. 61:6; Rev. 1:6; 5:10), the Reformers recaptured the high calling and responsibility of each individual believer before God—no matter how wise, literate, articulate, or socially prominent they are. To echo Peter, all of the individual "living stones" are built together into a "spiritual house." There is no suggestion from Peter of an individualism that opposes the community. Unfortunately, when the theological framework that supported this outlook was gradually weakened and removed, the Reformers' accent on the individual became untethered from what provided both content and limit to its expression. The result is the quasireligious form of individualism that Chesterton mocked in the quote above. But within its proper theological framework, the Reformers' affirmation of the individual is still valid.

---

39. Lewis, *Mere Christianity*, 185–86.
40. For more on the role of Christianity in the development of Western individualism, see Larry Siedentop, *Inventing the Individual: The Origins of Western Liberalism* (Harvard University Press, 2014).

In sum, there are countless ways of trying to recognize, value, and respect human individuals. Individualism is a radical strategy that seems to reduce everything to human individuals. When accounting for the intuition that people matter, that human life is significant, individualism grounds the intuition in the intuition itself. It insists that my life is significant for no other reason than because I think it is.

As we have seen in this chapter, this type of postmodern autonomy approach has its attractions but also faces serious problems. Perhaps the most serious problem is the difficulty of resolving disagreements. The subjectivism that individualism tries to use as a shield against the clashing value claims of groups who disagree with one another turns out to provide no protection. When two or more individuals' desires or values collide, something beyond the individuals is required to adjudicate.

The Christian vision of the world bases the worth and dignity of each human individual in God. In the areas of human moral status and the meaning of human life, Christian knowledge shines its light on the perspectives and values of each man and woman. It clarifies what is already good and true and beautiful, replaces the shadows of opinion with the illumination of truth, and informs the changing flow of human desire with the unswerving character and purposes of a divine being who is more than just an individual. Christianity is thus better able to recognize and affirm the genuine value of the individual than individualism itself.[41]

Further Reading

Bellah, Robert, Richard Madsen, William M. Sullivan, Ann Swidler, and Steven M. Tipton. *Habits of the Heart: Individualism and Commitment in American Life*. Berkeley: University of California Press, 1985. Updated with a new introduction in 1996.

This is an influential and controversial critique of American "individualism" (which the authors admit is a term used in numerous, sometimes contradictory senses). While chapter 6 is actually titled "Individualism," the whole book aims to fairly contrast four American traditions they call "biblical," "civic republican," "utilitarian individualist," and "expressive individualist."

Clark, Kelly James, and Anne Poortenga. *The Story of Ethics: Fulfilling our Human Nature*. Upper Saddle River, NJ: Pearson / Prentice Hall, 2002.

This is an excellent book on the history of ethics, and it is eminently readable, short, and academically rigorous. Its authors apparently possess but do not explicitly

---

41. I would like to thank John F. Kilner, Scott B. Rae, and Baker Academic editor David C. Cramer for their many charitable and insightful suggestions on earlier drafts of this chapter.

endorse a biblical worldview. Their fifty-page chapter "The Postmodern World" nicely covers the influence on moral philosophy of nine key figures from G. E. Moore to Richard Rorty.

Lewis, C. S. *The Abolition of Man*. 1943. Reprint, New York: HarperCollins, 2015. These three short evening lectures on moral subjectivism, delivered February 24–26, 1943, are a classic discussion that does not rely on distinctively Christian knowledge. Lewis explains how subjectivism has a range of serious practical and theoretical problems.

Metz, Thaddeus. *Meaning in Life: An Analytic Study*. Oxford: Oxford University Press, 2013. This is a longer and more detailed presentation of several of the main positions Metz sketches in his *Stanford Encyclopedia of Philosophy* article on "The Meaning of Life." In particular, his discussion of supernaturalism, naturalism (including subjectivism and objectivism), and nihilism is a good starting point for Christians wanting to understand these families of views.

Moreland, J. P. *The Kingdom Triangle: Recover the Christian Mind, Renovate the Soul, Restore the Spirit's Power*. Grand Rapids: Zondervan, 2007. Moreland's third chapter, "The Postmodern Story," is a particularly concise and incisive discussion of this movement, focusing on its troublesome approach to knowledge in general and moral knowledge in particular.

Willard, Dallas. *The Divine Conspiracy: Rediscovering Our Hidden Life in God*. New York: HarperCollins, 1998. Chapter 10 of this book, "The Restoration of All Things," is an excellent presentation of how meaning in life requires a certain cluster of conditions (e.g., a projected future for one's self and the cosmos) and how the biblical tradition richly meets those conditions.

PART 2

Grounding Significance in Science

5

More Than Meets the Eye

Naturalism and Human Significance

SCOTT B. RAE

Philosopher Thomas Nagel is both an atheist and a philosophical naturalist—meaning he believes that all reality can be reduced to the material world alone.[1] In his 2012 book *Mind and Cosmos*, he pronounces a stark conclusion regarding naturalism due to its inability to account for some key aspects of human experience that many believe make human beings significant. Those include consciousness, rationality, and morality or moral properties.[2]

With theism out of the question for Nagel, he attempts to maintain his naturalism and provide an adequate account for the above three things that many consider to be essential components of human nature. He concludes that mainstream evolutionary naturalism (the view that atheistic evolution alone accounts for the origin of all reality) fails in this attempt. Instead he tentatively proposes a rough form of teleology (that these components are somehow built into the design of the universe) as his best, but still largely

1. The terms "naturalism" and "evolutionary naturalism" will be further explained in the following section of this chapter.
2. Thomas Nagel, *Mind and Cosmos: Why the Materialist, Neo-Darwinian Conception of Nature Is Almost Certainly False* (New York: Oxford University Press, 2012).

exploratory, explanation for consciousness, rationality, and morality. He does recognize how significant a departure this is from the tradition of naturalism, which is still the dominant worldview in the academy, particularly in the sciences.

In his work on science and religion, *Where the Conflict Really Lies*, Christian philosopher Alvin Plantinga makes a similar argument about rationality, concluding that on an evolutionary, naturalistic account, there is little to suggest that our reason is reliable, especially when it comes to abstract ideas about the world.[3] Plantinga does not share Nagel's skepticism about theism, since he considers theism a much more comfortable "home" for rationality than is naturalism. Both Nagel and Plantinga (as well as many others) illustrate ongoing attempts to account for these important aspects of human experience.

This chapter is designed to assess the suitability of naturalism as a basis for understanding the world and for living life. Its goals are twofold: (1) to describe and assess different ways of grounding human significance attempted by naturalists and (2) to show that naturalism cannot adequately account for some of the features commonly regarded as central to the significance of human beings.

The first part of the chapter defines in greater detail what naturalism is and then considers the various ways in which naturalists attempt to understand and ground human significance.

- For some, the concept is outright denied, and they see nothing particularly significant about humans. For example, Peter Singer and others describe any attempt to see humans as more significant than any other part of the animal world as arrogant speciesism (the view that one's own species is the superior one).

- A second option is some form of rationalist autonomy, in which one of the properties that make humans significant is the use of reason—specifically people's capacity to set ends for themselves. Nicholas Wolterstorff offers a critique of this way of grounding human rights that is particularly helpful for the present discussion.[4]

- A third option is to see human significance as somehow grounded in an evolutionary framework through adaptability and survival, though

3. Alvin Plantinga, *Where the Conflict Really Lies: Science, Religion, and Naturalism* (New York: Oxford University Press, 2011).

4. Nicholas Wolterstorff, *Justice: Rights and Wrongs* (Princeton: Princeton University Press, 2008).

humans' place at the top of the evolutionary ladder could well be temporary. This outlook opens the door to a view that is the subject of the next chapter on transhumanism (the view that it might be possible for human beings to surpass their humanity and become something different than merely human).

- A fourth option is a type of naturalistic Platonism, which recognizes that some necessary things about human beings are built into the structure of the world but does not necessarily acknowledge that there is a designer who placed them there.

- A final option, which moves toward the discussion of postmodern individualism addressed in the previous chapter, would be to see the grounding for human significance collapse into some form of subjectivism. In this outlook, significance is a matter of personal preference or is conferred by some external authority such as the state.

The second part of the chapter involves an assessment of naturalism's ability to account for some of the features associated with human significance—particularly rationality and morality—that distinguish human beings from the rest of the created order. Foundational to rationality is consciousness and the capacity to engage in first-person reflection on oneself and the world. This has been the subject of considerable debate in the philosophy of mind, and some prominent naturalists recognize the difficulty in accounting for consciousness through neuroscience and evolutionary theory.

Rationality itself is just as difficult to account for on the basis of naturalism. Plantinga has argued that there is deep conflict between science and what he calls the "metaphysical add on" to evolution, the insistence it proceeded without any divine intentionality or direction.[5] Although there may be an evolutionary explanation for why basic beliefs about the world are necessary for survival, extending that argument to higher rational capacities such as abstract reasoning is harder to justify.

Another feature of people related to human significance has to do with morality or moral properties and how those could have arisen in a strictly material world reduced to chemistry and physics. Though evolutionary accounts of morality have been numerous (e.g., those of E. O. Wilson, James Rachels, and Michael Ruse), many naturalists recognize the difficulty of accounting for morality. As in the case of consciousness and rationality, morality and moral properties are arguably most at home in the theistic framework developed in part 3 of the present book.

5. Plantinga, *Where the Conflict Really Lies*, 79, 129.

Defining Naturalism

There is little doubt that in the academic world, and especially in the world of the sciences, the dominant worldview is philosophical naturalism. That is not to say that there are no theists among scientists. Many scientists have a real and vibrant faith. But for many believers in the sciences, faith is a private matter that has little impact on their work in science. The vast majority of the scientific community operates within the framework of the worldview of naturalism.

What is meant by the term *philosophical naturalism*? Essentially it presumes that all reality is subsumed entirely within the material world—that is, what can be appraised by one's senses and what can be empirically measured and verified. No ultimate reality exists beyond this material or physical world. In terms of metaphysics, there is nothing that is "meta" or beyond the physical world.

Put another way, according to naturalism the universe that exists in space and time—which consists of physical objects, physical properties, events, and process—is all there is, ever was, and ever will be. As a result, there is no room for immaterial human components that cannot ultimately be reduced to physical or material substances. For example, consciousness and self-awareness must be reducible to the neurological components in the brain or the behavior of the body. There is no room for spiritual and nonmaterial notions such as the soul and the image of God.

Naturalism also contains a story about how reality came to be. Naturalistic evolution is the "myth" or story about the origin of reality and a statement that reality is reducible to the physical world and ultimately to the laws of chemistry and physics. In this view, the universe is a closed system and all events in it take place according to the laws of nature.

In terms of epistemology (the branch of philosophy that deals with knowledge), all that can be known is what is scientifically verifiable. Such things are the only things that count as knowledge. This view of knowledge is known as *scientism*. What cannot be verified is counted as mere belief and is often in sharp contrast to what naturalists consider a proper form of knowledge. Scientism has established a knowledge hierarchy in which so-called scientific knowledge is either the only kind of knowledge we have or is vastly superior to nonscientific claims, which amount to private expressions of belief.

According to the naturalist, what counts for genuine *knowledge* is publicly accessible, verifiable, objective, and therefore able to make a claim to be truth. On the other hand, the naturalist considers *belief* to be private and subjective—something that cannot be tested. It is ultimately a matter of personal preference and can make no valid claim to truth or authority over someone else's belief. Thus for the naturalist the domains of religion, philosophy, and morality would be primarily in the realm of belief and would not count as knowledge.

Another critical component of naturalism is its view of the human being. According to the naturalist, human beings and all of life on earth are the result of the blind, random forces of evolution. There is no design or intelligence behind the world and no purpose or reason behind it that would invest life with significance. Human beings are the end product of billions of years of evolutionary change. According to some, human beings will likely be surpassed by a biotech creation in the future.

As a result of the evolutionary story of origins, there is no transcendent source of life's meaning or of human dignity. Such things are human creations according to the naturalist worldview, which today sometimes takes a postmodern tone, suggesting that notions of human dignity are fluid and changing as they reflect culture and power relationships. For the strict naturalist, no basis exists for human dignity or life's significance since all of life is the result of random forces. The naturalist tends to view human beings in a deterministic way, rendering free will an illusion.

The naturalist advances a similar view when it comes to morality. For the naturalist, there is no transcendent source that defines right and wrong. In fact, for the strict naturalist, morality is purely a human creation formulated to make society livable. Morality plays a positive role only in the sense that it enables individuals and societies to survive and even flourish. According to biologist E. O. Wilson, "Ethical codes have arisen by evolution through the interplay of biology and culture."[6] According to the naturalist, morality is the result of purely material processes and ultimately has merely a biological basis.

The view that human beings are nothing more than the sum of their physical parts and properties is called *physicalism*. This view commonly holds that human beings are nothing more than physical objects, reducible to their molecules and chemical reactions. Naturalist philosopher Paul Churchland puts it this way:

> The important point about the standard evolutionary story is that the human species and all of its features are the wholly physical outcome of a purely physical process. If this is the correct account of our origins, then there seems neither need, nor room, to fit any nonphysical substances or properties into our theoretical account of ourselves. We are creatures of matter. And we should learn to live with that fact.[7]

Finally, for the naturalist, history has no direction, goal, or purpose. It is simply the continuation of events begun randomly in the past. It is no more

6. E. O. Wilson, "The Biological Basis for Morality," *The Atlantic*, April 1998, 98–107.
7. Paul Churchland, *Matter and Consciousness: A Contemporary Introduction to the Philosophy of Mind* (Cambridge, MA: MIT Press, 1984), 21.

than the record of one event following another. Indeed, there is no design in history at all, and thus even human actions are not literally done for a purpose or end. However, within the scientific community there is often high optimism about scientific and technological progress. Nowhere is this more evident than in the biotech community. An incurable optimism about where the biotech revolution is going can lead members of the biotech community to minimize potential problems. But this optimism is not related to any overall view of where history is going.

It is difficult to imagine a worldview more at odds with Christian theism than philosophical naturalism. In a Christian understanding of metaphysics, God is the ultimate reality, and there is a realm of reality that is not material. In a Christian view of knowledge, what can be empirically verified does indeed count for knowledge, but knowledge is not limited to the physical realm. God reveals truth both through general revelation in the world and through special revelation in the Word. Those aspects of revelation also count for real knowledge and cannot be discounted or marginalized as mere belief.

From a Christian perspective, humans are made in God's image, the result of the intimate special creation by God, not random forces apart from divine intention and intelligence.[8] Humans have special significance by virtue of being in God's image, and life has purpose and meaning that revolves around bringing honor to and knowing God. Humans have genuine freedom that undergirds the notion of moral responsibility and criminal justice. Morality comes ultimately from the character of a transcendent God, who issues commands consistent with God's character. Right and wrong are not fundamentally human creations and are not fluid and changing with changing times and cultures. Moreover, history has a definite direction because God will bring history to its culmination with the return of Christ.

Naturalism and the Attribution of Significance

Accounting for human significance in a naturalistic framework presents some challenges. The terms used to describe the notion of human significance vary somewhat. Some people use (and critics would say overuse) the term *human dignity*, while others use the notion of *human rights* to safeguard the treatment of human beings who are said to be significant in some way. For example, the UN Universal Declaration on Human Rights asserts that human significance or dignity undergirds the specific affirmations of rights.

8. See John Kilner's chapter "Special Connection and Intended Reflection: Creation in God's Image and Human Significance" in the present book.

The preamble to the declaration begins by affirming that "recognition of the inherent dignity and of the equal and inalienable rights of all members of the human family, is the foundation of freedom, justice and peace in the world." Article 1 further affirms the equal dignity and rights of all human beings from birth.[9] Catholic philosopher Jacques Maritain, one of the contributors to the specific language of the declaration, recognized the importance of how human rights and human significance are grounded. He states pointedly, "We agree on these rights, providing we are not asked why. With the 'why,' the dispute begins."[10]

The assumptions of the naturalist, including a physicalist view of a human person, raise challenging questions about the *why* that undergirds the attribution of significance to humans. The scientist E. O. Wilson summarizes the naturalistic framework for viewing persons in this way: "The central idea (of naturalism) is that all tangible phenomena, from the birth of the stars to the workings of social institutions, are based on material processes that are ultimately reducible, however long and torturous the sequences, to the laws of physics."[11] What this means for human significance is widely debated.

Naturalist philosopher John Searle raises the important philosophical issue about human significance that follows from such a framework: "There is exactly one overriding question in contemporary philosophy . . . : How do we fit in? . . . How can we square this self-conception of ourselves as mindful, meaning-creating, free, rational, etc., agents with a universe that consists entirely of mindless, meaningless, unfree, nonrational, brute physical particles?"[12] Searle raises an interesting tension for the naturalist which, we will suggest in later chapters, is better addressed by Christian theism, with human significance grounded in such ideas as the creation of humans in the image of God.

Naturalist philosophers and scientists have essentially three ways of addressing Searle's question. First they can refuse to attribute any significance to human beings per se and "bite the bullet" by insisting that people's self-conception as meaningful is an illusion. A second response is to recognize human significance based on evolution or on the capacity of humans for rational agency. A third response is to argue that human significance is conferred as a part of social

---

9. Office of the High Commissioner for Human Rights, *Universal Declaration of Human Rights*, UN Department of Public Information, December 10, 1948.

10. Jacques Maritain, *Man and the State* (Chicago: University of Chicago Press, 1951), 77, cited in Paul Copan, "Grounding Human Rights: Naturalism's Failure and Biblical Theism's Success," in *Legitimizing Human Rights: Secular and Religious Perspectives*, ed. Angus Menuge (London: Ashgate, 2013), 11.

11. E. O. Wilson, *Consilience: The Unity of Knowledge* (New York: Knopf, 1998), 266.

12. John R. Searle, *Freedom and Neurobiology: Reflections on Free Will, Language, and Political Power* (New York: Columbia University Press, 2007), 4–5.

practices that bestow dignity and rights on all humans. Human significance in this view is a strictly human construction and, according to some, a sort of useful fiction maintained for utilitarian purposes. At times this view can lapse into a more subjectivist view in which human beings create their own significance and meaning, rendering it entirely self-conferred. These three responses to Searle's question each warrant more detailed consideration.

Perhaps the clearest diminishing of human significance comes from Peter Singer, who popularized the term "speciesism" (as a parallel to racism) to describe the view that human beings have special significance vis-à-vis the animal world. Singer rejects the notion that mere membership in the human species endows humans with any special significance, particularly over animals. He first used the term in his works on animal rights in the 1970s.[13]

Similarly, James Rachels outlines how in his view Darwinism has under-mined the notions of human dignity and the sacredness of human life. He rejects the idea that humans have any special significance because of their membership in the human species. He tries to reconstruct morality, especially bioethics, in view of the fact that humans have no special significance. In his introduction to *Created from Animals* he writes: "I shall argue that Darwin's theory does undermine traditional values. In particular, it undermines the traditional idea that human life has a special, unique worth."[14]

Singer and Rachels's sentiments are echoed by the stark statements of Richard Dawkins, who argues that a naturalistic universe consisting of "just electrons and selfish genes" has "precisely the properties we would expect if there is, at bottom, no design, no purpose, no evil and no good, nothing but blind pitiless indifference."[15] Dawkins refers to the ideas of human purpose and significance as illusions, yet interestingly he also admits to being a "pas-sionate anti-Darwinian when it comes to politics and how we should conduct our human affairs," perhaps reflecting uneasiness with "biting the bullet" on the full implications of naturalism.[16]

Instead of an outright denial of intrinsic human significance, other natural-ists attempt to account for or recognize significance in some way consistent with a naturalistic evolutionary framework. One example of this comes from the work of the political philosopher Ronald Dworkin, who argues that the

13. Peter Singer, *Animal Liberation* (New York: Harper Collins, 1975), 5.
14. James Rachels, *Created from Animals: The Moral Implications of Darwinism* (New York: Oxford University Press, 1990), 4.
15. Richard Dawkins, *River out of Eden: A Darwinian View of Life* (New York: Basic Books, 1995), 132–33.
16. Richard Dawkins, *A Devil's Chaplain: Reflections on Hope, Lies, Science, and Love* (New York: Houghton Mifflin, 2003), 10–11.

significance of human life is grounded in the processes of natural (evolutionary) and human creation. He grounds it in both the process of naturalistic evolution and the human contribution to making someone's life what it is.

Human beings, Dworkin suggests, are "creative masterpieces" that are the result of both "natural creation and self creation."[17] As he puts it, "The life of a single human organism commands respect . . . because of the complex creative investment it represents."[18] What Dworkin seems to argue is that the substantial natural and human "investment" put into each person (and what that investment produces) grounds human significance and thus human rights. In other words, human significance is *recognized* because of complex natural and human processes that produce human beings for what they are.

Rejecting the notion that rationality alone is the basis for human significance, University of Maryland philosopher Ben Dixon offers a somewhat different grounding for human significance within a naturalistic framework. Self-labeled a "Darwin-approved argument for human dignity," Dixon's view "centres on the idea that humans are the only creatures capable of creating, maintaining and expanding institutions for moral reasons."[19] Dixon is responding to Rachels's rejection of human dignity mentioned above and bases human significance on the recognition that evolution has produced human beings capable of what Dixon calls "the value-seeking and value-preserving nature of humans."[20]

Dixon suggests that the basis for conscience is humans' ability to value and that the way rationality combines with social instincts to produce something akin to conscience is unique to humans. Further the "interaction between robust rationality and conscience synergistically yields the human phenomena of forming, maintaining and expanding institutions that support what conscience affirms."[21] He concludes that "we have good grounds for thinking that our struggles to formulate, preserve and improve upon conscience-respecting institutions likely make us worthy of respect."[22]

This is only one example of capacities-based approaches to human significance, which argue that evolutionary forces produce capacities that set human beings apart from other creatures and thus ground their significance. As we will see later in this chapter, naturalism has difficulty accounting for some of

17. This summary of Dworkin is taken from Wolterstorff, *Justice*, 334.
18. Ronald Dworkin, *Life's Dominion: An Argument about Abortion, Euthanasia, and Individual Freedom* (New York: Knopf, 1993), 84.
19. Ben Dixon, "Darwinism and Human Dignity," *Environmental Values* 16, no. 1 (February 2007): 24.
20. Ibid., 34.
21. Ibid.
22. Ibid.

these critical capacities, such as consciousness, rationality, and morality, which many philosophers suggest set humans apart from other creatures and form the basis for their significance. The central issue the naturalist must address is: How do all these capacities arise if one begins with brute matter that is simply rearranged?

At the least, a capacities view of human significance runs into difficulty accounting for the dignity of severely disabled people. In addition, since capacities come in degrees, it follows that any view of human significance based on capacities must view human significance itself as degreed. This should be a caution even to the theist, who grounds significance in humanity's creation in the image of God. For if being in God's image is capacities based, then it is also degreed. Such an understanding stands in stark contrast to the biblical teaching that human significance is not degreed—an absolute that holds regardless of a person's functional abilities.

Rather than denying human significance altogether or recognizing it as grounded in some aspect of evolutionary adaptation, some naturalists insist that human significance is *conferred*. They see it as granted through social practices of treating human beings with dignity and respect. For example, Richard Rorty rejects what he calls "rights foundationalism," the view that human rights and dignity depend on something like a human nature that is common to all human beings. This would also apply to other foundations for human significance such as rationality or morality. As Nicholas Wolterstorff observes, on Rorty's view "there is no human nature for human rights to be grounded in. It is only the social practice of according certain rights to each and every human being that attaches rights to the status of being human. Human rights, as Rorty sees the matter, are all socially conferred. None of them is natural (in any sense)."[23]

One example of conferring human significance involves the personhood of the human fetus. Hilde Lindemann suggests that a pregnant woman calls her fetus into personhood and that this bestowal of personhood by the mother is the foundational social practice by which the fetus is imbued with significance:

> But to describe it (the pregnancy) in purely physical terms fails to capture the central role the woman is playing in the profoundly social activity of calling her fetus into personhood, making a place in the social world for the developing child to occupy when it is born. By the phrase "calling a fetus into personhood," I don't mean "giving birth" or "giving biological life." I view personhood as a

23. This summary of Rorty is taken from Wolterstorff, *Justice*, 321. He is citing Richard Rorty, "Human Rights, Rationality and Sentimentality," in *On Human Rights: The Oxford Amnesty Lectures 1993*, ed. Stephen Shute and Susan Hurley (New York: Basic Books, 1993), 112–13.

social practice—as, indeed, the most fundamental social practice, the one on which all other practices rest. It consists in the physical expression of human beings' intentions, emotions, beliefs, attitudes, and other manifestations of personality, as recognized by other persons, who then respond by taking up an attitude toward them of the kind that's reserved for persons.[24]

The mother is not the only one who is involved in calling a fetus into personhood. Lindemann sees here a social process that involves family members and others close to the mother, in addition to a variety of social practices, norms, and expectations that all serve to reinforce this call into personhood.[25] In other words, the significance that comes with the designation of a "person" is not something that is innate to the fetus, nor is it grounded in the fetus having a human nature. The significance of the fetus is not recognized as already existing; rather, with the mother as the active agent in the pregnancy, significance is conferred as the mother and others around her call the fetus into personhood.

Another example of such a conferral of human significance comes from psychologist Steven Pinker. In answer to the question of whether human dignity is "a useless concept," he responds, "Almost." But then as he goes on to describe what he means by dignity and where it comes from, what he outlines sounds considerably like humans conferring dignity upon other humans:

> Dignity is a phenomenon of human perception. Certain signals from the world trigger an attribution in the mind of a perceiver. Just as converging lines in a drawing are a cue for the perception of depth, and differences in loudness between the two ears cue us to the position of a sound, certain features in another human being trigger ascriptions of worth. These features include signs of composure, cleanliness, maturity, attractiveness, and control of the body. The perception of dignity in turn elicits a response in the perceiver. Just as the smell of baking bread triggers a desire to eat it, and the sight of a baby's face triggers a desire to protect it, the appearance of dignity triggers a desire to esteem and respect the dignified person.[26]

Rather than seeing human significance as something intrinsic, Pinker considers it to be an element of human perception. This judgment appears to put the notion of significance into the realm of the subjective, which may be

24. Hilde Lindemann, ". . . But I Could Never Have One: The Abortion Intuition and Moral Luck," *Hypatia* 24, no. 1 (Winter 2009): 45.
25. Ibid., 46. See also Ronald M. Green, "Conferred Rights and the Fetus," *Journal of Religious Ethics* 2, no. 1 (1974): 55–75.
26. Steven Pinker, "The Stupidity of Dignity," *New Republic*, May 28, 2008, 31.

one of the reasons why he holds that the notion of dignity has limited value and warrants only qualified respect.

Naturalism's Accounting for Rationality and Morality

Prominent among what many think sets humans apart from the rest of the natural world—and thus helps to account for the significance of humans—is the exercise of rationality and morality. Even if someone such as Rachels accepts that higher orders of animals have a limited capacity for rationality, humans typically have a far more sophisticated capacity. For Rachels, the most advanced animals have rationality comparable only to severely neurologically challenged humans, such as children with severe Down syndrome. Even if one accepts that some animals have rudimentary rationality, theirs is not comparable to the abstract reasoning engaged in by most humans, not to mention the most brilliant humans.

The same holds true for morality. Moral reasoning sets humans apart from the natural world. Even if one concedes a very elementary moral capacity on the part of the highest order of animals, sophisticated human moral reasoning, with its emphasis on motives and intentions, typically makes humans far more advanced morally than animals.

The argument here is that reducing reality to the laws of physics and chemistry as the naturalist must do cannot account for the rational and moral aspects of humanity that many think make humans different from the natural world and thus contribute to their significance. The point here is not that these capacities adequately ground human significance but only that they are widely recognized as part of what makes humans significant.[27]

Rationality

Any discussion of the rationality of humans would seem to presume that they possess nonmaterial mental states or consciousness. Thomas Nagel distinguishes between brain states and mental states and describes a mental state as partially composed of "the first-person, inner point of view of the conscious subject; for example, the way sugar tastes to you or the way red looks or anger feels, each of which seems to be something more than the behavioral responses and discriminatory capacities that these experiences explain."[28] This refers to the ability of one to engage in first-person reflection about experiences

27. Part 3 of this book offers more-holistic, constructive proposals for grounding human significance.
28. Nagel, *Mind and Cosmos*, 38.

and suggests that the nonphysical mental state and the physical brain state are not the same thing.

Nagel further distinguishes between that which is *produced* by the brain state (the experience of taste, color, pain, etc.) and that which is *constituted* by the brain state. He concludes, "Conscious subjects and their mental lives are inescapable components of reality not describable by the physical sciences."[29] He insists that humans have both physical and mental components, which are objective and subjective, respectively, and argues that the strictly physical, evolutionary account of the origin of consciousness is "complete fantasy."[30]

One common explanation for consciousness on naturalistic grounds is that it is an emergent property. In other words, it emerges when the physical conditions are right, analogous to how the property of wetness emerges when the conditions are right to bring hydrogen and oxygen into the chemically correct configuration. Wetness is not a property of either hydrogen or oxygen but emerges when they are combined. Nagel calls this "harmless emergence." He suggests that the example of liquidity depends on the "interactions of the molecules that compose the liquid. . . . But the emergence of the mental at certain levels of biological complexity is not like this," since consciousness is an entirely nonmaterial property, unlike wetness, which is fully physical.[31]

Nagel articulates the struggle with which many naturalists wrestle, that of accounting for nonmaterial consciousness on a strictly material view of the world. He seems to recognize that emergence is not a solution to this problem but only renames the problem. The question that still remains for the naturalist is how we got consciousness, rationality, and moral reason (mental properties) from matter alone. Portraying emergence as the answer begs other questions about how mental properties emerged from brute matter and, more importantly, how it could have happened at all. It is no wonder that naturalist Paul Churchland admits that a commitment to philosophical naturalism brings with it difficulties accounting for things like purpose, significance, consciousness, and value.[32]

Accounting for consciousness is necessary for an account of rationality that makes sense. What follows from viewing consciousness as mental states that are different from physical brain states is that I am the owner of my own mental states and experiences and that I am not identical to my experiences. In addition to nonmaterial consciousness, rationality also presumes that the person is an enduring self. Christian philosopher J. P. Moreland connects consciousness and rationality in this way: "We stand at the end of our deliberative

29. Ibid., 41.
30. Ibid., 51.
31. Ibid., 56.
32. See Churchland, *Matter and Consciousness*.

processes as intellectually responsible rational agents. . . . Intellectual responsibility seems to presuppose an enduring I."[33] Similarly, philosopher A. C. Ewing writes, "There must surely be a single being persisting through the (rationally deliberative) process."[34]

In addition, rationality necessarily includes the basics of our understanding of knowledge, such as evidence (and the weighting of such evidence), justification, explanation, and logic. Moreland calls these states "introspective knowledge," and insists that "reasoning itself requires direct access to one's own thoughts/beliefs/sensations in order to engage in rational treatment of these states."[35] Thus to have what he calls "epistemic success" requires that we are capable of first-person introspection of our mental contents. In other words, we must be able to engage in the mental steps necessary to either justify or falsify our concepts and propositions.[36]

Accounting for the attribute of consciousness that is necessary to exercise rational capacities is not the only difficulty that naturalism has with explaining rationality. Though it seems clear that a rudimentary ability for reasoning would be necessary for adaptive success, it is difficult to explain the origin and history of abstract rationality on strictly naturalistic grounds. As Christian philosopher Alvin Plantinga writes,

> The purpose of our cognitive faculties, from that [evolutionary] perspective, is to contribute to our reproductive fitness, to contribute to our survival and reproduction. Current physics with its ubiquitous partial differential equations (not to mention relativity theory with its tensors, quantum mechanics with its non-Abelian group theory, and current set theory with its daunting complexities), involves mathematics of great depth, requiring cognitive powers going enormously beyond what is required for survival and reproduction.[37]

Plantinga later describes how metaphysical beliefs, including the belief in naturalism itself, seem irrelevant to survival and reproduction.[38] Nagel pointedly suggests that the naturalist must explain how "innate mental capacities

33. J. P. Moreland, *The Recalcitrant* Imago Dei: *Human Persons and the Failure of Naturalism* (London: SCM, 2009), 72.

34. A. C. Ewing, *Value and Reality: The Philosophical Case for Theism* (London: George Allen and Unwin, 1973), 84.

35. Moreland, *Recalcitrant* Imago Dei, 79.

36. Ibid., 96–97.

37. Alvin Plantinga, *Where the Conflict Really Lie*, 286. Plantinga even suggests that such abstract reasoning may have been a *detriment* to survival, due to what he calls the "nerdiness factor" in which the only ones who found this kind of reasoning helpful for survival are professors concerned with achieving tenure!

38. Ibid., 349.

that were selected for their immediate adaptive value are also capable of generating, through an extended cultural evolutionary history, true theories about a law-governed natural order that there was no need to understand earlier."[39]

Not only is it difficult to account for abstract reasoning on a naturalistic basis; it is likewise unclear that evolutionary adaptability requires beliefs to be formed or to be necessarily true. Consider first that beliefs need not be formed for adaptive behavior to occur. Plantinga distinguishes between beliefs and what he calls "indicators," the neural structures that take in data from the environment that cause behaviors (such as fleeing predators) that enable the organism to survive. Plantinga cites the example of tiny bacteria, which have indicators that are connected to a propulsion mechanism that enables them to move toward waters in which they can survive. Those mechanisms do not require beliefs to be formed about those indicators. As Plantinga describes, "Fleeing predators, finding food and mates—these things require cognitive devices that in some way track crucial features of the environment and are appropriately connected with muscles; but they do not require true belief, or even belief at all. . . . Indicators need not be or involve beliefs. . . . The objector is right in pointing out that fitness requires accurate indication, but nothing follows about the reliability of belief."[40]

But even if we grant that humans rely not just on indicators but on beliefs for survival, there is no reason to suppose that adaptive behavior requires that beliefs be *true*—a point crucial to rationality since the formation of justified true beliefs is at the heart of epistemology. One can imagine all kinds of false beliefs that could nonetheless have adaptive value. Consider the early human who is face-to-face with a dangerous predator. Assuming he could hold beliefs, there is no reason to think that those beliefs must be true in order to produce the right adaptive behavior. He could believe any number of things that are false and still produce a response of flight from the predator. He could believe that the predator is friendly but that the best way for him to show his friendship to it would be to sing loudly to it from a distance. Or he could believe that if he gets close to the predator he will be eaten. Both beliefs cause the same behavior—that of flight from the predator. In fact, whether they are true or not is irrelevant to their ability to produce the behavior necessary to survive.

Nevertheless, do not true beliefs generally produce adaptive behavior while false ones do not? It is true that we generally trust our rational faculties and

39. Nagel, *Mind and Cosmos*, 76.
40. Plantinga, *Where the Conflict Really Lies*, 329.

act according to beliefs that are true. But the point here is that in a world with a naturalistic framework, there is no reason to presume that our rational faculties are necessarily reliable.[41] We generally hold that true beliefs cause beneficial actions by virtue of the content of those beliefs. But if naturalism is true, then belief is simply a neural structure that has neurophysical properties that cause the appropriate behavior; the content of the belief is irrelevant to producing that behavior. A variety of beliefs with different content may have neurophysical properties that cause the same behaviors.

Morality and Moral Properties

Accounting for morality and moral properties on the basis of naturalism is just as challenging as providing an adequate grounding for rationality on that basis. This discussion presumes the objectivity of moral values, starting with the notion that morality and moral properties are built into the fabric of the world. This is the view known as "moral realism." In this view, morality resembles truth about the sciences and mathematics, and morality is discovered, not created by human beings.[42] Admittedly there are other meta-ethical options, such as forms of moral subjectivism (morality is subjective to an individual's personal tastes and preferences) and noncognitive views of morality (morality is not fundamentally a matter of truth but resembles something like moral cheerleading). However, moral realism arguably fits best with people's experience of morality in the world, where there are moral demands that appear to be universal, such that failure to live up to those demands brings guilt and shame.

C. S. Lewis's investigations into morality led him to conclude that there "is a Something which is directing the universe, and which appears in me as a law urging me to do right and making me feel responsible and uncomfortable when I do wrong. I think we have to assume it is more like a mind than it is like anything else we know because after all the only other thing we know is matter and *you can hardly imagine a bit of matter giving instructions.*"[43] Even those who hold to nonrealist views of morality find it difficult to live consistently with such views. There is no satisfactory basis for maintaining that anyone else should recognize that something "ought" to be different than

---

41. The following argument is taken from ibid., 336–37.

42. For other examples of philosophers who argue for moral realism, see Russ Shafer-Landau, *Whatever Happened to Good and Evil* (New York: Oxford University Press, 2004); Louis P. Pojman, *Ethics: Discovering Right and Wrong*, 8th ed. (Belmont, CA: Wadsworth, 2011). See also a summary of these arguments in Scott B. Rae, *Doing the Right Thing: Making Moral Choices in a World Full of Options* (Grand Rapids: Zondervan, 2013), 48–56.

43. C. S. Lewis, *Mere Christianity* (New York: Macmillan, 1947), 22, emphasis added.

it now "is." As J. P. Moreland concludes, "Given evolutionary naturalism, we have no reason at all to believe the world has anything other than natural facts and subjective reactions to them."[44]

On a strictly naturalistic basis, objective morality would likely be construed as a product of evolutionary development. Sociobiologist E. O. Wilson insists that "ethical codes have arisen by evolution through the interplay of biology and culture." He cites the parallels in behavior between animals and human beings and claims that they originated similarly: "*Ought* is the product of a material process."[45]

Naturalist philosopher Michael Ruse puts it this way:

> The position of the modern evolutionist . . . is that humans have an awareness of morality . . . because such an awareness is of biological worth. Morality is a biological adaptation no less than are hands and feet and teeth. . . . Considered as a rationally justifiable set of claims about an objective something, ethics is illusory. I appreciate that when somebody says "Love thy neighbor as thyself," they think they are referring above and beyond themselves. . . . Nevertheless, . . . such reference is truly without foundation. Morality is just an aid to survival and reproduction, . . . and any deeper meaning is illusory.[46]

This view holds, then, that moral behavior is advantageous to survival of individuals and especially large groups. Traits such as cooperation, respect, civility, and toleration are deemed to make it easier to get along and survive.

This view has serious problems. Many moral values that are widely accepted as universal do not seem to have much adaptive value. Consider, for example, values such as altruism and self-sacrifice—especially the kind of sacrifice that societies have long held up as heroic, such as compassion, forgiveness, unconditional love, and giving up one's life for another. These can all be seen as putting both individuals and communities at a competitive disadvantage when it comes to survival and reproduction. Giving up one's life entails literally losing in the evolutionary battle for survival. In fact, many if not most moral obligations call for an explicit setting aside of one's self-interest in order to adhere to moral values that have intrinsic value apart from the advantage gained for someone or some community.

---

44. Moreland, *Recalcitrant* Imago Dei, 157.
45. Wilson, "Biological Basis for Morality," 58, emphasis in original.
46. Michael Ruse, "Evolutionary Theory and Christian Ethics," in *The Darwinian Paradigm* (London: Routledge, 1989), 262; cited in William Lane Craig, "The Indispensability of Theological Meta-ethical Foundations for Morality," paper presented at the American Academy of Religion, November 1996, http://afterall.net/papers/the-indispensability-of-theological-meta-ethical-foundations-for-morality.

The difficulty for naturalism goes deeper here. As with rationality, the mechanism of adaptability has little to do with truth. Whether or not our moral evaluations are true does not really matter. Nagel cites the examples of pain and pleasure, recognizing that the association of pain with injury and pleasure with sex has important adaptive value. However, the evaluative notions of pain as *morally* bad and pleasure as *morally* good are both irrelevant to the adaptive value of those phenomena. In other words, the aversion to pain has value for survival regardless of any negative moral assessment attached to that pain.

According to Nagel, "The mind-independent truth of (moral) judgments has no role to play in the Darwinian story: so far as natural selection is concerned, if there were such a thing as mind-independent moral truth, those judgments could be systematically false."[47] Nagel rightly distinguishes between factual judgments, which are essential for the perception necessary to adapt and survive, and value judgments, which he holds are irrelevant for survival: "A Darwinian account of the origin of our basic desires and aversions, has no implications as to whether they are generally reliable perceptions of judgment-independent value, or whether indeed there is such a thing."[48]

Naturalism can even support moral conclusions grounded in reproductive advantage that are considered heinous today. For example, the authors of *A Natural History of Rape* argue that sexual assault can be explained in reproductive terms. The desire to reproduce when no mate is available results in the drive to force oneself onto someone with whom one can reproduce. To be fair, the authors do not condone sexual assault, but it is not clear on what basis they claim it is immoral and ought to be prohibited, if the impulse to engage in such behavior is rooted in biological advantage.[49]

Grounding something in biological advantage is conducive to survival but not necessarily conducive to truth—similar to the predicament involving rationality.[50] By extension of this argument, Christian philosopher Richard Swinburne suggests that on a naturalistic basis, we should expect nothing more than what he calls "wantons." Swinburne uses the term to describe individuals who have no notion of duty but only act to satisfy their own desires. If

47. Nagel, *Mind and Cosmos*, 107.
48. Ibid., 109.
49. Randy Thornhill and Craig T. Palmer, *A Natural History of Rape: Biological Bases of Sexual Coercion* (Cambridge, MA: MIT Press, 2000). See also Paul Copan, "God, Naturalism, and the Foundations of Morality," in *The Future of Atheism: Alistair McGrath and Daniel Dennett in Dialogue*, ed. Robert B. Stewart (Minneapolis: Fortress, 2008), 141–61.
50. Moreland, *Recalcitrant* Imago Dei, 157.

naturalism cannot produce any adequately grounded moral properties, then we are left with a world full of wantons.[51]

Naturalism fails to account for the full texture of a moral universe that is part of the normal experience of human beings. We live in a world where we experience moral obligations and moral judgments when we fail to live up to our obligations. Many moral obligations result in net losses of benefit to those who keep those obligations: the moral obligations to rescue someone in need, repay a debt, keep a promise, refrain from stealing, and so on. One could even argue that *most* moral obligations conflict with sheer self-interest. In other words, people have moral obligations that do not provide them with any material good or benefit but only impose limitations and losses. Yet they still have these obligations. If people fail to keep them, they are subject to judgment and often experience shame. The greater the failure, the greater the sense that people are somehow defective in character.

Having those obligations only makes sense if, as Christian philosopher George Mavrodes puts it, "reality itself is committed to morality in some deep way. It makes sense only if there is moral demand on the world too, and only if reality will in the end satisfy that demand."[52] And on a materialist view of the world, reality cannot satisfy that demand; the radical demands of morality that most often bring losses to one's life seem absurd from this outlook.

In a world that seems to have morality deeply embedded in its fabric, the naturalist has difficulty adequately accounting for moral awareness, moral values, and the objective truth of those moral principles that characterize the world. As atheist philosopher J. L. Mackie concedes, "Moral properties constitute so odd a cluster of properties and relations that they are most unlikely to have arisen in the ordinary course of events without an all powerful god to create them."[53]

Conclusion

The analysis in this chapter helps set the stage for grounding human significance in a Christian worldview that says that human beings matter tremendously because they are created by a good and rational God, in the image of that God, whose infinite love was revealed in the life, death, and resurrection of Jesus.

51. Ibid., 153. See also Richard Swinburne, *The Evolution of the Soul* (Oxford: Clarendon, 1993), chaps. 11–12.
52. George Mavrodes, "Religion and the Queerness of Morality," in *Ethical Theory: Classical and Contemporary Readings*, ed. Louis P. Pojman (Belmont, CA: Wadsworth, 1998), 653.
53. J. L. Mackie, *The Miracle of Theism* (Oxford: Clarendon, 1983), 115.

A naturalistic framework for human significance fails to provide a compelling account of why people matter, both in general and in terms of key traits such as consciousness, rationality, and morality that set human beings apart from the rest of the world. Although naturalism is the dominant worldview in secular culture around the world, it is as much a matter of "faith" as any religious view of the world. In fact, a Christian worldview better accords with the reality of the world and has compelling reasons to commend it, as later chapters demonstrate.

Further Reading

Churchland, Paul. *Matter and Consciousness*. Cambridge, MA: MIT Press, 1984.
   Churchland is one of the most ardent defenders of philosophical naturalism, especially in the philosophy of mind. He attempts to account for all of reality by reducing it to the laws of physics and chemistry. This is a standard defense of consciousness from a naturalist framework.

Moreland, J. P. *The Recalcitrant* Imago Dei: *Human Persons and the Failure of Naturalism*. London: SCM, 2009.
   Christian philosopher Moreland describes how naturalism fails to account for consciousness, free will, rationality, morality, and the continuity of personal identity. He concludes by arguing that viewing humans as made in the image of God provides an adequate accounting for these human traits where naturalism fails.

Nagel, Thomas. *Mind and Cosmos: Why the Materialist, Neo-Darwinian Conception of Nature Is Almost Certainly False*. New York: Oxford University Press, 2012.
   Atheist philosopher Nagel indicts naturalism for its failure to ground consciousness, rationality, and value. After also rejecting theism as an explanation, he tentatively suggests some sort of teleological view that accounts for these aspects of humanity.

Plantinga, Alvin. *Where the Conflict Really Lies: Science, Religion, and Naturalism*. New York: Oxford University Press, 2011.
   Christian philosopher Plantinga argues that, despite superficial conflict between science and religion, there is deep agreement between science and the Christian faith and deep discord between naturalism and science. He particularly argues that naturalism gives no assurance that people's rational faculties should be considered reliable when it comes to matters of truth.

Wolterstorff, Nicholas. *Justice: Rights and Wrongs*. Princeton: Princeton University Press, 2008.
   Interacting with a wide variety of ways to look at justice, Christian philosopher Wolsterstorff addresses the concept of justice and its justification from the ground up. He offers a thorough treatment of the subject and deals with the idea that rights and justice come from the intrinsic value of human beings.

6

The Privilege of Being Human

Transhumanism and Human Significance

PATRICK T. SMITH

Many sci-fi fans have been captivated by such movies as *Gattaca*, *Transcendence*, and *Lucy*. These cinematic portrayals of possible futures for human life and societies are not merely the imaginations of science fiction. Although their story lines contain some unreasonable premises and incredible science for the sake of entertaining moviegoers, we should not let the overly fantastic aspects of these films distract us from the issues these movies raise.

Many serious scholars in various disciplines suggest that parts of these descriptions of human possibilities will become realities in the not so distant future. They see much of the technology in place already, and more is being developed. Emerging today is a posthuman vision that seeks "the radical removal of the constraints of our bodies and brains and the reconfiguration of human existence according to technological opportunities."[1] The movement that seeks to transform humans into posthumans is broadly known as *transhumanism*.[2]

For some proponents, this movement seeks to defy the limits of human finitude in a quest for (near) immortality by utilizing radical life extension

1. Fabrice Jotterand, "At the Roots of Transhumanism: From the Enlightenment to a Posthuman Future," *Journal of Medicine and Philosophy* 35, no. 6 (2010): 617.
2. See Brent Waters, *From Human to Posthuman: Christian Theology in a Postmodern World* (Burlington, VT: Ashgate, 2006), 50.

programs and other biotechnologies. Thus, in the words of philosopher John Gray, "the hope of life after death has been replaced by the faith that death can be defeated."[3] In this scheme, the focus is on what humans may become as they transcend previous limitations on the way to a posthuman future that is radically different from their current experience. To quote a line from Morgan Freeman's character Professor Norman in the movie *Lucy*, "It's up to us to push the rules and laws, and go from evolution to revolution."[4]

The revolutionary thrust of a posthuman vision raises fundamental questions for contemporary society about the nature and proper ends of humanity. That pressing anthropological questions must be asked in light of transhumanism and the possibility of a posthuman future was not lost on philosopher Hans Jonas three and a half decades ago. Concerning the idea of humanity being remade through a combination of ideology and technological power, he writes, "If and when *that* revolution occurs . . . , a reflection on what is humanly desirable and what should determine the choice—a reflection, in short, on the image of [humans]—becomes an imperative more urgent than any ever inflicted on the understanding of mortal [humans]."[5]

Elaine Graham correctly argues that "technologies and the work of material fabrication are indeed substantive and not simply an incidental part of being human."[6] Thoughtful reflection on the history of human civilization would go some distance in substantiating this claim. Technologies developed by humans have long been able to transform the natural environment and enhance various aspects of the human condition. Perhaps that much is uncontroversial. However, human engagement in the technological endeavor itself is not the primary issue. Some observers think humans are on the cusp of being able to alter their very selves in such profound ways that they will be able to fulfill dreams (or nightmares) of achieving near godlike status. They will overcome limitations that previously have either "plagued" or been part of human existence, depending on one's perspective.

Graham brilliantly captures the irony of the contemporary debates when she writes that "advanced technologies are both heralded as the means by which humanity might attain its most fundamental aspirations—the '*end*'

---

3. John Gray, *The Immortalization Commission: Science and the Strange Quest to Cheat Death* (New York: Farrar, Straus and Giroux, 2011), 207–8; quoted in Gilbert Meilaender, *Should We Live Forever? The Ethical Ambiguities of Aging* (Grand Rapids: Eerdmans, 2013), xi.

4. *Lucy*, written and directed by Luc Besson (Saint-Denis, France: EuropaCorp Distribution, 2014).

5. Hans Jonas, "Toward a Philosophy of Technology," *Hastings Center Report* 9, no. 1 (February 1979): 41.

6. Elaine L. Graham, "The 'End' of the Human or the End of the 'Human'?," in *God and Human Dignity*, ed. R. Kendall Soulen and Linda Woodhead (Grand Rapids: Eerdmans, 2006), 263.

of the human—and perceived as constituting an urgent threat to human dignity: the end of the '*human*.'"[7] What does it mean to be human? What, if anything, ought to be valued about human life as it is? On a posthuman vision, why should humans as they are now be considered to have significance (moral or otherwise)? The pursuit of a posthuman vision raises some profound philosophical and theological questions.

This chapter examines what is at stake for the significance of people today in light of the transhumanist movement's emphasis on what humans might become. The discussion begins by identifying transhumanism as both a techno-scientific and profoundly ideological project, which is also a diverse and complex movement. The chapter then identifies a contrasting vision to the one provided by transhumanism; in many ways, it is an ancient vision, which affirms that, despite their frailties and finitude, people have inherent worth as they are now.

The next section takes up how a posthuman vision challenges this ancient notion of human significance and has negative implications for ethics and human flourishing. The final section of the chapter acknowledges that people do yearn for transcendence. However, the kind of transcendence people aspire to is better explained on a Christian understanding than a transhumanist one. As this chapter concludes, Christianity provides an external transcendence which is achieved through divine grace that allows people to remain genuinely human in the process.

The Vision of Transhumanism

Transhumanism has gradually developed over the past three decades, though earlier forms of the movement can be traced back to the seventeenth and eighteenth centuries in the works of such thinkers as Francis Bacon, René Descartes, and Marquis De Condorcet.[8] The movement can be understood as "a class of philosophies of life that seek the continuation and acceleration of the evolution of intelligent life beyond its current human form and human limitations by means of science and technology, guided by life-promoting principles and values." "Posthuman" refers to "possible future beings whose basic capacities so radically exceed those of present humans as to be no longer unambiguously human by our current standards."[9] Theological ethicist

7. Ibid., 263–64.
8. See Max More, "The Philosophy of Transhumanism," in *The Transhumanism Reader: Classical and Contemporary Essays on the Science, Technology, and Philosophy of the Human Future*, ed. Max More and Natasha Vita-More (Malden, MA: Wiley-Blackwell, 2013), 3–17.
9. "What Is Transhumanism?," Transhumanist FAQ, http://humanityplus.org/philosophy /transhumanist-faq/.

Brent Waters thinks it is impossible to know exactly what a posthuman is since "no such creature yet exists, and there is little consensus among those who speculate on its emergence."[10]

Some in the movement assert that the only thing necessary for a being to be considered posthuman is that it have at least one posthuman capacity. A "posthuman capacity" is a general central capacity that greatly exceeds "the maximum attainable by any current human being without recourse to new technological means" in the areas of health span, cognition, and emotion.[11] As prominent transhumanist philosopher Nick Bostrom writes, "Transhumanists hope that by responsible use of science, technology, and other rational means we shall eventually manage to become posthuman, beings with vastly greater capacities than present human beings have."[12]

On Bostrom's account, a posthuman is a being that is radically different from current understandings and ways of being human. It is this "posthuman vision" that transhumanism as a movement seeks to realize. The emphasis here with respect to transhumanism seems to be nothing short of human metamorphosis through the use of biotechnologies, which include an ever-expanding range of mechanisms such as "drugs, gene therapy and manipulation, psychopharmaceuticals, hormones, organ transplants, new forms of orthopedic appliances, and neural implants."[13]

Two broad observations concerning biotechnology and the transhumanist movement are especially important. First, the transhumanist movement is a technoscientific endeavor. A wide array of current and developing technologies can help realize the posthuman goals of transhumanism. The development of biotechnologies such as orthopedic appliances and neural implants "will enable human beings to reengineer themselves without the need to involve genetic and reproductive mechanisms."[14] According to transhumanism, these biotechnologies can accomplish incredibly drastic enhancements with respect to existing ways of being human. Targets include the "radical extension of human health-span, eradication of disease, elimination of unnecessary suffering, and augmentation of human intellectual, physical, and emotional

10. Waters, *From Human to Posthuman*, 50.

11. Nick Bostrom, "Why I Want to Be a Posthuman When I Grow Up," in *Medical Enhancement and Posthumanity*, ed. Bert Gordijn and Ruth Chadwick (New York: Springer, 2008), 108–9.

12. Nick Bostrom, "Transhumanist Values," *Journal of Philosophical Research* 30, Issue Supplement (2005): 4.

13. Dennis Hollinger, "Biotechnologies and Human Nature: What We Should Not Change in Who We Are," *Ethics & Medicine: An International Journal of Bioethics* 29, no. 3 (2013): 173.

14. C. Ben Mitchell, Edmund D. Pellegrino, Jean Bethke Elshtain, John F. Kilner, and Scott B. Rae, *Biotechnology and the Human Good* (Washington, DC: Georgetown University Press, 2007), 3.

capacities."[15] Possibilities even include the development of superintelligent machines that may be in some respects humanlike but not biological.[16]

Not only is transhumanism a technoscientific project, but second, it is an ideological movement entrenched firmly in philosophies of the Enlightenment. Transhumanist sociologist James Hughes states, "The belief that science can be used to transcend the limitations of the human body and brain, is an ideological descendent of the Enlightenment, a part of the family of Enlightenment philosophies." He sees the Enlightenment as that intellectual movement developing from the early seventeenth to the early nineteenth century whose key thinkers "broadly emphasized the capacity of individuals to achieve social and technological progress through the use of critical reason to investigate nature, establish new forms of governance, and transcend superstition and authoritarianism."[17] The transhumanist movement, then, extends beyond the realm of "gadgets and medicine." Also involved are "economic, social and institutional designs, cultural development, and psychological skills and techniques."[18]

In light of these two observations, transhumanism's aim to strive for a posthuman future through medicine and biotechnology embodies what ethicist Gerald P. McKenny has called the Baconian project. As developed in the works of Francis Bacon and René Descartes, this project contains a moral-technological imperative "to eliminate suffering and to expand the realm of human choice—in short, to relieve the human condition of subjection to the winds of fortune or the bonds of natural necessity."[19] This appears to be the heart of transhumanism's posthuman vision. The next section identifies some of the various forms this vision takes.

Transhumanism as a Diverse and Complex Movement

In light of its close relationship to the philosophies of the Enlightenment, transhumanism's incredible diversity is not surprising. Transhumanism encompasses thinkers from numerous fields of discourse (e.g., sociology, philosophy, political science, economics, genetics, and other natural sciences) with varying

15. Bostrom, "Transhumanist Values," 3.

16. See Ray Kurzweil, *The Singularity Is Near: When Humans Transcend Biology* (London: Penguin, 2005).

17. James Hughes, "Contradictions from the Enlightenment Roots of Transhumanism," *Journal of Medicine and Philosophy* 35, no. 6 (2010): 623.

18. Bostrom, "Transhumanist Values," 3–4.

19. Gerald P. McKenny, *To Relieve the Human Condition: Bioethics, Technology, and the Body* (Albany: State University of New York Press, 1997), 2.

visions of a posthuman future. In some cases these posthuman visions are in direct conflict with each other. Since the movement is partly derived from Enlightenment philosophies, it bears the marks of the "inherited internal contradictions and tensions of the Enlightenment tradition."[20] To observe this is simply to acknowledge what transhumanists themselves recognize—that the movement is characterized by a significant amount of variance at key points. This variance is especially evident in two key areas.

First, consider the different views regarding the importance attached to the human body. Futurist Ray Kurzweil, considered an innovator in artificial intelligence, offers one such view. He forecasts a future where radical enhancement of human capabilities will be possible through technology, primarily GNR (genetics, nanotechnology, and robotics). Based on the *law of accelerating returns*—the claim that technologies improve at an ever-increasing rate—Kurzweil thinks it is inevitable that humanity will arrive at *the Singularity*. This term refers to a "period during which the pace of technological change will be so rapid, its impact so deep, that human life will be irreversibly transformed."[21] Such irreversible transformation for Kurzweil has as its end a melding of human with machine, which is to be a complete revolution of what was once human existence. This posthuman vision includes the possibility of uploading individual human minds into machines. Hence, Kurzweil thinks there will be actual opportunities to extend personal identity indefinitely in ways previously unimaginable.

Gerontologist Aubrey de Grey offers a view related to Kurzweil's, though with some differences. Like Kurzweil, de Grey is a notable proponent of radical enhancement for the purposes of a posthuman future. De Grey envisions a human existence that can have indefinitely long life spans. He is developing strategies whereby humans can engineer beings of what he calls *negligible senescence*, which are beings that essentially do not age. In some ways, these profound life-extension programs might be the most appealing aspect of radical enhancement. According to de Grey, his striving to engineer beings of negligible senescence should not be considered a quest for immortality. He observes, "Immortality means inability to die, i.e., a certainty of never dying. . . . There is always a non-zero probability of dying some time—and indeed a non-zero probability of dying in any given year. So . . . we will never make ourselves immortal."[22] Central to his program is the idea of *longevity escape velocity*, where people are able to push back their date of death further and further.

20. James Hughes, "Contradictions," 622.
21. Kurzweil, *Singularity Is Near*, 7.
22. As quoted in Nicholas Agar, *Humanity's End: Why We Should Reject Radical Enhancement* (Cambridge, MA: MIT Press, 2010), 86.

The posthuman views of Kurzweil and de Grey have points of convergence and divergence. While their views are far more complex and detailed than the brief description here conveys, one can already discern some broad points where their views converge.[23] Their proposals are not the same, and the technologies employed are of a different sort, but they nevertheless have at least one goal in common: radical life extension. Both views see limited life spans as a problem of the human condition that needs to be addressed by biotechnology.

At the same time, there is a significant point of discontinuity regarding the necessity of the body. For Kurzweil the body seems to have no lasting importance. It merely preserves human existence and personal identity until *the Singularity*, when technology will arrive for humans to upload their consciousness to machines if they so choose. However, for de Grey technology focuses on maintaining humans as biological entities while staving off the aging process or possibly even reversing it to some degree. Whether or not biological embodiment continues in posthumans is a significant point of divergence. It is also a matter of great importance from a Christian perspective, as we will see.

Another important area where transhumanist outlooks differ involves sociopolitical and moral philosophy. Many proponents of transhumanism are not working on the biotechnologies that have the potential to fulfill a posthuman vision but are instead addressing how society should operate in a posthuman future where presumably there could be both humans and posthumans. How can human societies be sure that radically enhanced beings will not oppress or wrongly oppose the unenhanced? How do societies keep the unenhanced from rising up against those perceived to be better off? Here again, there are tensions, diversity, and disagreement that reflect transhumanism's commitment to many of the values of the Enlightenment tradition. Hughes helps explicate these points, three of which this chapter addresses below.

The first point is whether human–posthuman societies should take the form of political liberalism or technocratic elitism. As already noted, a key element of the Enlightenment was the use of technological development and human reason to improve human nature. Moreover, it was believed that decisions for improvement are best left to individuals to make. A problem arises when people do not make decisions that are in their own best interests or that lead to improvement. Historically this problem validated the need for developing forms of authoritarianism such as "colonialism and scientific socialist dictatorships of the advanced proletariat" to impose on the masses methods of improvement that are in accord with reason.[24]

23. Ibid., 8–9.
24. Hughes, "Contradictions," 629.

Likewise, according to Hughes, in keeping with this Enlightenment impetus, "transhumanists are overwhelmingly and staunchly civil libertarian, defenders of judicial equality and individual rights."[25] Yet a number of transhumanists recognize a need for some sort of benevolent technocratic elitism to prevent "the inadvertent evolution of humanity in undesirable directions."[26] Accordingly, what would be required politically is a technocratic elitism, perhaps involving what transhumanist Nick Bostrom calls a "singleton." Drawing from set theory, he notes that the term refers to a "world order in which there is a single decisionmaking agency at the highest level. Among its powers would be (1) the ability to prevent any threats (internal or external) to its own existence and supremacy, and (2) the ability to exert effective control over major features of its domain (including taxation and territorial allocation)."[27]

A second philosophical difference among transhumanists concerns whether ethical relativism or forms of ethical universalism should inform posthuman moral discourse, both now and in the future. On Hughes's account, "The 1948 adoption of the United Nations' Universal Declaration of Human Rights was a milestone in the institutionalization of Enlightenment values." If so, then the ideal captured in the declaration requires some sort of ethical universalism both to undergird it and ground what is needed to establish the value of humans in a manner such that "ethics and law should apply equally to all persons."[28] So far so good, it would seem.

However, Hughes also recognizes that Enlightenment philosophies generated a "postmodern" critique, which challenges the claim that human rights are self-evident and absolute. Instead, many have claimed that ethical universalism is itself historically situated and not absolute. According to Hughes, transhumanists find themselves caught between these two approaches regarding moral discourse and application. Many of them would want to promote, as an ethical absolute, "the rights of all people to control their own bodies and brain and to take advantage of technological enablement. But they hesitate at the idea that humanity today should attempt to constrain the moral choices of humanity's descendants."[29] To do so would be folly, given that our descendants would be superior to us both morally and intellectually.

A third philosophical point, closely connected to the first two, concerns the question of whether or not biotechnologies will lead toward inevitable

25. Ibid.
26. Ibid.
27. Nick Bostrom, "What Is a Singleton?," *Linguistic and Philosophical Investigations* 5, no. 2 (2006): 48–54, http://www.fhi.ox.ac.uk/singleton.pdf.
28. Hughes, "Contradictions," 633.
29. Ibid., 633–34.

progress in the form of a utopian posthuman vision for society or toward a dystopian society. The exhilarating vision that through reason and science humanity will be able to continually improve itself and its environment—and eradicate most if not all of the social ills that plague human society—was a hallmark of the Enlightenment. Many transhumanists share in this Enlightenment confidence concerning the eventual outcome of their evolutionary engineering efforts to bring about a posthuman future. Consider the enthusiasm of transhumanist Simon Young, evident in his fervent exhortation that since humans have "the will to evolve, . . . let us cast away cowardice and seize the torch of Prometheus with both hands."[30]

At the same time, a contrasting posthuman vision suggests that faith in inevitable progress might very well be misplaced. For example, in contrast to Kurzweil's predictions of a utopian *Singularity*, the followers of transhumanist Eliezer Yudkowsky "believe that an apocalyptic outcome is much more likely than a utopian one and that any [artificial intelligence] researcher not trying to ensure 'friendliness' of his creations is an agent of human extinction."[31] The sociopolitical and moral implications of the transhumanist vision are of special concern to Christian ethics, with its theological perspective on how humans as creatures do life together and how they relate to other parts of the creation.

In sum, transhumanism does not speak with a single voice on every important topic that it addresses as an intellectual, scientific, political, and cultural program. These observations should be kept in mind when one is attempting to systematize the movement in a concise way. But regardless of the different emphases (and sometimes disagreements), there is a shared consensus amongst proponents of transhumanism that appears to hold the movement together. Brent Waters describes it as the "unwavering belief that the current state of the human condition is deplorable, and the only effective way to remedy this plight is for humans to use various technologies to radically enhance and transcend their innate and latent capabilities. The condition of humans is wretched because they are finite and mortal creatures. Consequently, the overriding goal is to overcome these limitations through a series of progressive transformations."[32] In other words, transhumanists seem agreed that in order to improve the human condition, humanity must commit to (1) alleviating suffering through biotechnology aimed at transcending the problems associated with human finitude, (2) increasing indefinitely the current human

30. As quoted in Maxwell J. Mehlman, *Transhumanist Dreams and Dystopian Nightmares: The Promise and Peril of Genetic Engineering* (Baltimore: Johns Hopkins University Press, 2012), 11.
31. Hughes, "Contradictions," 633.
32. Waters, *From Human to Posthuman*, 50.

life span, and (3) endorsing the freedom to diminish the importance of the body. Moreover, existing humans should employ whatever resources necessary to bring about a posthuman vision in order to address social ills and extant human suffering. The emphasis of transhumanism is on what humans *can* or *may become*, not on what they currently *are*.

A Contrasting Vision—the Inherent Worth of People as They Are

Transhumanism's description of the human condition and its locating human value in what people can become are distinctly different from views that consider people to have inherent worth as they are. Many thinkers from various disciplines have appealed to the language of dignity to denote such worth. To be sure, there is not universal agreement regarding what a term like "inherent worth" means and to what entities it applies. This is the case both in common discourse and in technical philosophical usage. So its meaning and that of related terms will need explication here.

For the purposes of this chapter, philosopher Paul W. Taylor's analysis can tell us something about the term's meaning. According to Taylor, things with inherent worth are "entities that have a good of their own . . . [irrespective] of any instrumental value an entity may have and without reference to the good of any other being."[33] What Taylor describes as *inherent worth* other thinkers have referred to as *intrinsic value*.[34] If people have inherent worth or intrinsic value, then a robust notion of dignity applies to them. The notion of dignity has the weightiest of moral implications for those entities that have it.

For example, an appeal to dignity has frequently provided a basis for human rights. As ethicist Dónal O'Mathúna observes, "Dignity is an underpinning idea that has been incorporated into various conventions of human rights that seek to practically improve the lives of all human beings."[35] The term appears five times in both the 1948 Universal Declaration of Human Rights of the United Nations and the European Convention on Human Rights and Biomedicine.[36] The term also plays an important role in the 2005 Universal

33. Paul W. Taylor, *Respect for Nature: A Theory of Environmental Studies* (Princeton: Princeton University Press, 1986), 75.

34. Mark Timmons, *Moral Theory: An Introduction*, 2nd ed. (Lanham, MD: Rowman & Littlefield, 2013), 8, 20n6.

35. Dónal O'Mathúna, "Human Dignity and the Ethics of Human Enhancement," *Trans-Humanities* 6, no. 1 (2013): 99.

36. Daniel Sulmasy, "Dignity and the Human as a Natural Kind," in *Health and Human Flourishing*, ed. Carol Taylor and Roberto Dell'Oro (Washington, DC: Georgetown University Press, 2006), 71.

Declaration on Bioethics and Human Rights, where the "member states endorsed universal principles governing human subject research in 'medicine, life sciences and associated technologies' to promote respect for human dignity, human rights and fundamental freedoms."[37]

Despite its widespread appeal, the concept of dignity is often maligned due to its ambiguity.[38] Steven Pinker criticizes the contributors of an edited volume on the subject by highlighting the ambiguity in the authors' use of the term. He claims that employing the idea of dignity is unhelpful since doing so leads to outright contradictions: "We read that slavery and degradation are morally wrong because they take someone's dignity away. But we also read that nothing you can do to a person, including enslaving or degrading him, can take his dignity away."[39]

Regardless of such criticisms, many recognize the ethical importance that attends to the idea of dignity. Ronald Dworkin highlights the moral significance of the term "dignity" when discussing political rights, despite its lack of clear meaning:

> Anyone who professes to take rights seriously, and who praises our government for respecting them . . . must accept at a minimum, one or both of two important ideas. The first is the vague but powerful idea of human dignity. This idea . . . supposes that there are ways of treating [humans] that are inconsistent with recognizing [them] as . . . full member[s] of the human community, and holds that such treatment is profoundly unjust. The second is the more familiar idea of political equality. This supposes that the weaker members of a political community are entitled to the same concern and respect of their government as the more powerful members have secured for themselves.[40]

Even political equality is ultimately based on something more fundamental and foundational: "the powerful idea of human dignity." Although something like this idea does in fact ground much moral discourse regarding how humans should be treated—and reflects the idea that they have inherent worth—the vagueness surrounding the term "dignity" needs attention.

Criticisms of human dignity such as Pinker's raise an important distinction that needs highlighting in any discussion of the concept of dignity—the

---

37. Fabrice Jotterand, "Human Dignity and Transhumanism: Do Anthro-Technological Devices Have Moral Status?," *American Journal of Bioethics* 10, no. 7 (2010): 45.

38. See, e.g., Ruth Macklin, "Dignity Is a Useless Concept," *British Medical Journal* 327 (2003): 1419–20; Michael Rosin, *Dignity: Its History and Meaning* (Cambridge, MA: Harvard University Press, 2012).

39. Steven Pinker, "The Stupidity of Human Dignity," *New Republic*, May 28, 2008, http://www.newrepublic.com/article/the-stupidity-dignity.

40. Ronald Dworkin, *Taking Rights Seriously* (Cambridge, MA: Harvard University Press, 1977), 198–99.

distinction between invariable and variable senses of the term. The *invariable* sense refers to something intrinsic to humans, whereas the *variable* sense refers to something that is contingent or fluctuates depending on some perceived status or ability or even on the context in view. We can refer to this latter sense of dignity as circumstantial dignity. An example would be giving higher regard or more honor to some people based on their accomplishments or social status (e.g., an Olympic gold-medal winner over against a groundskeeper).[41]

The invariable sense of dignity, though, is more powerful since it refers to why all people matter—simply because they are people. This is the sense that is most suitable for establishing what some have called the *principle of equal regard* in ethics and sociopolitical philosophy. Moreover, it provides the impetus for affirming human solidarity and serves as the basis for making moral deliberations about circumstantial dignity meaningful. As O'Mathúna has recognized:

> When we see people being treated in undignified ways, or who are unable to achieve their full potential, or who live in abject poverty, and we say their dignity is diminished, we do not thereby claim that they have less inherent dignity. Nor should we claim that it is ethical to treat them differently than those who live more dignified lives. Instead, because of their inherent dignity, we have an ethical responsibility to address the reasons for their diminished circumstantial dignity.[42]

This widely held idea that people have some sort of inherent dignity signifies that humans are to be valued for who they *are* as they *are*. This is distinctly different from focusing on what humans might become in the future through biotechnology according to a posthuman vision. The notion of dignity strongly affirms that people matter morally despite the limitations and vulnerabilities that come along with being finite and embodied beings. In fact, how we view and treat people precisely in the face of their human limitations and vulnerabilities is one of the most powerful means of affirming the value or inherent worth of all people.

Dignity denotes not only the inherent worth of humans but also that they are the kinds of entities that have a special moral status among the rich biological diversity of the biosphere (which has its own form of intrinsic value). Much debate surrounds what exactly about humans grounds this exalted moral status, their dignity. As political scientist Francis Fukuyama writes:

> If what gives us dignity and a moral status higher than that of other living creatures is related to the fact that we are complex wholes rather than the sum

41. For a discussion of these points see O'Mathúna, "Human Dignity," 101–3.
42. Ibid., 103.

of simple parts, then it is clear that there is no simple answer to the question, What is Factor X? That is, Factor X cannot be reduced to the possession of moral choice, or reason, or language, or sociability, or sentience, or emotions, or consciousness, or any other quality that has been put forth as a ground for human dignity. It is all of these qualities coming together in a human whole that make up Factor X. Every member of the human species possesses a genetic endowment that allows him or her to become a whole human being, an endowment that distinguishes a human in essence from other types of creatures.[43]

A certain mysteriousness attends the idea of dignity and the exalted moral status associated with it. One of the biggest questions of our day is what way of looking at the world best explains the widespread conviction that people matter—that they have dignity. More attention is given to this matter below. For now we have been able to clarify the definition of human dignity that reflects the invariable sense of the term. In the words of William Cheshire, dignity is "the exalted moral status which every being of human origin uniquely possesses. Human dignity is a given reality, intrinsic to the human substance, and not contingent upon any functional capacities which vary in degree."[44]

Objections to the Inherent Worth of People as They Are

Many biocentric environmental ethicists and animal rights advocates have balked at such notions as human beings having some exalted moral status compared with other members of the biosphere.[45] This anthropocentric claim, it is charged, is the source of untold environmental degradation and suffering on the part of animals. Holding to such a dangerous view of the exalted moral status of human beings over against other animals is a form of speciesism which is morally unjustified. Moreover, they add, many additional members of the biosphere could meet the criteria for having inherent worth as described by Taylor and others. These are serious claims against the idea that people as they are now have an exalted moral status. If there is a view that causes such harm when followed consistently, then it should be vigorously challenged. Is there an adequate defense for the claim that humans have a special exalted moral status?

43. Francis Fukuyama, *Our Posthuman Future: Consequences of the Biotechnology Revolution* (New York: Farrar, Strauss and Giroux, 2002), 171.

44. William Cheshire, "Toward a Common Language of Human Dignity," *Ethics & Medicine* 18, no. 2 (2002): 10; quoted in O'Mathúna, "Human Dignity," 100.

45. See, e.g., Paul W. Taylor, chap. 3, "The Biocentric Outlook on Nature," in *Respect for Nature*, 99–168, especially 129–56; Peter Singer, chap. 2, "Equality and Its Implications," and chap. 3, "Equality for Animals?," in *Practical Ethics*, 3rd ed. (New York: Cambridge University Press, 2011), 16–70; and Peter Singer, "Speciesism and Moral Status," *Metaphilosophy* 40 (2009): 568–81.

There are indeed both philosophical and theological ways to affirm that humans have an exalted moral status while also holding that respect can and should be shown for animals and the environment. In order to demonstrate that a biblical outlook does not jeopardize the nonhuman creation in its upholding of human dignity, the response here takes a decidedly Christian theological turn. There are a number of forms that a theological response can take. We will focus here on relevant aspects of Jesus's teaching.

In Matthew 12:11–12, Jesus says, "Suppose one of you has only one sheep and it falls into a pit on the sabbath; will you not lay hold of it and lift it out? How much more valuable is a human being than a sheep! So it is lawful to do good on the sabbath." Consider also the words found in Matthew 6:26: "Look at the birds of the air; they neither sow nor reap nor gather into barns, and yet your heavenly Father feeds them. Are you not of more value than they?" In these verses, one can discern that Jesus is using a well-established form of religious argument found in rabbinic literature. In commenting on this approach and the ethical implications that follow, Richard Bauckham writes:

> The references to animals in the sayings of Jesus . . . belong to a form of argument from the lesser to the greater. Since, it is stated or assumed, humans are of more value than animals, if something is true in the case of animals, it must also be true in the case of humans. If acts of compassion for animals are lawful on the Sabbath, then acts of compassion for humans must also be lawful. If God provides for birds, then he can be trusted to provide for humans also. [46]

Jesus is following the pattern of Old Testament creation theology affirming the greater value of humans with respect to nonhuman animals in God's economy. Bauckham makes a few observations that are relevant to how Jesus's sayings help us properly understand the exalted moral status of humans. First, Bauckham notes that the kind of "hierarchy within the community of creation" that serves as the background for Jesus's statements "is one in which humans and animals alike exist for God's glory . . . , such that, if some animals do serve humans, humans also have responsibilities of care towards those animals (Matt. 12:11; Luke 13:15; 14:5)."[47] As Agneta Sutton writes, "Humans have a special covenant relationship with God, which involves a caretaker responsibility for the rest of creation" (see Gen. 9).[48]

---

46. Richard Bauckham, *Living with Other Creatures: Green Exegesis and Theology* (Waco: Baylor University Press, 2011), 94.
47. Ibid., 97.
48. Agneta Sutton, *Christian Bioethics: A Guide for the Perplexed* (New York: T&T Clark, 2008), 132–33.

Second, Bauckham observes that "Jesus never uses the superiority of humans to animals in order to make a negative point about animals."[49] A very important aspect of Jesus's teaching here is that humans and animals are all creatures of God. While animals may not be moral agents, they should be regarded as moral subjects with some interests that are worthy of protection.[50] Third, Bauckham writes, "Jesus' arguments certainly presuppose that animals have intrinsic value for God. Otherwise it would make no sense to say that humans are more valuable."[51] This observation suggests that there can be a difference in intrinsic value within God's economy. What accounts for the varying levels of intrinsic value?

Some have appealed to the idea of "natural kinds" for justification. For example, Daniel P. Sulmasy describes a natural kind as "designating a category of entities, all members of which, by virtue of being brought under the extension of the kind, can be necessarily known to be that sort of thing."[52] Members of natural kinds have attributes (inherent capacities) that characterize members of a natural kind, enabling them to fulfill their *telos* or purpose. When they do so they are said to be flourishing.

According to Sulmasy, those members who belong to the human natural kind have certain attributes whereby the status of "dignity" is conferred on them. Some of the attributes of the human natural kind are "the highly developed kind-typical capacities for language, rationality, love, free will, moral agency, creativity, and ability to grasp the finite and the infinite."[53] Many critics, of course, dismiss the notion of natural kinds, especially if it is understood as denoting some kind of rigid, fixed nature of the different species—something thought to be indefensible in light of Darwin. Any differences between the species would be matters of degree and not of kind.

Regardless of how one assesses recent debates and controversies about the usefulness of "natural kinds" language in light of contemporary arguments in the philosophy of biology, there is a sense in which the idea behind natural kinds points in the right direction. In some ways, the idea of natural kinds seeks to disclose something about the reality of human beings and to help provide content to the widely held moral intuition that people matter morally. It helps explain why under certain conditions humans' interests are given greater consideration than those of other members of the biosphere.

A biblically based theological outlook, however, does not look at people and the world in themselves as much as it considers the purpose, meaning, and value

49. Bauckham, *Living with Other Creatures*, 96–97.
50. Mitchell et al., *Biotechnology and the Human Good*, 52.
51. Bauckham, *Living with Other Creatures*, 96.
52. Sulmasy, "Dignity and the Human," 76.
53. Ibid., 78.

of life under God. Accordingly, following Neil Messer, "it might be more promising theologically to think of ourselves, and other living things, as members of *creaturely* rather than natural kinds." The implication of this approach is that theological categories take precedence in understanding the unique value and inherent worth that human beings have. As Messer explains, "This will mean locating our talk of the goods, goals, and the ends proper to human kind within an understanding of the good purposes of the Creator, rather than trying to read claims about these goods and ends off modern biological accounts that tend methodologically to bracket out considerations of the good."[54]

In light of this insight, another attribute can be added to the kind-typical capacities listed above for the human *creaturely* kind, which is that people are said to be the kinds of entities that are uniquely made according to the image of God in Christ. This particular attribute—imaging Christ—is what *theologically* justifies ascribing dignity to humans. It also provides a clue as to what it means *theologically* for humans to flourish as the kind of creatures they are under God. Moreover, it can provide some theological content for Fukuyama's mysterious Factor X which confers on people such high moral status.

Dignity and its relation to the image of God, then, is not merely based on biology or psychology, but perhaps can best be understood as something that is "imputed" to human beings. This sketch (greatly elaborated in part 3 of the present book) suggests that there are theological reasons for thinking both that human lives have more value than the lives of other entities in the biosphere and that people must see themselves as fellow creatures who need to stand in a form of solidarity with the rest of creation. Such solidarity entails human responsibility toward the environment that rigorously and painstakingly seeks to avoid environmental degradation and abuse of animals.

Posthuman Undermining of Human Significance

Comparing this theological outlook with the focus of a posthuman vision is revealing. Like most people, transhumanists want to affirm that people in their current condition matter morally. However, it is not so clear, given a posthuman vision and the core commitments that hold the movement together, why human beings matter morally as they are *now*. The question is whether a posthuman vision undermines the inherent worth and intrinsic value of human beings as they are now, despite its claims to the contrary. The answer is that it does, even if in subtle ways that are contrary to its best intentions.

54. Neil Messer, *Flourishing: Health, Disease, and Bioethics in Theological Perspective* (Grand Rapids: Eerdmans, 2013), 167.

Furthermore, it marginalizes those virtues and experiences that are commonly thought to make human life meaningful despite its limitations.

The goals and posthuman visions of transhumanism do seem in the end to advocate a form of the eugenics principle, which many people consider an affront to human dignity. Francis Galton, who coined the term "eugenics," defines it as "variations on a simple theme: using our understanding of the laws of heredity to improve the stock of humankind."[55] It is based on the premise that "all creatures would agree that it was better to be healthy than sick, vigorous than weak, well fitted than ill-fitted for their part in life."[56] While the eugenics movement is most often associated with the horrors and atrocities of Nazi Germany in the early part of the twentieth century, its roots can be traced back even earlier to the United States.

Two broad tactics have characterized eugenics. One is *positive eugenics*, which is a strategy that seeks to maximize the number of people with superior endowments in order to produce a superior human race. The other is *negative eugenics*, a strategy that seeks to constrain, if not end, the reproduction of those individuals deemed undesirable in order to keep their genes from being passed on to future generations. The aim of eugenics programs has been to minimize suffering and alleviate burdens of society by giving "the more suitable races or strains of blood a better chance of prevailing over the less suitable than they otherwise would have had."[57] Eugenics has been thoroughly discredited and condemned because of the negative value judgments made about certain human beings and the many detrimental consequences that resulted from eugenics programs. Such consequences include the racism fostered by the movement, the loss of innocent human life, the mistreatment of human "research" subjects, and the coercive effects on human freedom of government-implemented eugenics.

Despite these consequences of eugenics programs in the past, more recently a new eugenics movement has emerged—one claimed to be different from the old movement in three ways. First, there is a shift in focus. The new eugenics focuses on human progeny through reproductive technologies, as opposed to targeting the parents as the old eugenics program did. Second, the new eugenics is less cumbersome. Due to scientific advances in molecular genetics and technological advances in medically assisted reproduction, the new eugenics is now able to do what older eugenics programs could not. People can intervene directly into the reproductive process to select the kind of offspring with

---

55. As quoted in R. Kendall Soulen, "Cruising toward Bethlehem: Human Dignity and the New Eugenics," in Soulen and Woodhead, *God and Human Dignity*, 108.

56. Ibid., 108–9.

57. Francis Galton as quoted in ibid., 109.

the desired traits that they choose in order to enhance future generations of people. Such interventions are increasingly efficient as technology continues to improve and to become less expensive.

Third, the new eugenics focuses on the personal autonomy of individuals choosing and using reproductive technologies in a way that hopes to avoid the coercion that attended the old eugenics. As R. Kendall Soulen observes:

> Early eugenicists appeal to duty and self-sacrifice to encourage couples to marry and propagate (or not), with eugenic ends at heart. Moreover, the old eugenics used coercive state power to achieve its ends. In contrast, the new eugenics harnesses the awesome power of contemporary notions of freedom. Eugenic decisions will be exercised by parents seeking what is best for their children in the context of a liberal state and its guaranteed liberties.[58]

Noticeable differences between the older and newer forms of eugenics do exist then. The third point is especially significant here in claiming a *moral* superiority of the new eugenics over the old. In fact, some proponents question if the new eugenics programs should even be considered eugenics at all because of the negative connotations associated with the word. However, Soulen argues that the new eugenics shares the same basic principle that guided the early eugenics movement. The essence of the *eugenics principle* as developed by Galton and that characterizes both movements is "*selection*, preferring the existence of some individuals over others on the basis of desired or undesired traits."[59] Admittedly, governmental coercion in the old eugenics was unfortunate and morally wrong, but *selection* not coercion was the essence of the eugenics principle.

Something very much like the eugenics principle undergirds the transhumanist program with its posthuman vision. There is a philosophical adage that "better implies best." Its point is that something can only be "better" if there is a standard external to it by which comparisons of better or worse can be made. Transhumanism has such a standard. As Celia Deane-Drummond writes, "The kind of human flourishing projected by transhumanism is one of perfectionism molded by a particular cybercultural set of values and concerns." Accordingly, Deane-Drummond concludes that a posthuman vision of transhumanism is "eugenic insofar as it is a deliberate strategy for affirming and maintaining indefinitely only some forms of human life."[60]

58. Soulen, "Cruising toward Bethlehem," 110.
59. Ibid., 113, emphasis in original.
60. Celia Deane-Drummond, "Taking Leave of the Animal? The Theological and Ethical Implications of Transhuman Projects," in *Transhumanism and Transcendence: Christian Hope*

To be clear, the claim here is not that transhumanism is in every way like eugenics programs. For example, a key aspect of transhumanism is its desire to merge people in some ways with machines and other forms of biotechnology. Thus it is not an overt eugenics program seeking to select certain characteristics of future humans primarily through genetics or reproductive technologies. However, as in all eugenics programs, there is a commitment to raise the group in question (here, humanity as a whole) to a higher level by eliminating weakness. Transhumanism presumably has a threshold that could, for good or ill, serve as an intended baseline for all such future "human" beings. As noted earlier, though, it is not clear exactly what a posthuman would be. There is a sense in which transhumanists are "flying blind" with respect to what will be lost and gained by achieving the posthuman vision of radically altered human beings.

The point is not that it is wrong to use technology to try to eliminate conditions that cause suffering (e.g., on the grounds that good may come out of these unfortunate circumstances). Rather, transhumanism and its posthuman vision take aim not at the eradication of certain disabilities or particular traits of existing human beings (as has typically been the case in eugenic programs) but at the whole of humanity. Humanity or the human condition is to be improved upon by humans becoming something other than they are—something judged to be better. Herein lies the most troubling aspect of transhumanism's posthuman vision.

What, if anything, is wrong with a eugenics-type principle that seems to guide the posthuman vision of transhumanism? Primarily it undermines the inherent worth and dignity of human beings both by calling into question human solidarity and by violating the principle of equal regard. Secondarily it provides a *principled* basis for a discreet form of coercion even if it is not government sanctioned.

Solidarity in humanity today is called into question by the transhumanist preoccupation with what people can become. In the end the goal is not so much to help the needy but to eventually eliminate them. According to Soulen, a posthuman vision guided by a eugenics-type principle "does not really require us to have hopes for our fellow *human* beings, to bear their infirmities, or to labor on their behalf. Rather, it requires us to exercise a preference for the sort of fellow human [or posthuman] beings we will have, namely, the kind who will be least likely to trouble us with their infirmities in the first place."[61] The shared human condition with all its frailties and liabilities that forms

---

in an Age of Technological Enhancement, ed. Ronald Cole-Turner (Washington, DC: Georgetown University Press, 2011), 124.

61. Soulen, "Cruising toward Bethlehem," 114, emphasis added.

the basis for human solidarity does not appear defensible on a posthuman vision. Rather, as Deane-Drummond observes, "The human itself is now being transformed away from its roots in shared creaturely being."[62]

At the same time, a posthuman vision guided by a eugenics-type principle calls into question the principle of equal regard. By preferring the existence of certain kinds of individuals above others—namely, posthumans above humans—transhumanism fosters negative value judgments about the moral status and inherent worth of existing human beings. By its posthuman vision of humanity being replaced through the use of various biotechnologies, it may subtly communicate that human lives as they exist now are lives not worth living. Such a message flatly contradicts the affirmation of human dignity and the principle of equal regard.

Meanwhile, although the new eugenics may not be government mandated, it can be just as coercive in another way. If the biotechnologies along with the values of the transhumanist movement were to become commonplace, notes Dean-Drummond, "those choosing not to take up such opportunities might be considered irresponsible." She adds that "a similar pressure already exists on families who choose not to undertake prenatal tests for certain genetic diseases."[63] Based on transhumanist values and posthuman visions, there is no reason, in principle at least, why such coercion would not materialize.

Existential Concerns

Beyond the various concerns raised above, some important existential considerations also raise doubts about transhumanism. A posthuman vision challenges those virtues and experiences that make finite human life meaningful for many. Consider the portrait painted by philosopher Martha C. Nussbaum in her essay "Transcending Humanity":

> There is a kind of striving that is appropriate to a human life; and there is a kind of striving that consists in trying to depart from that life to another life. This is what *hubris* is—the failure to comprehend what sort of life one has actually got, the failure to live within its limits (which are also possibilities), the failure, being mortal, to think mortal thoughts. Correctly understood, the injunction to avoid hubris is not a penance or denial—it is an instruction as to where the valuable things *for us* are to be found.[64]

62. Deane-Drummond, "Taking Leave of the Animal?," 124.
63. Ibid.
64. Martha C. Nussbaum, "Transcending Humanity," in *Love's Knowledge: Essays on Philosophy and Literature* (New York: Oxford University Press, 1992), 381.

On Nussbaum's account, it is the vice of hubris not to recognize the limitations inherent in the human condition. She thinks there is something to be said for embracing our mortality. The desire of some humans to transcend radically their condition and ordinary experiences, she suggests, is produced by an anxiety that is based on the vulnerability of human life that is associated with our limitations.[65]

Charles Taylor thinks one can discern in Nussbaum's arguments "two things wrong with this aspiration" of transcending humanity. The aspiration is both self-defeating (at least in some forms) and damaging to the pursuit of human fulfillment. With respect to the former, the aspiration begins "as a human desire to offset the limits which often make our lives miserable and our world threatening. But if comprehensively granted, the wish would lift us altogether out of the human condition."[66]

Taylor and Nussbaum find the classic story of Odysseus and goddess Calypso illuminating on this point. Although Odysseus had the option to stay on Calypso's island with guaranteed safety and peace, he rejects that so that he may attempt the dangerous quest to rejoin his mortal wife. When first considering the alternatives, Taylor (echoing Nussbaum) observes:

> We may think he is crazy; the fear and vulnerability in us leaps at the offer; but as we consider it further we see that human love, caring, mutual support is inseparable from the limited and threatened human condition. Calypso's unending, danger-free life lacks all the meaning that the once-for-allness of human existence, with its key turning points, its moments to seize or lose, in short its human temporality, confers.[67]

In other words, the limitations that come with human finitude are themselves valuable; to lose them is to lose the very fulfillment we seek to gain.

As noted above, for Taylor and Nussbaum the problem runs still deeper. Transcending humanity is also wrong because "it actually damages us, unfits us for the pursuit of human fulfillment . . . by inducing in us hate and disgust at our ordinary human desires and neediness. It inculcates a repulsion at our limitations which poisons the joy we might otherwise feel in the satisfactions of human life as it is."[68]

If this line of thinking is correct, then when humans embrace their mortality they are able then to identify those aspects of humanity that make

---

65. This is the case for Nussbaum, whether the desire of transcending humanity is based on a posthuman vision or various traditions of religion.
66. Charles Taylor, *A Secular Age* (Cambridge, MA: Belknap, 2007), 625.
67. Ibid.
68. Ibid., 626.

them and their experiences truly valuable. More meaningful lives will not necessarily be the result of finding ways through biotechnology to transcend human limitations. As A. W. Moore muses, "It is not even obvious that, if I were immortal, my life would have *more* meaning. Indeed it might have less. For my mortality does lend shape to my life. It lends shape to every project I undertake and every scheme I embark upon."[69]

Many people, nevertheless, do feel the pull to transcend certain human limitations, perhaps in ways that go beyond what Nussbaum's insightful critique and Moore's astute observations would commend. Many consider it right to attempt to minimize various forms of suffering when possible through biotechnological interventions. But people also commonly recognize the importance of acknowledging limits to the means that humans should employ in order to accomplish these goals.

Instead of humans being completely transcendent *or* totally immanent, perhaps they are best understood as semi-transcendent. As Gilbert Meilaender puts it, people are "strange, 'in-between' sorts of creatures—lower than the gods, higher than the beasts." They are a relation of the temporal and eternal—"not simply body, but also not simply mind or spirit; rather, the place where body and spirit meet and are united (and reconciled?) in the life of each person."[70] Christians affirm something very much like this. However, according to Christianity, sin has distorted human longings for the kind of transcendence that is in keeping with the kind of creatures that people are.

The irony here is that transhumanism has a palpably religious dimension to it. As Maxwell J. Mehlman observes, "Eternal life, perpetual happiness, and permanent youthfulness certainly seem worth looking forward to, and therefore it is not surprising that transhumanists articulate them as the goals attainable by controlling future human evolution. What is striking, however, is how closely the transhumanist vision resembles the images of heaven at the heart of most of the world's religions."[71]

Mehlman's comments about the religious dimension ring a little truer to the ancient heresy of gnosticism than they do to a historic orthodox understanding of Christianity. Nevertheless, many of the categories and aspirations of the transhumanist movement do offer a sort of alternative theology. Accordingly, Brent Waters argues that "transhumanism represents a late modern religious response to the finite and mortal constraints of human

---

69. A. W. Moore, *The Infinite* (New York: Routledge, 1990), 227.
70. Gilbert Meilaender, *Neither Beast nor God: The Dignity of the Human Person* (New York: Encounter, 2009), 4.
71. Mehlman, *Transhumanist Dreams*, 23.

existence."[72] Waters is cautious about transhumanism because its soteriological and eschatological vision is based on heretical Christian sources. Transhumanist convictions, he argues, are theologically inadequate and socially dangerous.[73]

Christianity has traditionally affirmed that what humanity should aspire to—including human flourishing based on the kinds of creatures they are—is found in the person and work of Jesus Christ. A posthuman vision of humanity is one where vulnerabilities such as aging, death, embodiment, and finitude are to be overcome through the use of biotechnology and freedom over one's very self, by trusting in the power of human reason and goodwill to achieve that. In contrast to a posthuman vision, Christian theologian Vinoth Ramachandra argues that in a Christian outlook "a perfected humanity is a Jesus-like humanity."[74] Jesus exemplifies what it truly means to be human in that his earthly life "embraced finitude, vulnerability, dependence, and even evil and death through the incarnation, crucifixion and resurrection."[75] The fact that the resurrected Jesus maintains his glorified body for eternity affirms the necessary place of the body in what human flourishing entails.

Humanity's unique creation according to the image of God in Christ gives dignity to people as they are now, independently of what they might become later. However, humanity's existence in God's image also explains people's deep-seated aspiration to become something greater than they are right now—a compelling alternative to the transhumanist account. The future entity that people are to become in transhumanism is undefined; in Christianity the model is the glorious resurrected body of Jesus Christ. That body may well enable us to be the best of all that transhumanists aspire to be, without our needing to become anything other than truly human. People must depend on human power to get where the transhumanists aspire to go; in Christianity people have the power of God to get there. Even if technology could give everyone bodies with half the abilities of the resurrected body—which is doubtful—it cannot free people from their sinful preoccupation with self. That preoccupation, rather than other inadequacies, will always be the source of people's greatest unhappiness.

72. Brent Waters, "Whose Salvation, Which Eschatology? Transhumanism and Christianity as Contending Salvific Religions," in Cole-Turner, *Transhumanism and Transcendence*, 164.
73. Ibid., 163–74.
74. Vinoth Ramachandra, *Subverting Global Myths: Theology and the Public Issues Shaping Our World* (Downers Grove, IL: InterVarsity, 2008), 197.
75. Ibid., 213.

Further Reading

Cole-Turner, Ronald, ed. *Transhumanism and Transcendence: Christian Hope in an Age of Technological Enhancement*. Washington, DC: Georgetown University Press, 2011.

This book addresses various facets of the transhumanist movement by using theological resources from diverse Christian thinkers who represent a wide array of Christian traditions.

McKenny, Gerald P. *To Relieve the Human Condition: Bioethics, Technology, and the Body*. Albany: State University of New York Press, 1997.

This work provides a robust philosophical and theological critique of the Baconian project driving contemporary bioethics and explores the moral-theological significance of the body.

Mitchell, C. Ben, Edmund D. Pellegrino, Jean Bethke Elshtain, John F. Kilner, and Scott B. Rae. *Biotechnology and the Human Good*. Washington, DC: Georgetown University Press, 2007.

This book is a rich theological engagement with and assessment of the role of biotechnology regarding human flourishing and the common human good. It provides resources for how to understand emerging biotechnologies from the perspective of a Christian worldview.

Pellegrino, Edmund D., Adam Schulman, and Thomas W. Merrill, eds. *Human Dignity and Bioethics*. Notre Dame, IN: University of Notre Dame Press, 2009.

This compilation of essays, based on the work of the 2001–2008 US President's Council on Bioethics, reflects a vast range of philosophical and ethical perspectives and opinions on the significance of the language of human dignity for the future of bioethics.

Waters, Brent. *From Human to Posthuman: Christian Theology and Technology in a Postmodern World*. Burlington, VT: Ashgate, 2006.

This text provides a sustained reflection on and critique of the aspirations of the transhumanist movement. Waters thinks that the movement, with its technoscientific and ideological aspects, provides an alternative theology that in the end is deficient from the perspective of historic Christianity.

PART 3

Grounding Significance in God

7

Special Connection and Intended Reflection

Creation in God's Image and Human Significance

JOHN F. KILNER

People matter because they are in the image of God. This is a powerful claim.[1] This theological affirmation of biblical-Christian understanding, with its origins in the Old and New Testaments, has long been a liberating force in the world by inspiring people to respect and protect the dignity of all human beings. Yet misunderstandings of it have at times neutralized its liberating power.

Accordingly, explaining how humanity's existence "in God's image" can provide an enduring basis for why people matter will require a five-part argument. The first part will demonstrate that being in God's image has indeed been a dynamic inspiration in human history. The next three parts will develop a biblically sound understanding of what it means for people to be in God's image. And the final part will suggest the profound implications of this understanding for why people matter.

---

1. For elaboration and further documentation of this claim, see John F. Kilner, *Dignity and Destiny: Humanity in the Image of God* (Grand Rapids: Eerdmans, 2015). The author is grateful to Eerdmans for permitting this chapter to draw upon some of the material presented there.

Image-Inspired Liberation

Sadly, people have often failed to recognize or live up to what it means for humanity to be in God's image.[2] However, where the status of everyone as created in God's image has been embraced, the poorest and weakest people in society have usually benefited the most. For example, acknowledging people in need as created in God's image—and Christian service as conforming to the image of Christ—has long been a powerful impetus to help people in poverty.[3] In the last century, North American Christian leaders such as Martin Luther King Jr. have demonstrated the power of mobilizing efforts to care for impoverished people by making countercultural appeals to their status as "in God's image."[4] At the same time international gatherings of Latin American Christian leaders such as the Puebla Conference have been calling for much greater attention to the needs and perspectives of impoverished people precisely because they are "made in the image and likeness of God."[5]

The recognition that sick people, too, are in God's image has similarly benefited those incapacitated by illness. From the earliest centuries of the church, Christians cared for those who were sick because "every stranger in need was a neighbor who bore the image of God."[6] This recognition motivated Christians to refuse to participate in the common practice of infanticide (frequently in the form of abandoning deformed or unwanted infants outdoors).[7] In fact, this notion also spurred the early church to go beyond nonparticipation in infanticide to rescuing abandoned infants and caring for them.[8] More recently it has inspired Christian efforts to care for people with disabilities and for those with socially stigmatized diseases such as HIV/AIDS.[9]

2. For ample evidence of this, see John F. Kilner, "Much Is at Stake: The Liberation and Devastation of God's Image," in ibid., 3–51.

3. Gary B. Ferngren, "The *Imago Dei* and the Sanctity of Life: The Origins of an Idea," in *Euthanasia and the Newborn: Conflicts regarding Saving Lives*, ed. Richard C. McMillan, H. Tristram Engelhardt, and Stuart F. Spicker (Dordrecht: D. Reidel, 1987), 32–33; Gary B. Ferngren, *Medicine & Health Care in Early Christianity* (Baltimore: Johns Hopkins University Press, 2009), 103.

4. Martin Luther King Jr., *Where Do We Go from Here: Chaos or Community?* (Boston: Beacon, 1968), 180.

5. John Eagleson and Philip Scharper, eds., *Puebla and Beyond*, trans. John Drury (Maryknoll, NY: Orbis, 1979), par. 1142.

6. Ferngren, *Medicine & Health Care*, 145.

7. Darrel W. Amundsen, *Medicine, Society, and Faith in the Ancient and Medieval Worlds* (Baltimore: Johns Hopkins University Press, 1996), 50–69.

8. Goran Collste, *Is Human Life Special?* (Bern: Peter Lang, 2002), 45.

9. A good example of the former is the multicampus Harvest Bible Chapel in Chicago, Illinois, where the name of the fellowship of people with disabilities is "In His Image." For the

Humanity's creation in God's image has also inspired initiatives to stop people from oppressing other groups such as Native Americans, enslaved Africans and their descendants, and women.[10] Consider a few representative examples. Regarding Native Americans, the Spanish colonization of the West Indies and other areas of the Americas during the sixteenth century provides an excellent illustration.[11] In the face of much oppression and brutality, many Spanish friars risked their lives for the benefit of indigenous people there. As theologian Richard Mouw observes, their motivation was simply "the abiding confidence that they would not encounter any human being in any rural compound or village or city who was not created in the image and likeness of the God and Father of Jesus Christ."[12] Back in Spain, leaders in the church and legal system, such as Francisco de Vitoria, were inspired by the same confidence. Recognizing that Native Americans, like Europeans, were in God's image served as what theologian Roger Ruston calls "the doctrinal starting point" for Vitoria and his colleagues to challenge attempts to justify the domination of indigenous peoples.[13] Among the most ardent defenders of such people in the West Indies and beyond was Bartolomé de las Casas. His driving inspiration was that God deeply cares for all people, "formed in his image and likeness."[14]

The image of God played a similarly significant role in liberating enslaved Africans and their descendants in the United States and elsewhere. According to Abraham Lincoln and Martin Luther King Jr., recognizing that all people are in God's image was a driving force behind the US Declaration of Independence.[15]

---

latter, see World Council of Churches, *Christian Perspectives on Theological Anthropology* (Geneva: WCC, 2005), par. 119.

10. These categories are used to identify various peoples who have been oppressed and do not indicate that all native peoples in the Americas are in the same people group, nor that all people from Africa enslaved elsewhere are the same people group.

11. In his book *Inhuman Bondage: The Rise and Fall of Slavery in the New World* (New York: Oxford University Press, 2008), David B. Davis identifies the belief that all people are in God's image as a "crucial variable" in undermining slavery in Venezuela and some other parts of Hispanic America (143).

12. Richard Mouw, "The *Imago Dei* and Philosophical Anthropology," *Christian Scholar's Review* 43 (2012): 264.

13. Roger Ruston, *Human Rights and the Image of God* (London: SCM, 2004), 63, 86.

14. Bartolomé de las Casas, "Tratado Comprobatorio del Imperio Soberano y Principado Universal que los Reyes de Castilla y León Tienen sobre las Indias," in *Obras Escogidas*, ed. Juan Pérez de Tudela y Bueso (Madrid: Atlas, 1958), 5:357.

15. As Lincoln observed: in opposition to "the doctrine that none but rich men, or none but white men, were entitled to life, liberty and the pursuit of happiness," the authors of the Declaration of Independence insist that "nothing stamped with the Divine image and likeness was sent into the world to be trodden on, and degraded, and imbruted by its fellows." See Lincoln's "'Speech at Lewistown, Illinois' (August 17, 1858)," in *The Collected Works of Abraham Lincoln*, ed. Roy Basler (New Brunswick, NJ: Rutgers University Press, 1953), 2:546. See also

During the next century, as the US Civil War approached, influential leaders such as Theodore Dwight Weld, William Ellery Channing, William Whipper, Frederick Douglass, William Garrison, Henry Garnet, and Gerrit Smith effectively undermined support for slavery in some quarters through appeals to God's image.

In the process, according to several scholars familiar with this period, those enslaved were themselves empowered as well. As Carl Ellis Jr. writes, enslaved people "began to get the notion that they were created in the image of God. This confirmed their sense of human worth and reaffirmed their awareness that being a slave was a contradiction to their dignity as human beings."[16] Dan McKanan observes that fugitives from slavery "discovered the *imago dei* in their own capacity to expose slavery's violence."[17] Renita Weems adds that enslaved women gained strength to nurture their families and reject oppressive ideas "because of their fundamental belief in their rights as human beings created in the image of God."[18]

Surveying the many arguments made against slavery in the decades leading up to the Civil War, pastor-educator Richard Wills concludes: "More than the secular rationale could admit, freedom had a moral quality that grew out of a theological worldview that sought to articulate what it meant to have been created in God's image. . . . It was this theological idea that rallied the social resistance against the forces of slavery so all those created in God's image might be included in 'We the people.'"[19] Because of the continuing influence of this idea, notes theologian Karen Teel, "the image of God thus provides the theological basis for black people's struggle for survival."[20] As Glenn Usry and Craig Keener argue, a society "that does not know how to value anyone as . . . a person made in God's image" is missing what historically has been one of the greatest protections against the dehumanization and corruption of African-American men and women.[21]

Martin Luther King Jr., "The American Dream," in *A Knock at Midnight*, ed. Clayborne Carson and Peter Holloran (New York: Warner, 2000), 79–88.

16. Carl F. Ellis Jr., *Free at Last? The Gospel in the African-American Experience* (Downers Grove, IL: InterVarsity, 1996), 44.

17. Dan McKanan, *Identifying the Image of God: Radical Christians and Nonviolent Power in the Antebellum United States* (New York: Oxford University Press, 2002), 150.

18. Renita J. Weems, "Re-reading for Liberation: African American Women and the Bible," in *Feminist Interpretation of the Bible and Hermeneutics*, ed. Silvia Schroer and Sophia Bietenhard (London: Sheffield Academic Press, 2003), 25.

19. Richard W. Wills Sr., *Martin Luther King Jr. and the Image of God* (New York: Oxford University Press, 2009), 13, 15.

20. Karen Teel, *Racism and the Image of God* (New York: Palgrave Macmillan, 2010), 72.

21. Glenn Usry and Craig S. Keener, *Black Man's Religion: Can Christianity Be Afrocentric?* (Downers Grove, IL: InterVarsity, 1996), 56.

Sadly, women of all races have also been subject to demeaning treatment because of their gender. Historically they have often discovered that their creation in God's image is one of the most powerful protections against such treatment. In the words of African theologian Mercy Amba Oduyoye, "Many women have claimed the biblical affirmation of our being created 'in the Image of God' both for the protection of women's self-worth and self-esteem and to protest dehumanization by others. . . . Without it the whole edifice of human relations seems to crumble and fall."[22]

According to Palestinian Jean Zaru, the "truth that we are made in the image and likeness of God" has emerged for women in her part of the world as the greatest hope for overcoming injustice, exploitation, and oppression.[23] The international Mexico Conference on Doing Theology from Third World Women's Perspective similarly affirmed the importance of living out the implications of "being created in God's image" if there is to be justice in society.[24] According to Korean theologian Chung Hyun Kyung, "Asian women use most frequently the teaching from Genesis that contains the message that men and women are created equally in God's image."[25] In light of the global impact of the affirmation that all people are in God's image, the conclusion of Zoe Bennett Moore of the Cambridge Theological Federation is perhaps not surprising: "There is a direct connection between the value given to human life and that life seen as made in the image of God."[26] As University of Chicago's Anne Carr observes, women in particular today are invoking and benefitting from that connection.[27]

The influence of the image-of-God concept is not likely to disappear soon, since it continues to shape the guiding documents of a wide range of Christian

22. Mercy Amba Oduyoye, "Spirituality of Resistance and Reconstruction," in *Women Resisting Violence: Spirituality for Life*, ed. Mary John Mananzan et al. (Maryknoll, NY: Orbis, 1996), 170.

23. Jean Zaru, "The Intifada, Nonviolence, and the Bible," in *Feminist Theology from the Third World*, ed. Ursula King (Maryknoll, NY: Orbis, 1994), 230–31.

24. Mexico Conference, "Final Document on Doing Theology from Third World Women's Perspective," in *Feminist Theology from the Third World*, ed. Ursula King (Maryknoll, NY: Orbis, 1994), 37–38.

25. Chung Hyun Kyung, "To Be Human Is to Be Created in God's Image," in *Feminist Theology from the Third World: A Reader*, ed. Ursula King (Maryknoll, NY: Orbis, 1994), 252, 258.

26. See her presentation at the December 1998 World Council of Churches Consultation in England, as discussed in Jean Mayland, "Made and Re–Made in the Image of God," *Modern Believing* 40 (1999): 61.

27. Anne E. Carr, "The New Vision of Feminist Theology," in *Freeing Theology: The Essentials of Theology in Feminist Perspective*, ed. Catherine Mowry LaCugna (New York: HarperCollins, 1993), 14.

traditions and denominations—Protestant, Orthodox, and Catholic.[28] Nevertheless it is always in danger of losing that constructive influence when people alter what it means, either consciously or unconsciously, in order to benefit themselves and to put down others.[29] Accordingly, looking carefully at what the Bible teaches about humanity in the image of God is important for the preservation and promotion of this concept's liberating power.

Christ Is God's Image

Defining God's image has more to do with who God is—it is, after all, the image *of God*—than about who people are. The clearest definitional statements about the image of God in the Bible are those that straightforwardly state that Jesus Christ is the image of God (2 Cor. 4:4; Col. 1:15; cf. Heb. 1:3).

The New Testament reveals that God's purpose all along has not been for humanity to develop into some sort of generic "God's image," but to conform specifically to the image of Christ. "For those whom [God] foreknew [God] also predestined to be conformed to the image of [God's] Son, in order that he might be the firstborn within a large family" (Rom. 8:29). However, since Christ *is* God's image, conforming to the model of who Christ is and what Christ does is tantamount to conforming to God's image. It is the fulfillment of God's determination in the beginning that people would be created "in" or "according to" God's image, living and growing in reference to God's standard for humanity. That image/standard is Christ, whose God-given glory—evidence of being God's image—was present "before the beginning" (John 17:5; cf. Jude 25).

Accordingly, although a discussion of humanity's creation "in God's image" could begin with the pithy references to that idea in Genesis 1, beginning there has led people in all sorts of conflicting directions. If today's discussion took place at a time before the New Testament was available, then it would make sense to begin with Genesis. However, that is not our point in history. Since Genesis indicates that people are "in" or "according to" God's image, we would do well first to obtain as much clarity as the Bible provides on what God's image is. We can then examine what it means for humanity to be "in" or "according to" that image.

28. Jürgen Moltmann, *On Human Dignity: Political Theology and Ethics*, trans. M. Douglas Meeks (Philadelphia: Augsburg Fortress, 1984), 12 (Protestant); Gabriel Habib, "The Universality of Human Rights," *Christian Social Action* (December 1998): 36–37 (Orthodox); Ruston, *Human Rights*, 270 (Catholic).

29. See Kilner, "Much Is at Stake," for many illustrations of the devastation caused by altering the biblical meaning of the idea of creation in God's image.

When the Bible talks about something being an "image," that means it (1) has a *connection* with something else in a way that (2) may also involve a *reflection* of it. Being the image "of God," in particular, means having a special connection with God as well as being a substantial reflection of God. Having a special connection is significant, since that means when one mistreats the image one is mistreating the original. Being a substantial reflection is significant, since that means the image displays attributes (capacities, traits, abilities, etc.) of the original.

"Image" is the most common translation of the Hebrew word *tselem*, which appears in various biblical passages addressing humanity's creation in the image of God. Why the Old Testament employed this term for "image" most likely has to do not with the term's precision but with its flexibility and range. In the Old Testament the range of meaning of *tselem* extends all the way from the very physical to the completely nonmaterial. As such, it works well in reference to people, who have physical form but are more than material.[30]

The idea that being an image signifies having a special *connection* is evident, for example, in Daniel 3, which reports Babylonian King Nebuchadnezzar erecting a large *tselem* in the province of Babylonia. Anyone who spurned the image was to be thrown into a blazing furnace (v. 6)—a threat that Nebuchadnezzar acted on in the case of Shadrach, Meshach, and Abednego (v. 21). The purpose of this image was to represent the original in a way so closely connected to it that to honor it was to honor the original and to dishonor it was to dishonor the original.

As in Daniel 3, kings in the ancient Near East would periodically erect an image (*tselem*) in order to establish their presence as rulers where they were not physically present.[31] Evidence exists of this practice in Mesopotamia, the setting of Daniel 3.[32] Images representing rulers also occurred in Egypt, as when Pharaoh Ramses II had his image hewn out of rock on the Mediterranean coast north of Beirut as a sign of his rule there.[33]

While images could directly represent human rulers—reminding people of the rulers they represented—images could just as easily have a god as the reference point. This concept of an image representing a god, common in the

30. Hans Wildberger, "Tselem/Image," in *Theological Lexicon of the Old Testament*, ed. Ernst Jenni and Claus Westermann, trans. Mark Biddle, vol. 3 (Peabody, MA: Hendrickson, 1997); Wildberger there notes the "remarkable flexibility" of this term (1081).
31. David J. A. Clines, "The Image of God in Man," *Tyndale Bulletin* 19 (1968): 87–88.
32. J. Richard Middleton, *The Liberating Image: The* Imago Dei *in Genesis 1* (Grand Rapids: Brazos, 2005), 104–7.
33. Hans Walter Wolff, *Anthropology of the Old Testament* (London: SCM, 1974), 160–61.

ancient Near East,[34] surfaces in Amos 5:26 (cited in Acts 7:43), where even the house of Israel appears to be worshiping Mesopotamian gods by worshiping their images (*tselem*).

The other element often present in an image is the way that it provides a *reflection* of certain attributes of the original. In Old Testament times, images often displayed something about a king. In Daniel 3 the great height and gold surface of the image reflected the king's grandeur and wealth. Similarly, the image of Ramses II in Egypt (like that of Ashur-nasir-pal II in Mesopotamia) appears to have been fashioned to look like the ruler, with size or attached words impressing the observer with some of the ruler's noteworthy attributes. Accordingly, the biblical authors would reasonably have assumed the core ideas of connection and likely reflection as the reader's basic understanding of the term.

Not surprisingly, the primary Greek translation of *tselem* in the Greek Old Testament, *eikon*—which is also the primary word for "image" in the New Testament—can have as wide a range of meaning as *tselem*. In the New Testament, *eikon* most often refers to physical representations, but what an *eikon* represents is far more than physical in nature.[35] Furthermore, the idea that the original is closely connected with or somehow present in the image— already suggested in the term *tselem*[36]—becomes even more evident in the term *eikon*.[37] This renders the latter a particularly appropriate term for talking about Christ's identity as the image of God.

A good place to begin an investigation of Christ as the image (*eikon*) of God is Colossians 1:15. There Paul straightforwardly affirms that Christ "is the image of the invisible God," signaling both special connection and substantial reflection. The special connection is striking. As the image of the invisible God, Christ gives people the opportunity actually to see God. Jesus himself had previously observed: "Whoever has seen me has seen the Father" (John 14:9; cf. 12:45), for "the Father is in me and I am in the Father" (10:38)—so much so that "the Father and I are one" (10:30). Moreover, Jesus is a substantial reflection of God—someone who can be seen, in contrast with the "invisible God." When people look at Christ they see an expression of all the divine

34. Gregory K. Beale, *The Temple and the Church's Mission: A Biblical Theology of the Dwelling Place of God* (Downers Grove, IL: InterVarsity, 2004), 88–90.

35. I. Howard Marshall, "Being Human: Made in the Image of God," *Stone-Campbell Journal* 4, no. 1 (2001): 50–51.

36. W. Randall Garr, *In His Own Image and Likeness* (Leiden: Brill, 2003), 134–35.

37. Hermann Kleinknecht, "The Greek Use of *Eikon*," in *Theological Dictionary of the New Testament*, ed. Gerhard Kittel (Grand Rapids: Eerdmans, 1964), 2:389.

attributes in a way that reveals who God is and models how God intends for people to be in the world.[38]

The second of the two New Testament verses that explicitly identify Christ as "the image [*eikon*] of God" is 2 Corinthians 4:4. Here the idea of close connection is also present, again to the ultimate degree in which two are really one. Whereas in verse 4 the focus is on "the glory of Christ, who is the image of God," verse 6 explains that this glory is the "glory of God in the face of Jesus Christ." Because Christ is God's image, God and Christ are so closely associated that the glory of one is essentially the glory of the other. As the image of God, Christ is the expression, revelation, and very presence of God. Yet the close association of glory (*doxa*) with image suggests that being God's image involves more than connection. The image shows something about what it is connected to.

In 2 Corinthians 3:7, Paul introduces the subject of glory by talking about how visible it was on the face of Moses. However, now there is a "greater glory" (3:10), the "glory of God in the face of Jesus Christ" (4:6). For Paul, Christ as God's image entails not only the closest connection with God but also the greatest manifestation of God's glory. That glory is a visible expression or reflection of who God is and how God acts. It radiates the splendor of the very attributes of God. Those attributes in Christ provide the standard for who people were always meant to be and still can become if they will conform to Christ (Rom. 8:29).

One example of such attributes is God's *reason*, more commonly spoken of as God's wisdom. God's wisdom is not self-centered or prideful, in the way that human wisdom shaped by sin is (cf. the contrast between human and godly wisdom in 1 Cor. 1:19–25). Christ's wisdom is not merely abstract but ultimately provides concrete guidance for godly living. To "learn Christ" is to develop minds that are not futile or darkened (Eph. 4:17, 18, 20).

A second example of an attribute that God intends for Christ to manifest as God's image is *righteousness*. Christ, who has never sinned, is *the* example of what God intends for true humanity. When Paul lifts up Christ as God's image (2 Cor. 4:4), according to which believers are to be transformed (2 Cor. 3:18), it is in terms of a particular manifestation of glory—right standing with God (2 Cor. 3:9).

A third example of Christ's image-related attributes involves *rulership* over creation. Following language early in Hebrews 1 that echoes Christ's image-of-God status, Hebrews 2:8–9 indicates that God's intentions for people's

---

38. David H. Kelsey, *Eccentric Existence: A Theological Anthropology* (Louisville: Westminster John Knox, 2009), 2:966.

rulership since the beginning have not come to fruition, "but we do see Jesus." Christ's life, deat̃h, and glorification are all mentioned here as part of a description of the power Christ successfully exercised over "the suffering of death."[39] Christ demonstrates what rulership can be when sin no longer has control.

One final illustration of the model Christ provides for humanity involves *relationship*. In Romans 8:29, Christ is the firstborn in a loving family. According to Colossians 3:10–11, when Christ serves as the image according to which Christians are renewed, that renewal does away with prioritizing people on the basis of their being Greek or Jew, circumcised or uncircumcised, slave or free. Christ as God's image demonstrates God's commitment to reconciling relationships that have been broken for whatever reasons, including relationships with the nonhuman creation.[40]

Setting the Stage

If Christ is God's image, then how does that help explain who people are? The best way to answer that is to set the stage with several observations regarding how the Bible speaks about people and the image of God:

- people are "in" or "according to" God's image;
- God's image is undamaged by sin;
- not only are individuals in God's image but humanity as a whole is as well;
- God's image has to do with people as a whole rather than with particular human attributes.

Regarding the first observation: in various parts of the ancient Near East people considered kings, priests, and monuments to *be* images of gods or kings, as we have seen. The biblical writings adopt the general concept but adapt it in various ways to fit the biblical message—for example, by applying it to all people.

Another important adaptation of the Bible's authors is the way they normally avoid stating that people *are* the image of God.[41] Rather, these authors

39. On the connection of Heb. 2 here with Christ as God's image, see Michael S. Horton, "Image and Office: Human Personhood and the Covenant," in *Personal Identity in Theological Perspective*, ed. Richard Lints, Michael Horton, and Mark Talbot (Grand Rapids: Eerdmans, 2006), 190.

40. On the nonhuman creation, see Nico Vorster, *Created in the Image of God: Understanding God's Relationship with Humanity* (Eugene, OR: Pickwick, 2011), 24.

41. On the importance of paying careful attention to the ways that the authors of the Bible adjust ideas they employ from their contemporary cultural context, see Paul Niskanen, "The

insert a preposition indicating that people stand in some relationship with God's image.[42] Whereas Christ simply *is* the image of God (no preposition; 2 Cor. 4:4; Col. 1:15), people are created "in" or "according to" God's image. All of the image-related passages in Genesis (1:26, 27; 5:1; 9:6) consistently insert a preposition—and not always the same one—between people and the image. Image-related passages in the New Testament directly or indirectly referring to Genesis (e.g., James 3:9; Col. 3:10) also insert a preposition.

It is not plausible that in each of these passages the author is simply saying that people *are* God's image, as if there were no prepositions there and no need to add them.[43] In fact, prepositions such as "in" or "according to" make quite a difference. Saying that someone *is in* the water is quite different from saying that someone *is* the water. Saying that a violin *is (made) according to* a paper blueprint is quite different from saying that the violin *is* a paper blueprint.

The Bible's authors use prepositions to distinguish the rest of humanity from Christ. With Christ not overtly in view as a reference point in the Old Testament, the recognition there would simply have been that people are not yet God's image but are created "according to"[44] the standard of who God is (in order to reflect God's attributes to God's glory).[45] In the New Testament it would become clearer that Christ as God's image is the standard to which people need to conform completely. James 3:9 is particularly significant on this point since it conveys a New Testament author's summary of how the Genesis idea should be understood—not just as reinterpreted in Christ but in its own right applying to all people. In the words of James, people are made *kata* (according to) the likeness (image) of God, just as Paul explains that people need further making *kata* (according to or toward) the image of their creator (Col. 3:10).

There are two New Testament books that comment on the image status of both Christ and people, and they consistently distinguish between Christ, who is God's image, and people who need transformative growth according

---

Poetics of Adam: The Creation of *Adam* in the Image of *Elohim*," *Journal of Biblical Literature* 128, no. 3 (2009): 420.

42. On prepositions in the Bible as basically signifying relationships between things, see Murray J. Harris, *Prepositions and Theology in the Greek New Testament* (Grand Rapids: Zondervan, 2012), 27.

43. For further explanation, see Philip E. Hughes, *The True Image: Christ as the Origin and Destiny of Man* (Grand Rapids: Eerdmans, 1989), 21.

44. The standard *Hebrew and Aramaic Lexicon of the Old Testament* by Ludwig Koehler and Walter Baumgartner (rev. Walter Baumgartner and Johann Stamm, trans. M. E. J. Richardson [Leiden: Brill, 2001],104) specifies that "according to" is the best rendering of both prepositions, *be* and *ke*, in image-of-God passages in Gen. 1 and 5.

45. On the importance of this distinction see Sean M. McDonough, *Christ as Creator: Origins of a New Testament Doctrine* (Oxford: Oxford University Press, 2009), 91.

to the standard of that image. In Colossians 1, Christ straightforwardly *is* the image of God (v. 15). However, two chapters later, when people are in view, they are not God's image but need renewal *according to* God's image in Christ (3:10).[46] Similarly, according to 2 Corinthians 4:4, Christ *is* God's image. Yet four verses earlier (3:18), when people are in view, they need transformation *into* the divine image.[47]

Failing to take seriously the distinction between Christ being God's image and humanity being *in* God's image has contributed to overlooking a second important observation—that sin has damaged *people* but not God's image. If people were God's image, then by damaging people, sin would plausibly damage God's image. However, if people are created in (i.e., according to the standard of) God's image, there is no damage done to the standard just because people are later damaged.

There is ample discussion and documentation in the Bible regarding the destructive impact of sin on people. Yet at the same time there is every indication that people remain "in God's image"—that no harm has been done to this status or to the image on which it is based. People retain a special connection with God (though their relationship with God is badly damaged), and God still intends for people to reflect likenesses to God (though in actuality they largely fail to do so). The image of God is the standard of who people are created to be—embodied in the person of Christ—and that standard is not diminished in any way because of sin.

The image-of-God passages in Genesis 1, 5, and 9 all affirm that people are created in God's image. Although people subsequent to the fall in Genesis 3 are sinful, there is not the slightest indication of any damage to God's image.

46. The parallel passage Eph. 4:24 similarly includes the preposition *kata*, suggesting that it is central to the concept. In support of translating *kata* in Col. 3:10 as "according to" the model/pattern of Christ—and for the renewal here as parallel to the original creation "according to" the image of God in Gen. 1:27—see Peter T. O'Brien, *Colossians, Philemon* (Nashville: Nelson, 1987), 191; Murray J. Harris, *Colossians and Philemon* (Nashville: B&H Academic, 2010), 133; McDonough, *Christ as Creator*, 90–91.

47. Just as Paul can envision some people as justified, glorified, and conformed to God's image in Rom. 8:29, he can also refer to some as being the glory and image of God in 1 Cor. 11:7. However, he is not affirming in Rom. 8 that people are already image-conformed or glorified, or in 1 Cor. that they are already God's glory or image. Rather, Paul is recognizing the present dignity connected with their ultimate destiny. Paul knows all too well, for instance, that "all have sinned and fall short of the glory of God" (Rom. 3:23)—in fact, they have given up the glory of God (Rom. 1:23). In 2 Cor. 3:18 he reminds the Corinthians that glory must increase before their transformation into God's image can be accomplished. See John F. Kilner, "Humanity's Creation in God's Image," in *Dignity and Destiny*, 85–133, for more detailed biblical and scholarly support. Others such as Hughes (*True Image*, 22) agree that 1 Cor. 11:7 does not affirm that anyone is already God's image, offering additional exegetical rationales.

In particular, the rationale for punishing murder in Genesis 9:6 depends on people continuing to be in God's image.

The closest New Testament parallel to Genesis 9:6 is James 3:9. That passage similarly grounds a current standard of moral conduct directly in humanity's creation according to the image of God. The point that James is making requires the affirmation that all human beings have the status of being in God's image. Long after the author of Genesis 9 employed this affirmation to forbid murder, James has heard Jesus teach that if murder (angry action) is wrong, so are angry words (Matt. 5:21–22[48]). So James appropriately updates the image-of-God teaching of Genesis. In order to explain why his readers are not to curse human beings, he must affirm who human beings are today. They are specially connected with God by virtue of being made in God's image.

Not only does this indicate that God's image has not been lost; it also strongly suggests that it has not been badly damaged by sin the way that people have been. Otherwise the predicament would be akin to a badly damaged foundation of a building. Having a badly damaged foundation is not as great a problem as having no foundation at all. But it is a serious problem in the face of storms. There may be other supports propping the building up—as other biblical teachings commend respect for people.[49] Nevertheless, perception is key in terms of how people view and treat others. If God's image is a crucial basis for human significance, and that basis is damaged, people cannot help but have less respect for the "least lovely" among them, as history has shown.[50] It is therefore no wonder that the Bible's authors never even hint that the image of God has been damaged.

Acknowledging that the biblical writings recognize no damage done to God's image does not weaken or question the gravity of sin and its devastating effect on the human race and beyond. If anything, sin is all the more heinous because of the way that it causes people to contradict who their creator intends them to be.

Is a damaged image restored, then, or are damaged human beings restored? It is important to read the texts carefully and not to read into them ideas that are not there. In Romans 8:29, no language indicates that any sort of image is changing. Rather, God is changing people, and the image of Christ (God's

48. Although Jesus was only addressing implications for the community of believers, James applies the expansive principle to the wider human context that both he and the author of Gen. 9:6 had in view.

49. For further biblical support for human significance, see the following chapter in this volume by David Gushee.

50. For numerous examples, see Kilner, "Much Is at Stake."

image who is Christ[51]) is that to which people are being conformed. If any-thing, it is the constancy of that image that provides a sure goal for humanity. Again in 2 Corinthians 3:18, the image does not change; people do. Here and elsewhere, a different term—"glory"—signifies what changes. People are transformed "from one degree of glory to another." Discussions of God's image often confuse or conflate the terms "glory" and "image," resulting in the biblically unsound assumption that God's image can be damaged or lost and then restored, the way that glory can be. Colossians 3:10 conveys an outlook similar to that of the Romans and 2 Corinthians passages. The new humanity that characterizes Christians "is being renewed in knowledge according to the image of its creator" (v. 10). The image is not being renewed; people are. The image is the standard or goal according to which people are being renewed.

The consistent way that the Bible speaks about the standard of God's image has led many scholars to affirm that the fall and ongoing sin have not damaged God's image. Some reach this conclusion on theological grounds,[52] while others reach it on the basis of a wide range of Old and New Testament teachings.[53] Still others find Genesis 9:6 and James 3:9 particularly compelling on this score.[54] Those who focus on the Old Testament are particularly supportive of this view,[55] to the point that some have claimed virtual consensus regarding it.[56]

A third observation to make regarding how the Bible speaks about the image of God concerns who exactly is in God's image. Is it particular people, humanity as a whole, or both? Genesis 1:26 introduces the creation of humanity using a singular noun, *adam*, to which verse 27 refers by using both a singular and a plural pronoun. In other words, there is a tension between the singularity and plurality of humanity. *Adam* here refers not only to a single man named Adam but also to humanity as a whole. Contemporary readers can easily miss this point if they are located in societies like the United States that emphasize individuals, personal freedom, and autonomy.

51. On the image of Christ and the image of God as essentially the same thing, see Victor P. Furnish, *II Corinthians* (Garden City, NY: Doubleday, 1984), 215; Kelsey, *Eccentric Existence*, 2:999.

52. Gerald L. Bray, "God and Our Image," in *Grace and Truth in the Secular Age*, ed. Timothy Bradshaw (Grand Rapids: Eerdmans, 1998), 49–50.

53. E.g., Mark J. Mangano, *The Image of God* (Lanham, MD: University Press of America, 2008), 10.

54. E.g., Anthony A. Hoekema, *Created in God's Image* (Grand Rapids: Eerdmans, 1994), 18–20.

55. E.g., Wayne S. Towner, "Clones of God," *Interpretation* 59, no. 4 (2005): 351. See also Garr, *In His Own Image*, 153.

56. E.g., James M. Childs, "On Seeing Ourselves: Anthropology and Social Ethics," *Word & World* 2, no. 3 (1982): 230–31; Gunnlaugur A. Jonsson, *The Image of God* (Stockholm: Almqvist & Wiksell, 1988), 224–25.

Adam is more than one human being or even a huge number of human beings; there is also a corporate entity somehow connected to the image of God. At the same time, other passages such as Genesis 9:6 and James 3:9 more directly suggest that particular people have "image" status with all of the protections that should afford because it is *individual* people who are at risk for being killed or cursed. Connecting God's image both to humankind as a whole and to each of the humans who constitute that "kind" guards against destructive overemphasis on individuals *or* collectives.[57]

A fourth and crucial observation about the biblical image-of-God idea is that being in God's image has to do with people as entire beings (whether humanity as a whole or its component members are in view). There is no suggestion that being in God's image is constituted only by particular attributes (e.g., abilities, traits, capacities) that people have or have had. Select attributes (even if godlike) are not what are in God's image; persons as a whole are.

In Genesis 1, 5, and 9, each image statement simply affirms that "humanity" (*adam*) per se, not a particular aspect of *adam*, is in God's image. James 3:9 reflects a similar outlook. James identifies those who apparently warrant cursing most—those with the least godlike attributes—as those who are in God's image. The understanding that God's image has to do with people in their entirety, rather than with their most attractive attributes, has been heralded as "a new consensus."[58]

Viewing attributes (likenesses to God or differences from animals) as the basis of human worth opens the door to reductionism—focusing only on those characteristics of people that one thinks are most important. Such an outlook in turn can all too easily lead to devaluing those who do not manifest those characteristics sufficiently. From that flows logically (though perhaps unconsciously) the demeaning and oppression of particular groups of people who are seen as not as much in God's image as others are.[59]

For example, consider people with disabilities. The (generally unspoken) logic is that since attributes like reason, sensory abilities, and strength are what make people in the likeness of God and thus worthy of protection, those deficient in such attributes are not as worthy as others. A similar logic is at work concerning degree of wealth, color of skin, and so on. Biblical affirmations that all people are created in the image of God provide a ringing denunciation of

57. For more on the destructive overemphasis on collectives or individuals, see the essays by Gilbert Meilaender, Amy Laura Hall, and Russell DiSilvestro in part 1 of the present volume.

58. Stanley J. Grenz, *The Social God and the Relational Self: A Trinitarian Theology of the Imago Dei* (Louisville: Westminster John Knox, 2001), 193–94.

59. Regarding this logic, see Marc Cortez, *Theological Anthropology: A Guide for the Perplexed* (London: T&T Clark, 2010), 20. See also Ruston, *Human Rights*, 282–83.

basing people's significance on their particular attributes—precisely because that image is not a matter of current attributes, which vary in degree from person to person. Defining being in God's image in terms of people's reason (or other mental or spiritual capacities), righteousness, rulership over creation, or relationship all fall short on this score.[60] As Martin Luther King Jr. once observed, "There are no gradations in the image of God."[61]

The Creation and Renewal of People in God's Image

Stating that something is "in God's image" is actually an abbreviated way of referring to the biblical idea of being "in God's image and likeness." Because two terms ("image" and "likeness") are involved here, some people have mistakenly thought that they refer to two different ideas. However, there is ample biblical and extrabiblical evidence to confirm that there is a single idea (with two aspects) here that falls within the range of meaning of each term. Either term alone is sufficient to refer to this idea.

Genesis 1:26 indicates that God intended to create humanity according to the divine "image [*tselem*] and likeness [*demuth*]." Nevertheless, the author considers *tselem* alone to be sufficient to describe that standard in Genesis 1:27 and 9:6 and *demuth* alone sufficient in Genesis 5:1. Elsewhere in the Old Testament—and outside the Bible as well—either term alone also appears sufficient to refer to the very same idea.[62]

New Testament authors can also refer to people in terms of either "image" (*eikon*) alone (e.g., 1 Corinthians 11:7) or "likeness" (*homoiosis*) alone (e.g., James 3:9). Accordingly, biblical commentators commonly conclude that there is no meaningful difference between the terms; they represent the same idea.[63] Nevertheless, the idea to which either term can refer throughout the Bible does have two aspects, related to *connection* and *reflection*.

First, some sort of special *connection* between God and people is in view here. Understanding who people are is not possible without recognizing this

---

60. For a discussion of both the biblical inadequacy of each of these attributes as the definition of what it means to be in God's image—and the historical figures who have championed them—see John F. Kilner, "Misunderstandings about God's Image," in *Dignity and Destiny*, 177–230.

61. Martin Luther King Jr., "The American Dream," 88.

62. For example, both terms can describe the same human figures on a wall in Ezek. 23:14–15 or on the same statue in the ancient Near East (e.g., the ninth-century BC statue of King Hadyisi from Tell Fakhariyeh in modern-day Syria). See Alan R. Millard and Pierre Bordreuil, "A Statue from Syria with Assyrian and Aramaic Inscriptions," *Biblical Archaeologist* 45, no. 3 (1982): 135–41.

63. E.g., Brevard S. Childs, *Biblical Theology of the Old and New Testament: Theological Reflection on the Christian Bible* (Minneapolis: Fortress, 1993), 567.

connection. Passages about God's image do not define "image," but they do suggest something essential about it. According to Genesis 9:6, for instance, murdering human beings is forbidden not simply because God forbids it but for the deeper reason that people are connected with God in a profoundly significant way: they are created in God's image. When one destroys a human being, one is affronting God. According to James 3:9, not just murdering but even cursing a person is wrong because a person is in the image of God.[64] Cursing people is tantamount to cursing God.

People are not (yet) the image of God. Rather, they are made *in* the image of God—created to become God's image. That alone gives people a close connection with God. It identifies them with God. Christ as the standard of what that image entails was not revealed per se until the New Testament. Yet even the Old Testament acknowledged that humanity is profoundly connected with God by virtue of God's eternal purposes for humanity. It affirmed that people are not just stone statues the way that so many ancient images were—created in the final form of the image they were intended to be. Rather, people are living beings who must grow before they are what the creator intended them to become. Perceiving this and altering the ancient Near Eastern concept to communicate it is one of the great contributions of the Old Testament.

The primary way that the biblical account adds the aspect of growth is by joining the idea of "likeness" to "image" in a distinctive way. The term "image" indicates the presence of a connection between an image and an original. However, an image may or may not have anything to do with being like (i.e., sharing the traits or other attributes of) the original. Including "likeness" with "image" communicates that the kind of image in view here somehow has to do with likeness to the original.[65] It ensures that *reflection* as well as connection is a part of the concept.

"Likeness" alone may or may not indicate that there is a reason for the similarity—that there is a connection between the two things that are similar. A rock in a river and an egg at a store may look nearly identical, but there may be no connection between the two things. Including "image" with "likeness" communicates that the kind of likeness in view is because of a connection between two things, where one is the original. As noted above, though, this likeness cannot be referring to ways that people are currently like God. There-fore we must carefully examine the biblical text for direction.

---

64. Although this passage refers to God's "likeness," it is addressing the same "image" concept in view here.

65. For elaboration see Clines, "Image," 92; Hughes, *True Image*, 7–8; Grenz, *Social God*, 202.

Whenever the "likeness" term appears there in reference to humanity and God's "likeness-image," it is explicitly in the context of how God created people to be. There is a verb and a preposition. People are "created in [or according to]" the likeness of God. That is not the case where "likeness" appears elsewhere in the Bible. Elsewhere one thing is simply stated to be a likeness of something else. It is not just created with the *intention* that it be like it. It simply *is* like it. By contrast, in Genesis 1:26, God's *intention* for humanity is at the heart of what creation in the likeness-image of God entails. Later references to people created in God's likeness in Genesis 5:1 and James 3:9 not surprisingly mention the same creational intention since that is a necessary context for understanding the meaning of the term.[66]

Humanity's creation, then, in God's "likeness-image" (often in Scripture simply "image" or "likeness") means the following. All people are created according to "God's image," which the New Testament identifies as Jesus Christ. From before the beginning of creation, God intended that humanity should conform to the divine image, to Christ. So God created humanity well along the way toward that end. Even before the fall, humanity had further to go before becoming a full reflection of Christ, with a transformed spiritual body and imperishability (not able to die).[67]

However, after the fall people lost most of their ability to reflect God. They nevertheless continue to be in God's image, unique among creation as those whom God intends and will enable to become conformed to the divine image. No image has been damaged, for God's image is Christ—it is the standard of what God has always intended humanity to become. Even "being in" God's image has not been damaged, for to be in God's image is to be created according to that image, accountable to that standard. People are no less accountable simply because they reject God's standard.

In other words, the tremendous significance of human beings is completely secure, rooted in God's unwavering intentions rather than in variable, current human capacities. Even with their many limitations, all people have a special connection with God, and all people are created and intended to be

66. Theologians ranging from Karl Barth to various Eastern Orthodox leaders recognize the central place of "intention" here, though their theologies differ in many other ways. See Barth, "The Doctrine of Creation," in *Church Dogmatics* III/1, ed. Geoffrey Bromiley and Thomas Torrance (Edinburgh: T&T Clark, 1958), 200. For Eastern Orthodox views, see Linda Woodhead, "Apophatic Anthropology," in *God and Human Dignity*, ed. R. Kendall Soulen and Linda Woodhead (Grand Rapids: Eerdmans, 2006), 237–38.

67. Christ, as the one who has the power to destroy death itself, is imperishable (1 Cor. 15:25–26); and Christ now has a spiritual body (1 Cor. 15:44–47). "Just as we have borne the image of the man of dust, we will also bear the image of the man of heaven" (1 Cor. 15:49)— including an imperishable spiritual body.

a meaningful reflection of God. Christians are a community of people who are on a transformative journey mapped out for humanity by their creator. They are inspired by a destiny that others do not see and a dignity that others cannot adequately explain.

Being in God's image is not unrelated to the actual capacities, relationships, and functions that people have. Having those things is what normally flows from being in God's image but is not what defines it. People who lack those things are not any less "in God's image" than anyone else because of what it means to be "in" (i.e., "according to") God's image. It means that God's image (revealed to be Christ in the New Testament) provides the standard for their existence and their growth. Regardless of how far they fall short of fulfilling that standard, God intends for them—and offers them the means—to grow into all that actually being God's image entails.

God provides everyone with the opportunity for transformation according to the image of God that is Christ (i.e., according to the image of Christ). Humanity gains a dignity even now simply by being the recipient of such an amazing offer. God does not want anyone to perish (2 Pet. 3:9). In that sense, God intends for all to reflect God-glorifying attributes. God has created all according to the divine image and wants all actually to become God's image in Christ.[68] The offer they receive to be renewed according to (Col. 3:10), conformed to (Rom. 8:29), and thus transformed into (2 Cor. 3:18) God's image in Christ means that all are loved by God even with their many short-comings. For all we know, any particular person's renewal according to God's image may begin this very day. They should be viewed and treated accordingly.

People Matter

The implications of all this for how best to view and act toward people are extensive. As we noted at the outset, these implications are not merely theoretical but have been lived out in history. They are the evidence of the inspirational potential of the idea that all people are in God's image. People matter precisely because they are in the image of God.

Human existence itself has great significance on these very grounds. Many people use some term such as "dignity" to describe the special significance that comes from being in God's image.[69] This is not the dignity that varies

---

68. For elaboration see Bernd Oberdorfer, "Human Dignity and 'Image of God,'" *Scriptura* 204 (2010): 238.
69. Christoph Schwöbel, "Recovering Human Dignity," in Soulen and Woodhead, *God and Human Dignity*, 53. See also Vorster, *Created*, 16, 22.

according to circumstances but the dignity that necessarily accompanies being human. To reflect that distinction, some people refer to the latter form of dignity as "natural" or "inherent." The danger of such language is that it can imply that dignity is intrinsic to humanity without any necessary reference to God. Such is not the case with the dignity resulting from creation in God's image. This dignity is literally God-given.[70]

People receive dignity as a gift of God's grace. However, it does not come without requirements. So in that sense it has an element of loan as well as gift to it. There is something that must in some sense be accounted for or repaid (though not in kind).[71] Being created in God's image has great benefits, but it comes with God's great expectations. The dignity of all who are in God's image neither depends on particular human attributes nor diminishes due to sin. Human limitations cannot weaken it. This dignity is as unshakable as God.

Since God's image has a corporate dimension to it and is not just something true of particular people by themselves, humanity's existence in God's image entails that everyone has this special significance. There is a basic equality among members of the human community. This does not mean that people should consider everyone to be equal or identical in every respect. Rather, it suggests, in the words of theologian H. Richard Niebuhr, "that they deal with each person as uniquely sacred and ignore all claims to special sanctity."[72] As disabilities ethicist Hans Reinders observes, humanity's creation in God's image signifies that "in the loving eyes of God . . . there are no marginal cases of being 'human.'"[73] People who are socially marginalized need not define themselves by their circumstances or the demeaning viewpoint of those who would oppress them. With the notion of equality comes the idea of a basic unity. All people together have a common origin and purpose.

People, then, have a dignity, sacredness, equality, and unity that are grounded in their identity as created in God's image. Accordingly, they ought to be treated with respect. If one would respect God, one must also respect people,

70. Joan Lockwood O'Donovan, "Human Dignity and Human Justice: Thinking with Calvin about the *Imago Dei*," *Tyndale Bulletin* 66, no. 1 (2015): 136.

71. On human life as loan as well as gift, see John F. Kilner, *Life on the Line* (Grand Rapids: Eerdmans, 1992), 67.

72. H. Richard Niebuhr, *Theology, History, and Culture: Major Unpublished Writings* (New Haven: Yale University Press, 1996), 155; Vorster (*Created*, 22) calls this "fundamental" equality; Christopher J. H. Wright (*The Mission of God* [Downers Grove, IL: InterVarsity, 2006], 423) calls it "radical" (root) equality.

73. Hans S. Reinders, "Human Dignity in the Absence of Agency," in Soulen and Woodhead, *God and Human Dignity*, 124.

for they are in God's image. Some would even say that a sort of reverence or veneration is due other people.[74]

Respect and reverence, though, can mean a lot or a little, depending on how concrete a difference they make in how people act. One way for them appropriately to mean a lot is for them to undergird specific human rights. Human rights refer to what people ought to receive or be protected from by virtue of being human beings. People are in the image of God, which means that how they are treated and to what they have access matters greatly. Because they are in God's image, they have dignity and sacredness that warrant according them human rights. In that sense, ultimately, rights "are by the *imago* anchored in the structure of the universe."[75] Not surprisingly, many denominational documents emphasize the direct connection between human rights and humanity's creation in the image of God.[76]

Tying rights closely to a clear sense of the dignity and sacredness of all people is important. Otherwise, rights claims can degenerate into mere assertion of self with no regard for others. Human rights are really God's rights over humanity more than one person's rights over another. God is every person's creator, so God is the one to direct how people treat one another. Being in God's image, people draw their significance from God's connection with them and from the divine reflection God intends them to be, not merely from any attributes they may have per se, however excellent those are. In other words, people have rights; but contrary to much secular thinking, they do not have a right to those rights. Those rights flow from the God-given dignity and sacredness rooted in creation in God's image.

Just as humanity is not merely a collection of separate people but is also an interrelated whole, so humanity's status as created in God's image has implications for the whole together. God has a connection with humanity as a whole, just as God intends divine attributes to be reflected in humanity corporately and not just in particular people. God intends justice to be a hallmark of human society, as it is of God's own character. Just treatment of all requires taking account of personal and societal relationships in which people live, rather than merely viewing people as individuals. Where there is injustice, liberation from that oppression is what humanity's status in God's image mandates.

74. E.g., Ian A. McFarland, *The Divine Image: Envisioning the Invisible God* (Minneapolis: Fortress, 2005), 30.
75. John N. Thomas, "'What Is Man?': The Biblical Doctrine of the Image of God," *Interpretation* 3, no. 2 (1949): 163.
76. As Ruston (*Human Rights*, 270) observes: "In the twentieth century it became routine in papal and conciliar documents to link the possession of rights with the image and likeness of God in all human beings."

While people never warrant less than what justice requires, they frequently warrant more, namely, love. Love is God's ultimate intention for relationships of people with one another and with the natural world as well.[77] Love involves giving more than the required minimum and entails more than utilitarian maximizing of social benefit. It generates true solidarity, fellowship, interdependence, inclusive community, and unified mission. Such social blessings are as much human rights as are personal protections and provisions. Again, the reason that people warrant love is not that people are so lovable in themselves but that love is the appropriate way to treat those in God's image—whether they be friend or enemy.

Perhaps the most obvious way to violate justice and love is to destroy someone who is in God's image. Nicholas Rowe's *Tamerlane* laments war precisely because it

> Lays waste the noblest work of the creation,
> Which wears in vain its Maker's glorious image.[78]

Genesis 9:6 explicitly invokes humanity's status as created in God's image in conjunction with forbidding murder. Destroying someone in God's image, in light of God's connection with humanity, is tantamount to attacking God personally. The "shedding of blood" here (whether literally or by extension) may encompass all life-threatening or bloody violations of a person.[79] According to James 3:9, violations of people created in God's image can include even abusing them using words alone.

There are many arenas where treating people correctly as created in God's image is particularly important in light of historical abuses. The existence of all humanity in God's image offers a potent rallying cry for respecting and protecting even the weakest and most marginalized of human beings. God would have people attend to the needs of those who are impoverished, for example, precisely because they are in God's image. Impoverished people are not more important than others; however, their special degree of need means

77. As John Calvin writes: "There is but one way in which to achieve what is not merely difficult but utterly against human nature: to love those who hate us. . . . It is that we remember not to consider men's evil intention but to look upon the image of God in them." See John Calvin, *Institutes of the Christian Religion*, trans. Ford Battles (Philadelphia: Westminster, 1960), 3.7.6.

78. From act 1, scene 1 in the version available to John Wesley. See John Wesley, "The Deceitfulness of the Human Heart," in *The Works of John Wesley: Sermons IV*, ed. Albert Outler (Nashville: Abingdon, 1985), 156.

79. Michelle A. Gonzalez, *Created in God's Image: An Introduction to Feminist Theological Anthropology* (Maryknoll, NY: Orbis, 2007), 126–27; Ferngren, "*Imago Dei*," 38 (discussing Clement of Rome).

that the equal regard due to all who are in God's image requires a special degree of care toward them. Since both particular people and humanity as a whole are in God's image, addressing poverty must take place at both a personal and a structural level.

Similarly, people with special needs due to disabilities warrant special care and welcome. They have an image-based dignity that does not waver, regardless of their ability or potential ability. Christ, God's image, models God's embrace of disability on the cross and through a resurrected but wounded body. All of humanity shares in such woundedness and vulnerability in a variety of forms—physical, mental, moral, spiritual—without losing the dignity of being created in the image of God. Whoever would treat those with disabilities as God does must view them in terms of their destiny as well as their dignity—in terms of God's intention for them to be a divine reflection as well as their special connection with God. Their glorious renewal according to God's image in Christ is sure if they are believers and still offered to them if they are not (yet).[80]

Because people in their entirety, including their bodies, are in God's image, particular bodily characteristics never warrant ascribing greater worth to one race or ethnicity than another. Slavery is a particularly outrageous example of making unwarranted distinctions. As theologian Leonard Verduin writes, "To make a slave of a fellow image-bearer is a contradiction in terms."[81] It is a violation of how God intends one person in the divine image to behave toward another and thus an offense against God. The goal is not just reconciliation but racial solidarity in which appreciation of the diversity of God's purposes for humanity in God's image is the norm. Affirming humanity's creation in God's image is a powerful way to mobilize the church to oppose racism in word and deed. With due appreciation for the extent of evil involved in racism, Christians will not be satisfied with bandaging the wounded but will insist on transforming the social practices and structures that perpetuate racism.

The same goes for overcoming the oppression of women. People, male and female alike, are created in God's image—not because women and men have the same attributes but because of God's connection with them and the divine reflection God intends them to be. Because demeaning women is an affront to people in God's image, it is an offense against God. Moreover, men and women alike participate in renewal according to God's image in Christ. To

---

80. No wonder Reinders ("Human Dignity," 133–39) contends that a secular outlook cannot provide comparable warrant for the special care due to people with disabilities.

81. Leonard Verduin, *Somewhat Less Than God: A Biblical View of Man* (Grand Rapids: Eerdmans, 1970), 37 (though his view of being in God's image is somewhat different from the view presented here).

oppress women is for humanity to forfeit much of the blessing of diversity and interdependence that God has intended to characterize its existence in the divine image from the beginning. Women warrant far better than that. They must be treated with the dignity, rights, love, and all other blessings appropriate for those created and called to renewal in God's image.

Recognizing that a person or group is in God's image, then, has huge implications. So does recognizing oneself as created in God's image. Most discussion about the implications of being in God's image centers on who we see others to be; however, in some ways who we understand ourselves to be is more important.

Jesus highlights this difference in Luke 10. Whereas the man questioning him is preoccupied with the status of others ("Who is my neighbor?" [v. 29]), Jesus was more concerned with the questioner's own status (was he *being* a [good] neighbor? [v. 36]).[82] People preoccupied with the question of who else qualifies as "in God's image" can easily fail to consider carefully what it means to be in God's image themselves. They are loved by God—able to love all people as God does, simply as people—independent of the particulars of who they are and what they do. They can empower others to love themselves—and their neighbors as themselves—by helping them to recognize everyone as created in God's image.

The implications for pastoral care, counseling, and evangelism are immense. Even the weakest person—morally, emotionally, spiritually—has a special connection with the God of the universe. Moreover, God intends for that person increasingly to become a meaningful reflection of God en route to a glorious eternal life as the image of God in Christ. People's existence as created in God's image can give them meaning and hope even in the depth of despair.[83] The special connection and intended reflection that constitute being in God's image are God's enduring promise to them that so much more is possible if they are willing to let God break the power that sin has over them.

Much is lost when counselors and other caregivers fail to encourage and challenge hurting people with the glorious truth that they are created and continue to be in God's undamaged image. People need to hear the message that even though, like many others, they may be rather flawed in terms of

82. For more on this dynamic in the image-of-God concept, see Dónal P. O'Mathúna, "The Bible and Abortion: What of the 'Image of God'?," in *Bioethics and the Future of Medicine: A Christian Appraisal*, ed. John Kilner, Nigel Cameron, and David Schneidermayer (Grand Rapids: Eerdmans, 1995), 205.

83. See Christoph C. Schonborn, *Man, the Image of God*, trans. Henry Taylor and Michael Miller (San Francisco: Ignatius, 2011), 42. Schonborn here affirms the teaching of John Paul II that only because of creation in the image and likeness of God does humanity have meaning in this world.

rational, moral, relational, or other attributes, their special connection with God and intended reflection of God—their existence in God's image—is not about their current limited attributes. Despite all that is wrong with them, their existence in God's image is a constant that has not deteriorated.[84] It is irrevocably grounded in God's pronouncement voiced in Genesis 1:26 before the beginning of the creation of humanity and echoed in Romans 8:29. In fact, while people are already created in God's image, so much more is possible for those who will trust God to renew them in Christ according to that image. What wonderful news that is!

Effective ministry flows from recognizing oneself and those among whom one is ministering as together in God's image. That recognition fosters humility in the one ministering. It also engenders a sense of responsibility to reflect God's character and priorities well. Image-inspired ministry involves speaking constructively and working for the liberation of others from oppression. It entails acting redemptively. For example, overcoming racism is not just a matter of recognizing that people who are "different" are in God's image. It includes living out one's status as created in God's image in a way that allows God to overcome one's self-centeredness and enables seeking the well-being of all as God does. Similarly, overcoming gender bias requires more than acknowledging women as created in God's image. It also necessitates men understanding and living more fully the implications of their own creation in God's self-sacrificial image.

Ultimately, then, why do people matter? It is because they have a special connection with God and are intended to be a meaningful reflection of God. They have the dignity and destiny of those made in God's image.

Further Reading

Berkouwer, G. C. *Man: The Image of God*. Grand Rapids: Eerdmans, 1975.
   A classic theological anthropology that combines discussion of major historical figures and movements with systematic theological and biblical perspectives on what it means for humanity to be in the image of God.

Hoekema, Anthony A. *Created in God's Image*. Grand Rapids: Eerdmans, 1994.
   A biblical presentation from a Reformed theological perspective of the nature and destiny of human beings, reflecting structural and functional aspects of being created in the image of God.

84. Like the very person of God, the image of God remains "untarnished by the tragic" in the words of Thomas E. Reynolds, *Vulnerable Communion: A Theology of Disability and Hospitality* (Grand Rapids: Brazos, 2008), 187.

Howard, Thomas, ed. *Imago Dei: Human Dignity in Ecumenical Perspective.* Washington, DC: Catholic University of America Press, 2013.

A collection of three essays on human dignity and humanity in the image of God, one each from three major Christian traditions: Eastern Orthodox, Catholic, and Protestant.

Hughes, Philip E. *The True Image.* Grand Rapids: Eerdmans, 1989.

A biblically rooted Christian account of humanity structured in terms of people's creation in the image of God, the impact of sin and redemption on the image, and the connection of anthropology with Christology.

Kilner, John F. *Dignity and Destiny: Humanity in the Image of God.* Grand Rapids: Eerdmans, 2015.

A detailed examination of the primary biblical passages and vast secondary literature on the image of God, documenting the liberating power of this idea and the devastation caused by misunderstandings of it.

McFarland, Ian A. *The Divine Image.* Minneapolis: Fortress, 2005.

A theological account of Christ as revealing the invisible God and of human beings whose existence in the image of God tells us not what they are but what they need to do if they would know God.

Middleton, J. Richard. *The Liberating Image: The* Imago Dei *in Genesis 1.* Grand Rapids: Brazos, 2005.

A study of humanity's creation in the image of God as it appears in Genesis 1, examining its meaning in the text, insights from consideration of its sociocultural context, and its implications for ethical issues such as peace and generosity.

Smail, Thomas A. *Like Father, Like Son.* Grand Rapids: Eerdmans, 2006.

A discussion of what people's relationships with God and others should be like since people are in the image of the trinitarian God—Father, Son, and Holy Spirit.

8

Nothing Human Is Merely Human

Various Biblical Bases for Human Significance

DAVID P. GUSHEE

When a man or woman wrongs another, breaking faith with the LORD, that person incurs guilt and shall confess the sin that has been committed.

—Numbers 5:6–7

This obscure text illuminates the most important contribution of the Bible to the conviction that human life has God-given dignity.[1] The text implies that no human interaction is merely a human interaction. Every encounter between human beings is simultaneously an encounter with a God who cares deeply about what happens between human beings. The Christian tradition that human life has dignity, and the rich repertoire of moral expectations associated with that tradition, has for centuries hinged on the assumption embedded in Numbers 5:6–7 and echoed throughout the biblical drama. Meanwhile, every moral tradition that has abandoned belief in God but still seeks to encourage

1. The present author is grateful to William B. Eerdmans Publishing Company for permitting this chapter to draw upon some of the material presented in his larger work *The Sacredness of Human Life: Why an Ancient Biblical Vision Is Key to the World's Future* (Grand Rapids: Eerdmans, 2013).

human beings to serve rather than exploit each other must find a different basis for its exhortations.

Four primary elements of the witness of the Old Testament foster the view that human life has great dignity: its creation theology (including the *imago dei* or "image of God" theme), its depiction of God's compassionate care for human beings, its covenantal and legal materials, and its prophetic vision of a just wholeness (*shalom*) for Israel and all creation in the promised eschatological future.

In the New Testament, three primary elements also contribute to a human dignity ethic: the nature of Christ's ministry, the meaning of the career of Jesus (incarnation, cross, resurrection, ascension), and the ethos and moral vision of the early church.

This chapter will sketch the main contributions of each of these biblical elements to a Christian human dignity ethic.

Creation and Humanity

Human life has dignity because it was created by God. Genesis 1–2 tells us that humans do not come from nowhere but are the creative handiwork of God, and this by itself elevates human worth and dignity. What is true about humans as creatures of their creator is also true about all other creatures on the planet in their own way. Humans are a part of a *community* of God's earth-creatures; other creatures have divinely ascribed status as well.

At the same time, God says uniquely about humans, "Let us make human-kind in our image."[2] This theme explicitly includes "male and female" (Gen. 1:26–27) and implicitly includes every male and female. God is *equally* the creator of *all* humans. The dignity, blessings, and tasks given to human beings are given to all. There is one God who makes one humanity. According to biblical creation theology, then, there is at least an implicit primal human egalitarianism and unity.

Genesis 2 adds another important element. It tells a story in which God begins to create humanity by creating one person first. God creates human-kind by creating a first man. The first woman is then formed out of the first man. From these first parents come absolutely everyone else. In this sense all people are kin, all part of one vast human family. As Paul states in his speech at Mars Hill: "From one ancestor he made all nations to inhabit the whole

---

2. For a more comprehensive examination of this theme, see John Kilner's chapter "Special Connection and Intended Reflection: Creation in God's Image and Human Significance" in the present volume.

earth" (Acts 17:26). All people have the same divine creator and the same earthly forebears.

Genesis 1 and 2 teach a primal human unity and equality. By virtue of their common origin, all people are one race—the human race. There is one universal human family. These claims equalize human status and teach people to value one another far beyond those most closely connected to them. All are God's creation, all are children of Eve, and all are part of one human family.

Every worldview (even purportedly Christian ones) based on an ontologically divided or fundamentally hierarchical view of humanity poses a threat to this theology of creation, which in turn poses a threat to such worldviews.

Adolf Hitler, for example, once wrote: "The Jew is the creature of another god, the anti-man. . . . He is a creature outside nature and alien to nature."[3] For Nazi ideology, the higher "Aryan race" shared neither a common origin nor a common humanity with Jews. Only the Aryan race was in the image and likeness of God. In fact, Nazi instruction to primary school students emphasized the fundamental and irrevocable division of humanity into separate and hierarchically ordered "races."[4] There was no such thing as a common humanity, only distinct races and peoples competing with one another for supremacy on the planet. History has demonstrated the consequences of that antibiblical ideology.

Few concepts have been more important than all humanity's creation by God in God's image for elevating and equalizing the status of human beings, birthing a human rights tradition, and dignifying human life. Herein lies the first essential biblical warrant for human dignity.

God's Compassionate Care and Liberating Deliverance

The Old Testament reveals a God who cares for humans with deep compassion, for despite their ascribed grandeur, people are physically vulnerable creatures, subject to great misery and suffering. Examples of God's care for rebellious yet beloved human creatures abound in every book of the Bible. The numerous examples of God's care for needy and suffering human beings have impressed themselves deeply on the consciousness of those peoples and cultures most affected by the biblical witness and especially those whose suffering has been the gravest.

3. Quoted in Leni Yahil, *The Holocaust: The Fate of European Jewry, 1932–1945* (New York: Oxford University Press, 1990), 44.
4. *The Nazi Primer: Official Handbook for Schooling the Hitler Youth*, trans. Harwood Childs (New York: Harper & Brothers, 1938), see especially chap. 1, "The Unlikeness of Men."

The Bible records that God's universal care for humanity took a more focused form in God's compassionate response to the suffering of God's people Israel when they were enslaved and threatened with the mass murder of their children in Egypt. God's deliverance from that slavery and infanticide profoundly shaped the Jewish people. The Hebrew community, apparently a peaceable alien minority amid the Egyptian population, was forced into backbreaking slavery. The situation took a decisive turn for the worse when Pharaoh moved from enslavement to a policy that can only be described as genocidal: "Every boy that is born to the Hebrews you shall throw into the Nile" (Exod. 1:22). The text states that "the Israelites groaned under their slavery, and cried out. Out of the slavery their cry for help rose up to God. God heard their groaning, and God remembered his covenant with Abraham, Isaac, and Jacob. God looked upon the Israelites, and God took notice of them" (Exod. 2:23–25).

But then, continues the narrative, God selects Moses as the means by which the Israelites will be delivered. Under God's direction Moses embarks on an escalating confrontation with Pharaoh that finally leads to their miraculous escape out of Egypt through the waters of the sea, with their pursuers "dead on the seashore" (Exod. 14:30) when the waters come crashing down. Liberation has come, as God's gift. The text celebrates the death of Israel's pursuers, the tragic though apparently necessary cost of Israel's liberation.[5]

This founding narrative of God's compassionate deliverance has been fundamental to Jewish life and thought for three thousand years or more. As Old Testament scholar James Muilenburg notes, "The hour of the Exodus was the birth of a people, the people chosen and called to a destiny. Israel's consciousness of being a people was first awakened at the Exodus."[6] Its echoes resound through later Old Testament writings and in every generation of Jewish life. "Remember that you were a slave in the land of Egypt. and the LORD your God redeemed you" (Deut. 15:15). This memory instructs Israel as to the character of God: one who keeps covenant promises to the chosen people, one who looks with compassionate love on Israel, and one who delivers Israel when it appears that all is lost. God is a God of justice who fights for Israel's liberation when the people are victimized. God's character also demands that Israel's way of life as a people reflect a responsive covenant fidelity, compassionate love, and justice, a central theme in both the law and the prophets.

5. In a world gone so terribly wrong, human dignity is often defended through the defeat and punishment of those who violate it. I am grateful to Sondra Wheeler for this insight.
6. James Muilenburg, *The Way of Israel: Biblical Faith and Ethics* (New York: Harper & Row, 1961), 50.

This Exodus-shaped vision has been embraced by many suffering peoples in human history. Michael Walzer has shown the endless fecundity of the Exodus texts for inspiring social revolutions in the name of justice.[7] This motif surfaced quite powerfully during the turn toward liberation theology in developing nations. Latin American, Asian, and African Christians toiling under conditions of colonialism and oppression turned to the God who hears the cries of the oppressed for dignity and a decent life. Catholic theologian Gustavo Gutiérrez helped set the tone when he argued that the Exodus account is paradigmatic of a God who acts to liberate the oppressed from their political subjugation and to deliver them to a life of freedom in community. God's action in history is fundamentally concerned with such liberation of the oppressed, and the Exodus-Sinai narrative reveals that "to love Yahweh is to do justice to the poor and oppressed."[8]

Catholic authorities resisted elements of liberation theology, notably its flirtations with Marxist ideology, but did weave into the teaching tradition of the church the idea of God's "preferential option for the poor." God chooses to side with impoverished people precisely because God is a God of compassion and justice and because failure to side with those who are poor means siding with their oppressors by default. God demands that all who would be God's people must do the same—especially those who hold social power: "Give justice to the weak and the orphan; maintain the right of the lowly and the destitute. Rescue the weak and the needy; deliver them from the hand of the wicked" (Ps. 82:3–4).

Perhaps the paradigmatic case of an Exodus motif surfacing in the North American context is in African-American life. No biblical narrative proved more important for those in the bondage of slavery or for the development of the black church tradition; and the Exodus remained influential all the way through the civil rights movement.

As enslaved Africans and their descendants toiled in seemingly endless servitude under their supposedly Christian masters, the subversive power of this narrative offered sustenance and revolutionary hope and undercut the false version of Christianity which blessed slavery as God's will.

In the days of Jim Crow, when slavery had given way to legalized segregation and second-class status, black Americans again found great strength in the Exodus narrative of a delivering God. Theologian James Cone provocatively describes what they found there: "In the Exodus-Sinai tradition Yahweh

---

7. Michael Walzer, *Exodus and Revolution* (New York: Basic Books, 1985).

8. Gustavo Gutiérrez, *A Theology of Liberation: History, Politics, and Salvation* (Maryknoll, NY: Orbis, 1973), 194.

is disclosed as the God of history, whose revelation is identical with his power to liberate the oppressed. There is no knowledge of Yahweh except through his political activity on behalf of the weak and helpless." The biblical God, continues Cone, is a "God of the oppressed," which means that "God discloses that he is the God of history whose will is identical with the liberation of the oppressed from social and political bondage."[9] This sets a foundation for black theology and according to Cone applies to all legitimate Christian theology, which is not just private but public, not just personal but political, and not just impartial in situations of social injustice but engaged on behalf of the oppressed.

The concept of a God who demonstrates impartial love for all people may seem to contradict the idea of a God whose ear is inclined to the oppressed. This tension has kept many from accepting a divine "preferential option" for the subjugated and victimized, and it was often articulated as a reason for rejecting liberation theology. But in a sinful and unjust world, justice requires special divine (and human) help for those who experience oppression and victimization. Some must be lifted up from the dust—even at the price of confrontation—to join the ranks of others who already have the privilege of standing up straight. Moreover, while God's revelation and will involve more than liberation, they never involve less than that. The lawgiver and liberator are one and the same God.

Biblical Law and Human Dignity

The Old Testament narrative moves from Exodus to Sinai, from God's miraculous deliverance of the covenant people to God's articulation of the laws that shall govern Israel. Several warrants for a strong human dignity ethic can be noted in biblical law.

First, God is the ultimate source of law in Israel, and God holds the people accountable for their obedience. From Exodus through Deuteronomy the text depicts God as literally dictating the laws that shall govern Israel—beginning memorably with an awe-inspiring, indeed terrifying, divine appearance at Sinai.[10] There is a profound role given in the Old Testament to teaching a proper fear of God as lawgiver, who holds Israel accountable for compliance with his laws.[11]

9. James H. Cone, *God of the Oppressed* (New York: HarperCollins, 1975), 65.

10. Patrick Miller, "Divine Command and Beyond: The Ethics of the Commandments," in *The Ten Commandments: The Reciprocity of Faithfulness*, ed. William P. Brown (Louisville: Westminster John Knox, 2004), 15.

11. Texts like this one abound: "Do not be afraid; for God has come only to test you and to put the fear of him upon you so that you do not sin" (Exod. 20:20). There is a reason people used to be called "God-fearing" and a reason they are no longer often called that.

If God is the source of law, then the full weight of God's sovereign majesty and power falls upon the laws thus offered. God's own dignity transfers to the law. The law therefore carries profound holiness and authority. God commands; humans must obey—beginning with Israel, God's chosen people. And there are severe consequences for disobedience.

The very idea that there is a divinely given moral law that governs Israel—and perhaps governs more than Israel—is itself a major contribution to a human dignity ethic. Human moral obligation is ultimately rooted in God's will.[12] As Old Testament scholar Walter Kaiser notes, "The foundation for all morality . . . is the character and will of God [who] is supreme and without any competitors. . . . There will be no higher standard of obligation."[13] God's revealed will establishes a transcendent reference point by which all life is to be governed and by which all human laws and actions can be evaluated and critiqued.

Certainly a variety of complexities can be identified related to an ethics rooted in God's will, most especially complexities related to adjudicating between different interpretations of that will and applying of a particularistic understanding of God's will in a pluralistic society and world. But for now the point is to suggest that such a formulation of ethics at its best causes humans to consider the divine source of moral obligation and therefore the great responsibility before God to meet that obligation.

Second, this elevation of a transcendent legal and moral standard over human life provides further momentum toward human equality before the law. In many cultures, the ruler defines the law and is above the law. No one in ancient Egypt could hold Pharaoh accountable. But the kings of Israel found that they were indeed accountable to the same divinely given moral law that governed everyone else. As J. David Pleins writes, "We . . . see in these formulations of the Ten Commandments the makings of a subtle critique of monarchy and an attempt to limit its powers. . . . Unlike elsewhere in the ancient Near East, where law was a royal prerogative, [here] each and every member of the community has a religious, moral, and social duty toward the nation's deity."[14]

The many kings who were tempted to forget that their will was not absolute in Israel often ended up paying a serious price for their pride and disobedience.

---

12. See Richard J. Mouw, *The God Who Commands: A Study in Divine Command Ethics* (Notre Dame, IN: University of Notre Dame Press, 1991); cf. Remi Brague, *The Law of God: The Philosophical History of an Idea*, trans. Lydia G. Cochrane (Chicago: University of Chicago Press, 2007).

13. Walter J. Kaiser Jr., *Toward Old Testament Ethics* (Grand Rapids: Zondervan, 1983), 85.

14. J. David Pleins, *The Social Visions of the Hebrew Bible: A Theological Introduction* (Louisville: Westminster John Knox, 2001), 48.

But the only context in which that could happen was in a society that believed in divinely given moral law and the accountability of all to God's law, with a socially acknowledged role for prophets who could demand compliance in God's name.

The power of law to level the playing field in human life has the effect of weakening those who are strong and strengthening those who are weak. The standard is clear: all stand equal before the law and before those human courts charged with enforcing it. No favoritism (Lev. 19:15) or partiality (Deut. 1:17) is to be shown toward those who are "great." If any member of a particular political community is understood to have moral and legal rights, all have such rights.[15] In Israel, where law was seen as divinely given, a failure to administer justice to all was treated as a direct affront to the God who authored the law. This is one reason why so much attention is given in biblical law to the functioning of the justice system itself, beginning with the command in the Decalogue against bearing "false witness" (Exod. 20:16), which has a primary reference to the necessity of truthful testimony in the administration of justice (cf. Exod. 23:6–8).

Third, the grounding of all moral obligation in God's law had a deep impact on the understanding of human law. A just society lives not by royal fiat but under the rule of law; and law itself must be anchored in the will of God, or it can become cruel and arbitrary. A long tradition of Jewish and Christian thinking about law developed, which came to argue that no human law carries authority if it stands in fundamental contradiction to divine law. On this view, laws that violate the moral order are illegitimate and without binding force, requiring a response of disobedience and resistance.

Such reasoning still continues to surface in surprising ways. Schooled in the tradition of Western Christian thought, Martin Luther King Jr. argued for civil disobedience to segregationist laws during the struggle for African-American equality in the United States.[16] As King famously states, "An unjust law is no law at all." When God's will is understood as the ultimate foundation of legitimate human law, it creates an understanding of law that goes far beyond a mere social contract.

Fourth, the leveling and inclusive nature of Old Testament law is reinforced by the narrative framework in which it is offered. Law begins in Israel with

15. The question then becomes: Who counts as a member of a political-legal community? The first step is to say, "Every member of this political community stands equal before the law." The second step is to include more and more people in the agreed political community. Thanks to Sondra Wheeler for reminding me of this critically important point.

16. Martin Luther King Jr., "Letter from Birmingham City Jail," in *A Testament of Hope: The Essential Writings and Speeches of Martin Luther King, Jr.*, ed. James Melvin Washington (San Francisco: Harper & Row, 1986), 293.

these words: "I am the LORD your God, who brought you out of the land of Egypt, out of the house of slavery" (Exod. 20:2). Every subsequent word of command carries an implicit "therefore." The entire narrative of merciful deliverance that we have already discussed serves as the framework and wellspring of Israelite law.[17] The God of compassion, kindness, and justice has delivered his covenant people Israel from destruction and established them in a great and fruitful land. This means that God the Deliverer is God the Lawgiver, and so God's law is characterized by a commitment to love, mercy, and justice, understood again as focused especially on behalf of vulnerable and victimized people, who are most in need of receiving it.

This means that God's law itself is an expression of grace and further evidence of God's care, which also has implications for the writing and administration of human law. Simple gratitude on Israel's part will require that love, mercy, and justice must characterize Israel's life as a people and must be felt in Israel's legal system. Israel's constantly reinforced memory of her own hour of desperate weakness and God's mercy on her behalf at that critical hour will serve as the motivational wellspring for Israel's obedience to a legal code especially designed to protect those who are weak.

The Prophetic Demand and Yearning for Shalom

One of the Old Testament's key resources for an ethics of human dignity is found in the demand and yearning for a transformed world of justice and peace. The concept of shalom names that state of affairs in which human beings flourish in community and the dignity of each and every human life is finally honored. Often defined simply as well-being or as a "just wholeness," shalom, as Walter Brueggemann so memorably put it, is "the dream of God" for a redeemed world and an end to human "division, hostility, fear, drivenness, and misery."[18] The prophets both demand shalom now and yearn for it when the time comes that God finally prevails.

Ethicist Karen Lebacqz has argued that an ethics of justice is often developed most profoundly amid the experience of a particular injustice.[19] The Old Testament yearning for shalom begins with the particular, especially Israel's experiences of wrenching violence and injustice. Prophets speak about shalom

17. Cf. Kaiser, *Toward Old Testament Ethics*, 83.
18. Walter Brueggemann, *Living toward a Vision: Biblical Reflections on Shalom*, 2nd ed. (New York: United Church, 1982), 16.
19. Karen Lebacqz, *Six Theories of Justice: Perspectives from Philosophical and Theological Ethics* (Minneapolis: Augsburg Fortress, 1987).

for Israel from within the cataclysm of war (cf. Jer. 33). From exile they speak of the land and people of Israel coming back from the dead (Ezek. 36–37).[20] They yearn for a New Jerusalem from within the experience of Jerusalem's destruction (cf. Isa. 65).

Earlier prophets, prophesying in times when all appeared secure, warned that the violations of shalom within the Jewish community would someday bring upon Israel judgments that were hardly imaginable. Thus the prophetic writings left a legacy both of particularity and universality. The prophets speak to specific events, injustices, and dreams of the Jewish people while also evoking powerful demands and yearnings on the part of many for the kind of world that they envision.

The narrowest translation for the Hebrew word *shalom* is "peace," as in the opposite of war, and peace as commonly understood is certainly an ingredient of shalom. The prophets demand peace from the covenant people Israel when they decry Israel's violence and murder (Mic. 7:2–3) and her turn to military alliances and military might (cf. Isa. 31:1; Hosea 1:7; Mic. 5:10).[21] They envision a time when "there shall be endless peace" (Isa. 9:7), and "they shall beat their swords into plowshares, and their spears into pruning hooks" (Mic. 4:3; cf. Zech. 9:9–10).

Shalom means peace, as in straightforward security from physical threats to bodies, homes, and communities. God promises just such a "covenant of peace" in which threats even from animals no longer exist (Isa. 65:25; Ezek. 34:25; cf. Num. 25:12). Shalom happens when the sixth commandment is obeyed and people stop murdering each other, but it extends to a time when even "legitimate" killing is no longer undertaken in human society. "Violence shall no more be heard in your land, devastation or destruction within your borders" (Isa. 60:18). Security is so complete that "your gates shall always be open; day and night they shall not be shut" (Isa. 60:11), for there are no more security threats at last (cf. Jer. 33:6, 15; Mic. 5:4–5). Eventually shalom in this sense is so complete that God "will destroy on this mountain the shroud that is cast over all peoples" and "will swallow up death forever" (Isa. 25:7–8).

Taking shalom seriously points us strongly toward what it really means for human beings to flourish. The prophets speak most often in a voice that is specific to a particular time and audience, but they leave a legacy relevant to all of us. The prophets of the exile, for example, speak of the liberation

20. Waldemar Janzen, *Old Testament Ethics: A Paradigmatic Approach* (Louisville: Westminster John Knox, 1994), 170.
21. Walter Brueggemann, *A Social Reading of the Old Testament: Prophetic Approaches to Israel's Communal Life* (Minneapolis: Fortress, 1994), chap. 15.

and return of the dispersed Jewish people (cf. Isa. 60–61; Jer. 16:14–15; Ezek. 34:11–13; Amos 9:14–15), scattered to the four winds by war and the deliberate policies of exile, imprisonment, and enslavement by imperial powers such as Assyria and Babylon. The slaves, prisoners, and exiles shall be set free at last (cf. Isa. 61:1). The prophets dream of the rebuilding of a glorious Jerusalem and the return of a growing and vibrant community to Israel's most important city (Isa. 61:4; Jer. 30:18–22; Ezek. 36:10). The people will come back, rebuild their homes and public buildings, and live securely there in a newfound unity. The vision of shalom thus includes the (re)building of community.

Shalom means not just rebuilt community but inclusive community. Egalitarianism and universality surface in powerful new ways here. Shalom overcomes ethnic divisions, as even the "foreigner" who lives in covenant faithfulness before God becomes a full and honored member of the Jewish community. The eunuch, previously considered inferior and unclean, is also welcomed as a full member of the community (Isa. 56:3–6). All are welcomed on the same basis; all "who choose the things that please me and hold fast my covenant" (Isa. 56:4) will be welcomed into the house of the Lord (Isa. 56:5). The temple will become "a house of prayer for all peoples" (Isa. 56:7) as all nations will come to worship God in Jerusalem.[22] Shalom restores the original unity of humankind at last. All people made in the image of God finally come together in one peaceable human community.

Shalom means that everyone has enough to eat and drink. There can be no vibrant human community for long if some have enough to eat while others starve to death. Shalom means abundant material well-being and prosperity fairly distributed to all (Isa. 60:5–7; 66:12; Jer. 31:12; Ezek. 34:14–15, 29; Joel 2:23–24; Amos 9:13–14; Zech. 9:17), in a flourishing land of ecological health and well-being that also symbolizes spiritual renewal in Israel (Isa. 32:15–20; 45:8).[23] Shalom means that those who work on the land will not have their produce stolen from them but will instead "eat it and praise the LORD" (Isa. 62:9; cf. Isa. 65:21–22; Jer. 31:5).

Shalom means economic justice, where everyone has the means necessary to work successfully to meet their material needs, and no one is permitted to take away from anyone either the means of production (mainly land) or the goods it produces. The prophetic vision of a restoration of economic justice (Ezek. 34:16) and an end to economic oppression finds rich complement in

22. Watson E. Mills and Richard F. Wilson, eds., *Mercer Commentary on the Old Testament* (Macon, GA: Mercer University Press, 2003), 613.

23. William P. Brown, *Ethos of the Cosmos: The Genesis of Moral Imagination in the Bible* (Grand Rapids: Eerdmans, 1999), 254–56.

the Levitical Holiness Code, which unexpectedly includes commands such as the Jubilee year provision (Lev. 25), intended to give every Israelite family a chance to regain access to its land every fifty years.

Shalom means the healing of broken bodies and spirits. According to God's words to Isaiah, "Then the eyes of the blind shall be opened, and the ears of the deaf unstopped; then the lame shall leap like a deer, and the tongue of the speechless sing for joy" (Isa. 35:5–6a); "I have seen their ways, but I will heal them; I will lead them and repay them with comfort" (Isa. 57:18); "your days of mourning shall be ended" (Isa. 60:20), as God promises to "bind up the brokenhearted" and "comfort all who mourn" (Isa. 61:1–2). Likewise, Ezekiel hears God saying, "I will seek the lost, and I will bring back the strayed, and I will bind up the injured, and I will strengthen the weak" (Ezek. 34:16). Those who are sick will be set free to move toward their full human flourishing and their full inclusion in community.

Shalom means both human and divine delight. It means joyful smiles and deep satisfaction, for "as a young man marries a young woman, so shall your builder marry you, and as the bridegroom rejoices over the bride, so shall your God rejoice over you" (Isa. 62:5). Shalom means that after endless suffering, humans will receive "a garland instead of ashes, the oil of gladness instead of mourning, the mantle of praise instead of a faint spirit" (Isa. 61:3). Shalom is like a party: "Out of [the city] shall come thanksgiving, and the sound of merrymakers" (Jer. 30:19); "their children shall see it and rejoice, their hearts shall exult in the LORD" (Zech. 10:7).

Finally, shalom means obedience to God and is therefore linked to the covenantal themes considered earlier. According to the prophets, disobedience is the source of Israel's suffering, and obedience will therefore be central to Israel's healing and the healing of the world. The problem had been that "justice is turned back, and righteousness stands at a distance; for truth stumbles in the public square, and uprightness cannot enter" (Isa. 59:14). Peace, justice, inclusive community, restored human unity, food for all, joy and delight—all come as God's gracious response to people who "maintain justice, and do what is right" (Isa. 56:1).[24]

The nations will stream to Jerusalem to worship and serve the one Lord of all (Mic. 4:1). "These I will bring to my holy mountain, and make them joyful in my house of prayer" (Isa. 56:7; cf. Zeph. 3:9). God promises that in the time of restoration, "I will put my spirit within you, and make you follow

---

24. On the other hand, God's abundant blessings can be seen as coming first, leading to obedient response, leading to further blessing. "I have seen their ways, but I will heal them" (Isa. 57:18a).

my statutes and be careful to observe my ordinances. Then you shall live in the land that I gave to your ancestors; and you shall be my people, and I will be your God" (Ezek. 36:27–28; cf. Zeph. 3:11–13).

The Old Testament ends with these glorious promises unfulfilled. But then comes Jesus Christ. In the ministry of Jesus, the church's theological reflection on the meaning of the incarnation, and the character and ministry of the early church, the incalculable value of human life gains powerful, even overwhelming affirmation. The witness of the New Testament helped shape a Christian church in which for two thousand years some believers have always been found demonstrating their conviction that every human life has dignity.

The Teaching and Example of Jesus Christ

Jesus carried forward in profound ways all four themes noted above. He articulated a creation theology affirming God as creator and God's sustaining care for human beings, while employing his power over creation to manifest that care in healing, rescuing, and raising people from the dead. He taught and exemplified the compassionate deliverance for suffering people that God had exhibited to Israel. He offered a rendering of Jewish legal and ethical norms that affirmed and heightened the protections offered there to human life. And he both voiced and embodied the prophetic vision of an eschatological shalom in God's coming future.

An abundance of examples could be cited from the ministry of Jesus to demonstrate the numerous ways in which he taught and consistently embodied the reality of a transformed world in which each and every life is hallowed as God wills. The themes set forth below are some of the most germane patterns in the ministry of Jesus.

Jesus's Consistent Opposition to Violence and His Teaching of the Way of Peace

A central commitment in the human dignity ethic is to protect human life from wanton destruction. Jesus rejected cycles of human violence despite the abundant provocation to violence that existed for all Jews under Roman occupation.[25]

Jesus rejected violence as a way to deal with personal affronts, conflicts, or assaults and as a political response to the humiliation of Roman subjugation

---

25. Howard Thurman's *Jesus and the Disinherited* (Richmond, IN: Friends United, 1981) remains deeply influential for me and helps shape this account.

(cf. Matt. 5:38–48). He rejected violence when it was proposed by James and John as a response to Samaritans who blocked his entry (Luke 9:54–55). He rejected it yet again when swords were flashed at the time of his arrest, saying that "all who take the sword will perish by the sword" (Matt. 26:51–52). He rejected it when he could have called legions of angels to save him rather than heading to the cross (Matt. 26:53). In his several comments on Jerusalem (cf. Luke 13:34–35; 19:41–44; 21:5–6; 23:27–31), Jesus seems to reject both the everyday violence of Jewish and Roman rulers and the guerrilla violence of rebels, and he foresees the coming terrible destruction of the city.

Jesus's earliest disciples saw that violence had no part in the way he lived and died and thus that it could not be a part of their own way of life as his followers. This is quite striking, not just because of their context of oppression but also because of the elements of the Old Testament that seem to permit violence for liberation from oppression. The early church, originally an entirely Jewish movement, became convinced that such violence did not fit a community seeking to imitate and obey Jesus.

But Jesus did not just say no to violence. He taught his followers how to find creative alternatives that could bring deliverance from violence. He taught transforming initiatives, such as going the second mile with the Roman soldier's pack, turning the other cheek as an unexpected response to being struck, and taking the first step to make peace by finding one's adversary and beginning the conversation (Matt. 5:23–24, 39, 41).[26]

He taught that forgiveness should be extended repeatedly to those who wound us (Matt. 18:22), and he embodied such forgiveness throughout his ministry, perhaps most notably when he prayed for his persecutors even from the cross (Luke 23:34). He characterized God his heavenly Father as offering such gracious forgiveness in the same way, calling his listeners to the imitation of God and warning them against withholding forgiveness (Matt. 6:14–15; Luke 17:3–4).[27]

He described God the Father as showering love rather than violence on God's enemies (Matt. 5:43–48), as one who seeks after those who walk away from him (cf. Luke 15).[28] Jesus's harshest words of judgment are reserved for

26. On "transforming initiatives," see Glen H. Stassen, ed. *Just Peacemaking: The New Paradigm for the Ethics of Peace and War* (Cleveland: Pilgrim, 2008).

27. For a very thoughtful Christian theological reflection on forgiveness, see L. Gregory Jones, *Embodying Forgiveness: A Theological Analysis* (Grand Rapids: Eerdmans, 1995).

28. On Jesus as peacemaker and the peacemaking theme in the New Testament, see Joseph A. Grassi, *Jesus Is Shalom: A Vision of Peace from the Gospels* (New York: Paulist Press, 2006); Perry B. Yoder and Willard M. Swartley, eds., *The Meaning of Peace: Biblical Studies* (Louisville: Westminster John Knox, 1992); Willard M. Swartley, ed., *The Love of Enemy and Nonretaliation in the New Testament* (Louisville: Westminster John Knox, 1992); Willard M.

those who turn religion itself into an instrument of violence, judgmentalism, and exclusion (cf. Matt. 23).

Jesus's Inclusive Ministry

A key element both of the kingdom of God and of human dignity is its expansive inclusiveness, its hospitable universality. Every individual is called, claimed, and welcomed; no groups are diminished vis-à-vis other groups; no categories of people are the privileged recipients of God's love. Everyone matters, especially those who seem to matter the least. Jesus embodied that inclusiveness throughout his ministry. His example pushed Christians toward the development of love for each and every human being, without exception, as a fundamental element of a Christ-following way of life.

In a religious culture in which women were consistently shunted into second-class status, Jesus spoke and traveled with women, touched and healed women, and taught and ministered to women (cf. Matt. 15:21-28; John 4; 20:15).[29] In so doing he laid the foundations for an elevated role for women within the church and within cultures later affected by Christianity.

In a religious culture in which major religious leaders had developed a reading of Jewish law which tended to elevate religious separatism in the interest of ritual purity (cf. Matt. 12:1-14; 15:1-20; Mark 7:1-23; Luke 13:10-17), Jesus consistently acted to welcome and care for the "impure" and the "unclean," thus demonstrating a reading of religious obligation that elevated the worth of all people. Holiness for Jesus meant justice, mercy, and welcome for the excluded, not an exclusionary practice that protected purity by rigid separation.[30]

Swartley, *Covenant of Peace: The Missing Piece in New Testament Theology and Ethics* (Grand Rapids: Eerdmans, 2006); Ulrich Mauser, *The Gospel of Peace: A Scriptural Message for Today's World* (Louisville: Westminster John Knox, 1992); Lisa Sowle Cahill, *Love Your Enemies: Discipleship, Pacifism, and Just War Theory* (Minneapolis: Augsburg Fortress, 1994); Daniel L. Smith-Christopher, *Jonah, Jesus, and Other Good Coyotes: Speaking Peace to Power in the Bible* (Nashville: Abingdon, 2007); J. Massyngbaerde Ford, *My Enemy Is My Guest: Jesus and Violence in Luke* (Maryknoll, NY: Orbis, 1984).

29. See, e.g., Richard L. Bauckham, *Gospel Women: Studies of the Named Women in the Gospels* (Grand Rapids: Eerdmans, 2002); Mary Ann Getty-Sullivan, *Women in The New Testament* (Collegeville, MN: Liturgical Press, 2001); Elisabeth Schüssler-Fiorenza, *In Memory of Her* (New York: Crossroad, 1987); Ben Witherington III, *Women in the Ministry of Jesus: A Study of Jesus' Attitude toward Women and Their Roles as Reflected in His Earthly Life* (New York: Cambridge University Press, 1987).

30. On the contested meanings of purity and holiness, see Stephen C. Barton, ed., *Holiness: Past and Present* (London and New York: T&T Clark, 2003). See also Marcus J. Borg, *Conflict, Holiness and Politics in the Teachings of Jesus* (Harrisburg, PA: Trinity Press International, 1984). It is, however, important to avoid disastrous anti-Pharisee and anti-Jewish stereotypes in interpreting these difficult texts. On this point, see Amy-Jill Levine,

In a religious culture in which obvious "sinners" were often treated as beyond the reach of God's love, Jesus purposefully welcomed such people at his dinner table (cf. Matt. 9:10–13; Luke 5:29–32). He ate with tax collectors and prostitutes, and he taught many times about God's welcoming and forgiving love toward those who have been on the wrong path but repent (cf. Luke 15:11–32; 19:2–9). His "open table" hospitality embodied God's redemptive love rather than angry rejection of those who stray. This "prodigal" (prodigious!) divine love mandates every effort to include rather than exclude, to convert rather than destroy.[31]

In a culture in which children were held of little account, Jesus welcomed and honored children—touched and held and cared for them (cf. Matt. 18:1–9; 19:13–14; Mark 9:33–40).[32] He taught his reluctant disciples to welcome rather than reject children, and he said that "whoever welcomes one such child in my name welcomes me, and whoever welcomes me welcomes . . . the one who sent me" (Mark 9:37). This saying, which in a powerful way echoes Matthew 25:31–46, teaches disciples to see in the face of each child the face of Jesus.

In a religious context in which sick and disabled people were often cast out from community or blamed as sinfully responsible for their own maladies, Jesus spoke with, touched, and healed thousands of sick ones, attending not only to their physical well-being but also their spiritual needs and their restoration into community (e.g., Matt. 4:23–24; 8:16–17). His example set the church on a historical trajectory of intensive commitment to health care ministries and to disabled people all around the world.[33]

In a political context in which the occupying Romans were hated, Jesus ministered to and spoke with Roman soldiers, and on one occasion he even honored a Roman centurion for his great faith (Matt. 8:5–13; Luke 7:1–10). He was somehow able to see in the Roman soldier more than an enemy

---

The Misunderstood Jew: The Church and the Scandal of the Jewish Jesus (New York: HarperOne, 2006).

31. Marcus J. Borg and John Dominic Crossan have clarified the significance of Jesus's own table fellowship as central to his ministry. See Marcus J. Borg, *Jesus: A New Vision; Spirit, Culture, and the Life of Discipleship* (San Francisco: Harper & Row, 1987); John Dominic Crossan, *The Historical Jesus: The Life of a Mediterranean Jewish Peasant* (New York: HarperSanFrancisco, 1991), chap. 13; cf. N. T. Wright, *Jesus and the Victory of God* (Minneapolis: Fortress, 1996), chap. 7.

32. Judith M. Gundry-Volf, "The Least and the Greatest: Children in the New Testament," in *The Child in Christian Thought*, ed. Marcia J. Bunge (Grand Rapids: Eerdmans, 2001), chap. 1.

33. Stevan L. Davies, *Jesus the Healer: Possession, Trance, and the Origins of Christianity* (London: SCM, 1995); cf. John P. Meier, *A Marginal Jew: Rethinking the Historical Jesus*, vol. 2, *Mentor, Message, and Miracles* (New York: Doubleday, 1994), chap. 21.

and was able to respond to soldiers as individuals loved by God rather than merely as national enemies hated by his people.[34] His example has been continually imitated as oppressed believers in various settings have sought to rise above their all-too-natural hatred of and thirst for vengeance against their persecutors.

Against a historic backdrop of tensions between Jews and Samaritans, Jesus spoke with and ministered to a Samaritan woman—and through her to her community (John 4). He also elevated a compassionate Samaritan to a memorably praiseworthy role in perhaps his most widely quoted parable (Luke 10:25–37). In so doing, Jesus worked to overcome one of the most powerful tensions of his context, setting an example always available to people whenever they have been prepared to listen and to follow.[35]

In an economic context in which a woman alone in the world faced desperate financial challenges, Jesus compassionately raised a widow's son from the dead and restored him to his mother, thus restoring her to economic and social well-being (Luke 7:11–17). The profound compassion of this particular story leaves an indelible impression. Here is one who grieves with and responds to bereft widows.

Jesus's response to the widow who gave her very last penny (Luke 21:1–4) strikes the same chord. His anger at a religious system that would demand that last penny of her (Luke 20:46–47) is also important—to value vulnerable ones means to confront those who exploit them.

In a political context in which socioeconomic divisions were acute, Jesus preached "good news to the poor" (Luke 4:18), welcoming the desperate into his band of followers (cf. Matt. 5:1–12). He taught rich people to share with people living in poverty and to live in simplicity rather than to be greedy, to hoard, or to ignore poor people (cf. Matt. 6:19–24; 19:16–24; Luke 12:13–21; 16:19–31). To tax collectors who collaborated with the hated Romans and extorted fellow Jews, he ministered in such a way that some were moved to cease extorting, make restitution, and follow him (Matt. 9:9–13). He also told a memorable parable about self-righteousness in which a penitent tax gatherer is described as justified before God (Luke 18:9–14).

In short, Jesus treats poor people with dignity, proposes a way of life in which everyone has enough and no one has too much, calls rich people and especially those unjustly rich to repentance, and creates an egalitarian community of economic sharing and justice. The powerful impact of Christ's

---

34. An early, quite sensitive discussion of how Jesus related to Roman soldiers is found in Thurman, *Jesus and the Disinherited*, 80–88.
35. See Wright, *Jesus and the Victory of God*, 305–7.

treatment of impoverished people and his vision of a just and dignified economic community has been felt through the centuries and up to today.[36]

Jesus's Teaching about God's Love for Human Beings

In a variety of different ways, Jesus taught the very good news that God loves human beings with an immeasurable love. The theme resonates through the pages of the Gospels in a way that has left a profound imprint on the church.

Jesus declared the divine decision to love people when, for example, he announced the coming reign of God (Matt. 4:17; Mark 1:14–15), which is nothing other than God's loving decision to save humanity and the world rather than leave everyone to their own destructive devices. This gracious divine decision was in a sense first announced in Genesis 8–9, when God made a covenant with Noah and all creatures after the flood, declaring that he would bear with people despite their sinfulness (Gen. 8:21–22). Jesus declared that God continues to love humanity—and not just those who return that love but those who reject it as well (Matt. 5:43–48).

Jesus said that God pays attention even to the life of a sparrow and all the more attends to providing for people's material needs—therefore freeing them to trust him and serve others (Matt. 6:26). He described God as a loving Father who can be counted on to give good gifts to his children—which authorizes and encourages people to ask for what they need and trust that it will be provided (Matt. 7:7–11; Luke 11:13; 18:1–8). He said that all children have angels in heaven who intercede for them before the Father (Matt. 18:10) and that God is like a shepherd who goes after the one lost sheep even if he has the ninety-nine at hand (Luke 15:3–7).

Jesus frequently offered reminders of God's special care for those who especially need it—people who are young, poor, abandoned, sick, hungry. These reminders were often accompanied by teachings requiring all who would be his followers to imitate this preferential love or face judgment for failing to do so (cf. Matt. 25:31–46). Love attends especially to those who need love the most, and God will hold us accountable for doing that.

"For God so loved the world that he gave his only Son, so that everyone who believes in him may not perish but may have eternal life" (John 3:16). The

---

36. See Obery M. Hendricks Jr., *The Politics of Jesus: Rediscovering the True Revolutionary Nature of Jesus' Teachings and How They Have Been Corrupted* (New York: Doubleday, 2006); see also Shane Claiborne and Chris Haw, *Jesus for President: Politics for Ordinary Radicals* (Grand Rapids: Zondervan, 2008). Much contemporary work on the economics of Jesus is indebted to John Howard Yoder, *The Politics of Jesus: Vicit Agnus Noster* (Grand Rapids: Eerdmans, 1972; 2nd ed., 1994).

bottom line of the New Testament is this divine saving love for the world—for humankind and for each and every individual human. This is an essential foundation of Christian belief in human dignity.

The Work of Jesus Christ

The Incarnation

"The Word became flesh and lived among us" (John 1:14). The Word, which in the beginning was "with God" and "was God" (John 1:1), became human in Jesus the Christ. The New Testament writers consistently marvel at the divine condescension, in which God stooped low to take on frail, humble flesh, carry human nature, suffer humiliation and death at the world's hands, and bear people's sins as God's suffering servant (cf. Phil. 2:1–11).

The paradox of the incarnation is that when divinity stooped low and took on humanity, humanity revealed its desperate debasement and yet was elevated through God's mercy. And it was elevated forever, for this moment in God's history marked an irreversible change in God's relation to humanity and the world. In the incarnation, God is the one who became a human to save people in Jesus Christ. Humanity itself must be fundamentally transfigured and permanently elevated through its association with the God-man Jesus Christ.

Christian theologians have often been moved to proclaim that if God became human, the status of the human changes. No human can be seen as worthless. No human life can be treated cruelly or destroyed capriciously. Human dignity can never again be rejected or confined to only a few groups or individuals of supposedly higher rank. The incarnation elevates the status of every human being everywhere on the planet at any time in human history. It elevates the worth of every human being at every stage of their lives, because the arc of Jesus's own life included every stage of existence including resurrection, which is human destiny.

There is a paradox here in Christian thought that must not be evaded. Many voices in the Christian tradition find in the incarnation confirmation of desperate human unworthiness rather than worthiness. But the depth of human sin, as Barth says, only highlights the even greater depth of God's love for humanity: "The Church and all Christendom looks in its message at this immeasurable and unfathomable fact, that God has given Himself for us."[37] Christian thought proclaims the immeasurable, incalculable value of the human person not because of any intrinsic goodness on humanity's part but

---

37. Barth, *Dogmatics in Outline* (New York: Harper & Row, 1959), 86.

because God has acted in so many ways to communicate his own immeasurably, incalculably great love for human beings. The deeper and more realistic people's understanding of the fallenness of the human condition, the more they find confirmation of the immeasurable God-given dignity of human life.

One particular teaching of Jesus has proven especially influential in linking the incarnation to human dignity: the eschatological judgment parable from Matthew 25. The King and Son of Man (presumably Jesus himself) sits on his throne with all nations gathered before him for the final judgment. He separates "sheep" from "goats," approved from disapproved, on the basis that "I was hungry and you gave me food, I was thirsty and you gave me something to drink, I was a stranger and you welcomed me, I was naked and you gave me clothing, I was sick and you took care of me, I was in prison and you visited me" (vv. 35–36). The "sheep" have no memory of having cared for him in this way, and so he tells them, "Just as you did it to one of the least of these who are members of my family, you did it to me" (v. 40).[38]

Jesus here suggests that God enters humanity not just in one human but in many people, especially those who are most needy. Jesus teaches us to see in the face of other people his own face. This judgment parable especially instructs us to see Jesus Christ in and through the faces of those who are suffering, those who are among "the least of these," enumerated here as people who are hungry, thirsty, strangers, naked, sick, or imprisoned.[39]

The incarnation forever elevates human embodiment. What happens to human bodies matters to God and must matter to us. What happens to people's bodies must matter to us because God came in a body in Jesus Christ. This reality is a powerfully important contributor to Christian commitments to human dignity as these relate to the protecting and flourishing of human life, which is bodily life.

The Cross

The body of Jesus Christ was nailed to a cross. On that cruel Roman cross Jesus suffered and died. The implications of the cross for human dignity are

---

38. While the full scope of people in view here is a matter of some debate, what is particularly striking about this text is whom Jesus singles out. When Jesus talks about the importance of how people are viewed and treated, he does not exalt those most likely to be exalted by the world but those most likely to be left out of consideration.

39. Vladimir Lossky has relatedly written: "Only the eyes of faith recognize the form of God beneath the form of the slave and, deciphering beneath the human face the presence of a divine person, learn to unveil in each face the mystery of the person created in the image of God." See Vladimir Lossky, *Orthodox Theology: An Introduction* (Crestwood, NY: St. Vladimir's Seminary Press, 1978), 102.

abundant. One place to begin is with Christian anguish over Christ's anguish. It is right that Christians should anguish over Christ's bodily humiliation, suffering, and death—especially as he embodies the suffering of humanity. The cross serves as a resource for honoring life's dignity when it motivates compassionate concern and intervention on behalf of all those who suffer in their bodies.

That concern can be sharpened and extended in appropriate ways if we focus more closely on the details of Christ's suffering and death and look around today's world for parallels.[40] This could lead us to special concern for those whose victimization occurs at the hands of the state; who are victims of unjust legal processes; who suffer humiliation, abuse, and torture; and perhaps especially those who have done nothing worthy of such cruelty, punishment, or death. In other words, Christ's suffering and death lead to concern about the violation of human dignity caused by those who hold political power and use it to oppress and abuse the innocent or defenseless.

Consider the connections between the cross and the disastrous turn toward prisoner abuse by the United States after 9/11. The endorsement by American Christians of not just abuse and cruelty but even outright torture in the interests of "national security" has arguably marked a fundamental repudiation of the ethical meaning of the cross.[41] The cruel torture and death of Jesus Christ should sensitize people rather than inure them to similar cruelties inflicted on others. During the American torture debate, some Christians intuited the connection between torture and the cross, but many were unable or unwilling to see the link.

Jesus's death is always portrayed as an evil. This is a reminder that abusing or killing anyone is not good. And yet the New Testament teaches that this particular death somehow brought the salvation of the world. "By his bruises we are healed" (Isa. 53:5), and "God so loved the world that he gave his only Son" (John 3:16).[42]

God stopped at nothing to reach out to humanity. God in Christ suffered and bled and died. What more could God do to demonstrate love for the

---

40. For one attempt to provide such a parallel, see James H. Cone, *The Cross and the Lynching Tree* (Maryknoll, NY: Orbis, 2011).

41. For documentation of such torture, see US Senate Select Committee on Intelligence, "Official Senate Report on CIA Torture" (New York: Skyhorse, 2015); cf. "Report of the Constitution Project Task Force on Detainee Treatment" (Washington, DC: Constitution Project, 2013).

42. Christians who love their lives often have been willing to lay them down if that is what fidelity to Christ requires. Christian martyrs such as these help clarify that what matters ultimately in Christian perspective is faithfulness to Christ. This does involve a proper valuing of one's own and others' embodied lives. But it may involve a willingness to sacrifice one's own life, as Jesus did.

world? Belief in human dignity is deepened considerably by reflection on the ultimate nature of the price God paid at the cross. The incalculably terrible suffering and death of Jesus Christ and the demonstration in that suffering and death of how very much God values each and every human being have contributed profoundly to a Christian moral tradition that exalts the immeasurable worth of the human being.

The Resurrection

And then Christ rose from the dead. It is significant that Christ rose in a body. It was a new, different kind of body. But it was still a body. This was a body that could be seen and touched. In this body Jesus ate and drank. Human life never ceases to be bodily, even at the resurrection. Christians never escape embodiment and its implications.

The resurrection of Christ also signifies the victory of God over evil, including the evil that took Jesus to the cross. In the resurrection God signals that in the end God will triumph over Satan and all forces that bring suffering and death; even death itself is destroyed (1 Cor. 15:25–26).[43] When the resurrection is fully realized, human dignity will be part of this ultimate victory of God over the evil that has harmed and destroyed so many human lives.

The resurrection marks the triumph of life. In the resurrection Jesus lives again, God wins, and therefore life wins. God is for life.[44] All that wars against life is enemy to God, and God has defeated it proleptically for all time at the cross. This demands that God's people participate in combating and with God's help defeating all that wars against life until Christ comes again.

The Ascension

The historic confession of the church is not just that Jesus rose from the dead but that he ascended to heaven, where he now sits at the right hand of the Father, and from where he shall come to judge the living and the dead. Jesus who rose from the dead was fully God and fully human; this means, as Barth writes, "the real mystery of Easter is not that God is glorified in it, but that man is exalted, raised to the right hand of God and permitted to triumph over sin, death and the devil."[45]

43. I first encountered this formulation in J. Christiaan Beker, *Paul the Apostle: The Triumph of God in Life and Thought* (Philadelphia: Fortress, 1980). Since then it has become a familiar concept, linked to the kingdom of God.
44. This theme has perhaps never been expressed more profoundly than by Pope John Paul II, *The Gospel of Life* (New York: Times, 1995), chap. 2.
45. Karl Barth, *Dogmatics in Outline*, 115.

God stoops low so that humanity can be exalted even to the right hand of God. Human beings must be viewed and treated as those whose divinely intended destiny is to dwell eternally in the presence of God the Father along with Jesus the Son. Humanity was made for an eternal destiny. Those who belong to Jesus Christ will follow him to the throne of God. They come from God and are returning to God. Jesus blazed the trail.

The Expansive Reach of the Body of Christ

The book of Acts depicts a rapidly growing church led by the Holy Spirit toward an ever more inclusive and hospitable community ethos. What had initially been a "Hebrew" Jewish community of Christ-followers rapidly expands to include large numbers of "Hellenists," that is, Greek-speaking Jewish Christians (Acts 6:1). The gospel next spreads through the ministry of Philip to neighboring Samaria (Acts 8). The barrier between Jew and non-Jew is shattered as the gospel is taken to gentiles, beginning with the conversion of the Roman centurion Cornelius (Acts 10–11). The rest of Acts and much of the rest of the New Testament tell the story of the progressive spread of Christian faith to both Jews and gentiles throughout the ancient world.

Paul offers an expansive theological effort to defend this revolutionary transformation of relationships between Jews and gentiles. His oft-quoted words in Galatians 3 are nothing short of breathtaking in their context: "There is no longer Jew or Greek, there is no longer slave or free, there is no longer male and female, for all of you are one in Christ Jesus" (Gal. 3:28). The epistle to the Ephesians expands on this theme. Christ "has made both groups into one and has broken down the dividing wall, that is, the hostility between us" (Eph. 2:14). If even Jews and gentiles can now be "one new humanity" (Eph. 2:15), other distinctions can and must also fall—between male and female,[46] slave and free,[47] and so on. In Christ, God has begun to reclaim this divided world and to bring peace to its warring members.

46. The literary witness of the early church shows that it did not fully eliminate the second-class status of women as found in Judaism and the Greco-Roman world, but it did make real progress in that direction. Women's dramatic inclusion in communities of early Christians did not eliminate questions about and differences regarding leadership roles in the life of the church, nor did it create a fully or universally egalitarian understanding of male and female roles in marriage, though it did soften the hard edges of patriarchy. The literature on this issue is vast. One especially valuable work is Craig S. Keener, *Paul, Women and Wives* (Peabody, MA: Hendrickson, 1992). See also David P. Gushee and Glen H. Stassen, *Kingdom Ethics: Following Jesus in Contemporary Context*, 2nd ed. (Grand Rapids: Eerdmans, 2016), chap. 12.

47. New Testament teachings enjoining slaves to obey their masters (e.g., Col. 3:22) were employed by Christian slaveholders in North America and elsewhere to compel submission to

The early church's ecstatic experience of the Holy Spirit, poured out upon sons and daughters, young and old, slave and free (Acts 2:17–18)—combined with its Spirit-led decision to shatter the Jew–gentile boundary line and perhaps also with the special appeal of its message to those most hurting and vulnerable—created powerful momentum toward radically inclusive and egalitarian community. This would be a community that would not accept the dehumanization and degradation of any category of people as occurred all around it in the Greco-Roman world.

This would also be a community committed to pressing toward enemy love. What mattered was not how enemies treated Christians but how Jesus responded when he was mistreated (1 Pet. 2:21–25). When reviled and abused, Christ-followers must not return evil for evil but should instead walk "in his steps" (1 Pet. 2:21) in patient endurance and forgiving love.[48] Reminded that "while we were enemies, we were reconciled to God through the death of his Son" (Rom. 5:10), Christians are both grateful for that reconciliation and called to their own "ministry of reconciliation" (2 Cor. 5:18). This is why "we regard no one from a human point of view" (2 Cor. 5:16).

What ultimately emerged in the early church were congregations that believed that in their own experience of transformed human relations lay the beginnings of the redemption of the world. Church leaders addressed their congregations with such seriousness on these points because so very much was at stake. These communities would seek to live in love toward one another and toward all. They would contribute only good to their neighbors—beginning with their near neighbors in Christian community but extending far beyond "the household of faith." They would do so until Christ returned.

---

their often cruel rule. These slaveholders often overlooked that the same New Testament texts urged first-century masters to be kind and just and to remember that "you also have a Master in heaven" (e.g., Col. 4:1)—undercutting cruel absolutism and tyranny. Paul's letter to Philemon is a fascinating example of this undercutting process at work as is his counsel to slaves to seek freedom from slavery if they can (cf. 1 Cor. 7:21). Christian leaders whose writings made it into the canon urged a softening of the cruelties of slavery while offering a logic of God's sovereignty and every person's worth that undercut the logic of slavery altogether. See William J. Webb, *Slaves, Women, and Homosexuals: Exploring the Hermeneutics of Cultural Analysis* (Downers Grove, IL: InterVarsity, 2001), for one fine treatment, as well as Willard Swartley, *Slavery, Sabbath, War, and Women: Case Issues in Biblical Interpretation* (Scottdale, PA: Herald, 1982).

48. The book of Revelation does not seem to exude the patient love described here. It is the work of a church under persecution, enduring extreme suffering, understandably hurt and angry at the cruelties and martyrdoms it was experiencing. Notably, the apocalyptic holy war imagined in Revelation involves Christ's death ("the lamb who was slain") and the church's continued faithfulness to his way rather than a call for Christians to take up arms. It was a word of encouragement, comfort, and promise to a martyred church as well as a stark condemnation of imperial Rome and its cruelties. See Richard Bauckham, *The Climax of Prophecy: Studies on the Book of Revelation* (Edinburgh: T&T Clark, 1993).

This communal ethos formed a powerful foundation for an ethic of human dignity in Christianity that lives on to this day.

Further Reading

Barth, Karl. *Dogmatics in Outline*. New York: Harper & Row, 1959.
Barth's theology includes rich theological ethics and profound reflection on dogmatic themes relevant to human dignity.

Bonhoeffer, Dietrich. *Discipleship: Dietrich Bonhoeffer Works IV*. Minneapolis: Fortress, 2003.
Bonhoeffer is another legendary Nazi-era Christian theologian who dug deeply into the wellsprings of Christology to ground opposition to Nazi desecrations of human life.

Brueggemann, Walter. *Living toward a Vision: Biblical Reflections on Shalom*. 2nd ed. New York: United Church, 1982.
The author's seminal treatment of the *shalom* theme in the Old Testament helped lay the foundation for other scholarship on the subject. Brueggemann shows that the *shalom* concept relates strikingly well to kingdom-of-God themes articulated by Jesus.

Gushee, David P. *The Sacredness of Human Life*. Grand Rapids: Eerdmans, 2013.
This comprehensive work on the sacredness of life traces the origins and meaning of the term, offers reflections on its biblical foundations, examines the career of the concept and its practice in Christianity, explores secularizations of the idea in modern thought, and considers applications to contemporary issues.

Stassen, Glen H., ed. *Just Peacemaking: The New Paradigm for the Ethics of Peace and War*. Cleveland: Pilgrim, 2008.
This work offers a strong focus on Jesus as peacemaker, an important theme for the biblical materials considered here.

Thurman, Howard. *Jesus and the Disinherited*. Richmond, IN: Friends United, 1981.
One of the very first works by a black theologian to be read widely in white Christian circles, this work sharpened every reader's understanding of Jesus as a Savior of and for the disinherited.

Conclusion

Why a Christian Outlook Matters

Comparing Grounds for Human Significance

JOHN F. KILNER

The conviction that people matter is one of the most basic things that virtually everyone has in common. It can provide common ground in many of the most divisive debates today. Upon reflection, most people would consider anything that undermines that conviction to be both wrong and destructive. Nevertheless, five of the most widely held outlooks on life—utilitarianism, collectivism, individualism, naturalism, and transhumanism—do exactly that. They undermine the conviction that people matter. They also foster much disagreement over important ethical issues by leading people in many different directions from the common starting point that people matter.

However, there is hope. If someone can help people who approach life from one of these outlooks to see the harmfulness of their way of thinking, then greater agreement about ethical issues is possible. The prospects for agreement are especially great if those who question their own outlook adopt instead a biblically based Christian outlook. Of course, the ability of such a Christian outlook to provide a satisfying account of why people matter may not be sufficient to persuade a person to affirm that account—that is, if the person rejects the gospel. But that ability can provide a compelling reason to (re)consider the gospel, with its capacity to help people make sense of the world in a way that other outlooks cannot.

Before highlighting some of the primary ways that each of the five outlooks falls short and the ways that a biblical-Christian outlook is comparatively better, it is worth noting a common feature of the five outlooks. Each recognizes and champions something important that is missing in other ways of thinking. However, each is dangerously reductionistic by making that missing element the all-encompassing focus of its approach. An *ism* at the end of an outlook's name signals such a preoccupation.

Utilitarianism recognizes that some individuals or groups try to impose their preferences on others without taking others' preferences into account. In response, utilitarianism insists that everyone's preferences should be considered. Considering everyone affected by a decision is important; but when anything can potentially be done to a minority if the majority of preferences are satisfied, many problems result.

Likewise, collectivism recognizes that trying to understand people based on their unique personal characteristics all too easily means overlooking the ways that groups to which they belong shape who they are. In response, collectivism calls for more attention to people's social context. Context does matter; but when individuals get lost and devalued in favor of focusing on the groups of which they are often unwittingly members, many problems again result.

The pattern continues with the other three outlooks. Individualism recognizes that society (or a subgroup) sometimes oppressively tries to impose its values on people. In response, individualism champions the importance of the individual. Individuals are indeed important; but when everything ultimately becomes a matter of what the individual wants, many difficulties arise.

For naturalism, a driving force is recognizing that many difficulties in society stem from people making decisions based on beliefs that have no empirical basis. In response, naturalism insists that for something to be a valid basis for decisionmaking, it must involve what all people can perceive, measure, or otherwise verify. Empirical verifiability is good; but when what cannot be verified in this way has no validity without it, many important things get lost in the process.

Finally, transhumanism recognizes that many people are stuck in the assumption that they can basically only be what they are now. In response, transhumanism maintains that biotechnology can enable people to become so different that they become something other than human. People do need to grow and improve; but when being human itself becomes a cause for dissatisfaction, serious problems arise.

In other words, each of the five outlooks is aware of something important. However, by letting that observation become the driving force of everything, it produces a problematic reductionism. Legitimate concern for individual*ity*, for instance, becomes individual*ism*, in which the preferences of the individual ultimately trump everything. In the case of each outlook, its reductionism opens the door to many problems—some more general in nature and some specifically related to why people matter. It will be helpful to recapitulate here some of those problems that received more detailed analysis in parts 1 and 2—so that the comparative strength of a biblical-Christian outlook (part 3) can more clearly come into view.

Utilitarianism

As Gilbert Meilaender discusses in chapter 2, utilitarianism insists that people act in a way that takes everyone's well-being into account, not just their own. The goal is to produce as much good as possible for as many people as possible. "The greatest good for the greatest number," the classic utilitarian credo goes. Every action is to be evaluated not according to the preferences of the actor (individualism) or of a group that defines them (collectivism). Maximizing the good of society is instead the governing criterion for how people should be and act.

Meilaender notes, however, that despite utilitarianism's aspiration to do good, it is beset with problems—some general and some more specific to why people matter. Here we can briefly recount key examples of both types. First, in terms of general difficulties, utilitarianism has an unrealistic view of people. By requiring people to make decisions based on which alternative will produce the greatest good for the greatest number of people, utilitarianism assumes that people have a godlike ability to know how their actions will affect people throughout the world over endless years. One might object that of course all that can reasonably be expected of people is to consider the relatively immediate impact of their actions on those relatively close at hand. But once one admits that this is all that people can do—and recognizes that utilitarianism defines right action in terms of all future impacts on all people—one must acknowledge that utilitarianism cannot really tell people what is right or wrong. Such an admission renders the outlook useless in practice.

Several other features of utilitarianism also render it impractical. In order to calculate which of several alternative actions is the right one to do, one must be able to locate them all on the same scale. Each positive consequence must produce a specific number of units of utility. While one can envision assigning a specific number of positive units to the benefit of economic prosperity, exactly how many negative units on the same scale should be attributed to the harm of killing a person? The utilitarian assumption that such a number could be assigned leads to the highly dubious conclusion that if killing a person enables enough people to get the benefit of economic prosperity, then that killing can be justified. The assumption that one could know how many units of utility each person would assign to economic prosperity is far-fetched enough. However, even the possibility that enough prosperity could justify killing someone renders the outlook dangerous.

Taken together, these various difficulties with utilitarianism all reflect a deeper mistaken assumption: that people are individually responsible for the overall well-being of the world. In other words, this outlook assumes that the greatest possible universal well-being is the necessary criterion for each person's every action. Utilitarians rarely emphasize such sweeping responsibility, for it is unbearably daunting. However, they cannot disavow it without abandoning utilitarianism in favor of a collectivism that is only concerned with the well-being of a particular subset of humanity. Making the world's greatest well-being the criterion for one's every action fails to recognize that people's place in the world is actually more limited. Individuals each have a role to play that is governed by their location—geographical, relational, vocational, and more. To place on people responsibility for the entire world is a burden that no one can bear.

In addition to these general difficulties with utilitarianism, Meilaender identifies a number of aspects of this outlook that more directly undermine the widespread conviction that people matter. The difficulty here stems from utilitarianism's exclusive focus on society as a whole. If individualism takes concern for the individual too far, utilitarianism does not take it far enough. In utilitarianism, it is irrelevant how individuals are viewed and treated, as long as society as a whole receives as much benefit as possible. However, while communities are important, so are individuals. Individuals are not merely means to be used for the community's ends.

Utilitarianism is concerned merely about generating as much well-being overall as possible, and so it ultimately sees people as mere generators of well-being. It does not matter who generates or benefits from that well-being; all people are interchangeable. This is a mistaken view of who people are, for a person is a "someone" rather than a "something." A someone has a story and relationships and warrants some measure of personal attention; a something is marked by various properties that are significant only to the extent that they are valuable enough to enough other people. Utilitarianism fails to recognize that people legitimately have commitments and ideals to which they are personally committed. They are not morally bound to give up everything whenever the majority considers something else to be more beneficial.

By justifying anything that will produce the greatest good for the greatest number, utilitarianism can justify punishing people far more than their crimes deserve if it will deter others in the future from breaking the law. In fact, there is no need for the one being punished even to have committed a crime, if punishing him or her for it will sufficiently deter others. Moreover, why not remove one living person's organs if the organs can be used to save the lives of many in need? If such practices could be done in a way that would work out well for the majority—would produce the greatest good overall—then utilitarianism would encourage them. If such practices seem hopelessly misguided before even beginning to undertake a utilitarian calculus, it is because people are not simply interchangeable in such ways. Utilitarianism demeans—actually denies—human significance by overlooking that fact.

When a utilitarian outlook comes to control scientific research or social policy, rather than just guiding individuals, the results can be disastrous. Fictional accounts such as Aldous Huxley's *Brave New World* have long portrayed this predicament. However, sometimes real life can be more gruesome than fiction. Various analyses have described the way that people justified deadly human experimentation in Nazi Germany in terms of the alleged greater good that could be generated for Germany and the world.[1] In the United States, many others long justified slavery on the grounds of the greater good (economic benefit) that it was producing for the country. In the twentieth century, the Tuskegee syphilis study appealed to a different greater good (medical benefit) to justify denying treatment to 399 poor black men in Alabama with syphilis, resulting in the early death of many and the infection of wives and babies.[2]

Utilitarian thinking helps open the door to such atrocities in multiple ways. For instance, it passes no judgment on what people consider beneficial. If people are not bothered by mistreating certain groups and relish the benefits of doing so, then plenty of positive units of utility are added to the utilitarian calculus. Moreover, utilitarianism maintains that it is the overall common

1. For example, a court reporter at the Nuremburg trials, Vivien Spitz, has provided detailed accounts of those experiments. Note the utilitarian bent of the justifications that the overseeing physicians offered at the time: "the good of humanity" (Gerhard Rose), "the service of my beloved Fatherland" (Oskar Schroeder), "devotion to the community" (Karl Brandt). See Vivien Spitz, *Doctors from Hell: The Horrific Account of Nazi Experiments on Humans* (Boulder, CO: Sentient, 2005).

2. See Susan M. Reverby, ed., *Tuskegee's Truths: Rethinking the Tuskegee Syphilis Study* (Chapel Hill: University of North Carolina Press, 2000). See also Jay Katz, "Addendum to the Final Report of the Tuskegee Syphilis Study Ad Hoc Advisory Panel," submitted to the US Department of Health, Education, and Welfare on April 28, 1973.

good that matters, not people per se—not particular people. The expression "common good" can be misleading, since it does not necessarily refer to a good that all people share in common. Rather, a small minority can be required to pay a severe price as long as the result is that the large majority benefits sufficiently. Those whom society considers to be least beneficial are the most expendable in such situations. Sometimes they are least beneficial because they have borne the brunt of terrible discrimination. In those cases, utilitarianism encourages rather than discourages compounding that discrimination. Given this problem and the others discussed above, utilitarianism is quite an inadequate answer to the question of why people matter.

Collectivism

Another outlook that loses sight of the importance of each person is collectivism. As Amy Laura Hall describes in chapter 3, rather than seeing people in terms of overall society as with utilitarianism, the focus of collectivism is on the groups, or collectives, that constitute what matters about people's identity. People are members of an ethnic group, an age demographic, and so on—seen, as it were, only "from a distance." Much marketing fosters and thrives on such an outlook. All that needs to be known about people and considered in decisionmaking is a function of their group identities.

Social context does matter; but as Hall argues, when individuals get lost and devalued in favor of focusing on the groups of which they are often unwittingly members, many problems result. Some of those problems are general and some more specific to why people matter. In terms of general difficulties, collectivism is based on faulty thinking—on the idea that the only way to understand people is from far enough above the masses of humanity that individuals can no longer be seen. Only the groups to which they belong are in view. Ironically, this attempt to understand everyone makes it impossible to understand anyone in particular. Moreover, while recognizing certain hive- or herd-like behavior in people, collectivism commonly confuses what "is" with what "ought to be." Particular people are not limited by the characteristics of groups of which they are members. They constantly and somewhat unpredictably aspire to more. And aspiration to what is better is to be encouraged rather than discouraged by leaving it out of account.

In collectivism, love (if we can call it that) within a group becomes a force that stifles individual growth in order to foster one group's agenda over that of another group. Life is reduced to a competition between groups, such that obedience to the values and ways of the group becomes essential. Other people no longer are friends or neighbors. They are members of some other group that threatens our group's access to needed resources in a world marked by scarcity and ruled by the necessity of winning.

People who understand themselves primarily in terms of a collective to which they belong not only seek to further the interests of that collective, but they easily lose accountability for their actions. Their actions become "the group's" actions rather than their own. Such is the case especially when people see themselves as members of an elite group that has special responsibility for achieving some admirable end or preventing some despicable harm. Amy Laura Hall's chapter recounts the poignant story of one famous US leader who was gradually drawn into committing war crimes as he increasingly understood himself as "part of a mechanism." A collectivist way of thinking caught him up and carried him away.

While collectivism is problematic as a general way of looking at the world, it undermines in particular the notion that people matter. One way it does so is by emphasizing group identities to the exclusion of individual differences. For example, some studies reduce people to such categories as Asian versus Western and suggest that one knows who people are by knowing what category they fit into. Other studies liken people to clusters of ants or bees. By overlooking the particular significance of particular people, such an outlook diminishes the significance of all. Every person is too inscrutable to be neatly categorized and explained by the groups to which others would assign them.

And who are these others who are doing the categorizing? Perhaps the most disturbing aspect of a collectivist outlook on life is the fact that one of the groups in the overall scheme of things is the group doing the categorizing. Just as one of the great threats to human significance in individualism is the prideful self-assertion of one individual over another, so collectivism typically involves one group pridefully asserting itself over others. The stakes may be relatively benign, as when marketers identify particular groups or types of people, claim to "own" them, and then manipulate them into buying their products. However, observers see a dynamic at work here similar to that which underlay the rise to power of more sinister collectives such as Hitler's Nazi party. In Germany's Third Reich, the Nazis mobilized an entire apparatus of science, medical authorities, and popular writings to classify people into groups—the master race, inferior races, and those whose bodily weakness rendered their lives "not worthy of living." Such thinking led to the Nazi Holocaust.

There are other relatively benign forms of collectivism today. For example, the "authoritative communities" movement in the United States seeks to make every child a world leader in terms of academic achievement. Proponents cite the superior test scores of children in China as a motivation and model. However, the commitment to promoting one group at all costs has a darker side to it as well. According to observers, the Chinese feudal system and Maoist initiatives that have yielded superior achievement have done so through such practices as requiring the abortion of any children beyond the first child born to a husband and wife and confining children to specialized or inferior educational opportunities based on early government testing. One group excels, but the idea that all people matter is severely damaged in the process.

What facilitates the elevation of some groups in collectivism at the expense of others is the typical unwillingness of a collectivist outlook to impose standards of right and wrong on any particular group. Just as in individualism the individual is the sole judge of what is acceptable behavior for that person, so in collectivism the group itself is the sole judge of its own behavior. In light of the self-centeredness of groups, particular groups may decide that part of their unique place in the world is to influence or even determine the role that other groups will play in the world. When such is the case, it is difficult in practice to find any vantage point in collectivism outside of the various groups in society from which to assert that a dominating group's agenda is wrong. Collectivism, then, can hardly serve as an adequate ground for the universal conviction that people matter.

Individualism

If utilitarianism and collectivism are inadequate grounds for human significance, we might think that their apparent opposite, individualism, could better serve as that ground. But as Russell DiSilvestro argues in chapter 4, such is not the case. With its exclusive focus on individual values and preferences as the basis of what is good and right, today's individualism is preoccupied with a recent (so-called postmodern) understanding of autonomy. On this view, there are no objective truths or standards binding on all, since personal choice is the prevailing standard.

DiSilvestro concedes that individualism is attractive to many due to its affirmation of the importance of the individual, especially when it comes to making decisions about one's life. However, he argues that, as with the other outlooks, individualism too is beset with problems—some general and some more specific to why people matter—that we can summarize here.

In terms of general difficulties, individualism depends on the mistaken assumption that individuals are fundamentally independent of all other people—that community is optional rather than essential for human flourishing.

Accordingly, an individualistic mind-set can lead some people to avoid relationships in the mistaken belief that those will hamper rather than enrich life. However, for the majority who not only unavoidably exist in relationships but want relationships as well, an individualistic outlook does not serve them well. Individualism says that the right thing to do or be is ultimately a matter of what one wants, not what the other person in a relationship wants. Resolving disagreements with another individualistic person can be next to impossible, because there is nothing outside each individual's values and preferences that the two can appeal to as common ground. Sometimes two people's values and preferences coincide, but sometimes they do not.

What complicates this picture is human nature. In theory people could all be virtuous and caring, such that living on the basis of their own perspectives would work out well for others also. However, ample evidence appears every day that "the heart is devious above all else; it is perverse—who can understand it?" (Jer. 17:9). The daily news is full of illustrations. Most people would acknowledge that they experience it in their interactions with others and observe it in themselves. People are self-centered, with a bent to put their own interests over those of others. Individualism encourages that.

The difficulties of individualism include not just the problems with relying on one's own perspectives. They also involve the denial of other important considerations. Individualism holds that there are no values, duties, or moral guidelines other than what the individual chooses to adopt. Justice, impartiality, truth, and caring have no standing if the individual does not want to abide by them. In fact, the entire world could agree that some particular action is heinous; but if one individual disagrees and considers it morally acceptable to do, then individualism supports that individual in acting contrary to all others. The dangers of self-delusion and destructive perversity are huge here. Rather than there being values in the world that all people ought to live by, individuals create their own values. Their own thoughts and desires are the causes rather than the effects of value in the world. Gone are any duties to help anyone with anything if one does not want to do so. Accordingly, individualism undermines community.

Ironically, individualism is not particularly helpful for the individual either. It justifies individuals choosing anything they want, based on their values. However, at some point they must wonder, "What values should I hold?" Individualism can only advise people to "value whatever they value"—not particularly helpful counsel. Even those who have adopted particular values cannot be very confident that those values really represent their own convictions. The fields of psychology and sociology (not to mention theology) have produced ample studies documenting the many ways that internal and external influences shape what people think. The idea that people are "free" and "independent" to formulate choices that are truly "their own" is wishful thinking. Even were they able to formulate such choices, the subjective values on which choices are based can vary widely over time. Choices made today for the future, based on today's values, may well limit people's own future options based on values they no longer hold when that future arrives. In other words, individualism is unable to ensure that people will be able to act in the future in a way that is in line with their own values at that time.

A host of difficulties thus raise general questions about whether individualism can successfully account for human significance. However, as DiSilvestro observes, there are several other considerations that confirm more directly that individualism is inadequate to ground the widespread conviction that people matter.

One such consideration is that for people to have significance, in the sense that their lives have meaning, their lives need to have a context larger than themselves. The necessary relationship between context and meaning is apparent in the realm of reading. We cannot know what the letter *I* means unless we know if there are other letters nearby and what those letters are. If an *n* is close at hand, then *In* will mean something quite different than *I*. If *ch* follows the *n*, then the meaning (of *Inch*) will be quite different again. So it is with people's lives. The meaning or significance of those lives requires a broader context and can vary considerably depending on that context. When people wonder if their life has any meaning or significance, they typically are looking for something beyond themselves. They seek a larger story in which they have a significant part. Significance requires more than individualism can deliver.

Individualism is not merely inadequate, though; it is dangerous. It cannot provide the safeguards for oneself or others that are necessary if the widely held conviction that people matter is true. Individualism cannot protect people from harm that others want to inflict on them. A society that encourages me to act as I choose encourages others to do so as well. Sometimes others can gain by harming me. That means I should expect harm to occur and in fact be promoted in such a society.

The problem here is not just a matter of one person harming another. Individuals are also not protected from harming themselves. Individualism insists that the significance of one's life is whatever one considers it to be. According to individualism, there is no such thing as having too high or too low a view of oneself; the view one has of oneself is right by definition. Accordingly, if some people do not value their lives at all, then their lives have no value. If they want to harm themselves, there is no reason for anyone to try to prevent that, for nothing of value is at stake. In light of this difficulty (as well as the others discussed above), individualism is unable to offer a plausible account of why people matter.

Naturalism

A rather different way of thinking—including thinking about why people matter—is naturalism. As Scott Rae describes in chapter 5, according to this outlook all that exists is the material world alone: that which can be scientifically, empirically measured and verified. No design or intelligence lies behind the world's past or future. Human beings and other life on earth are the result of the blind, random forces of evolution. All immaterial human capacities such as self-awareness emerge from material substances. People are merely physical objects. Therefore, whatever significance they possess is a function of whatever useful characteristics they may have, such as rationality or morality, to the extent that such characteristics are explainable on a purely material basis.

Empirical verifiability is good; but when nothing has validity without it, many important things get lost in the process—including the significance of people. But before we recall the implications of naturalism for human significance, some more general problems with this outlook warrant recollection.

Most importantly, Rae argues that naturalism cannot adequately account for two central features of human existence: rationality and morality. If those are central to why people matter, as most naturalists hold, then this inability renders naturalism unable to justify human significance. If human significance must be grounded in something other than such human capacities, then naturalism simply gives an inadequate account of human life in general.

First, regarding rationality: consciousness and the self are its foundations, and naturalism cannot explain their origins. If physical organisms change due to their interaction with their environment over time, then they would become different and perhaps more complex physical organisms but not something that is nonphysical. Naturalists sometimes cite such examples as the interaction of hydrogen and oxygen molecules to produce something different—wetness—as an illustration of how consciousness could have emerged. However, wetness is itself a physical property, so the illustration gives no credibility to the idea that something nonphysical could result from merely physical interactions. In addition to depending on consciousness, rationality also depends on there being an enduring self that can analyze and justify or reject possible courses of action. Naturalism denies that there is such a nonmaterial self; naturalism typically sees the person as merely an accumulation of experiences.

According to naturalism, mental processes developed via evolution as a means of facilitating survival. However, that view is unable to account well for abstract reasoning and beliefs. Even if some degree of reason is necessary for survival, the reasoning involved in advanced physics, for example, is hardly required for survival and can even divert attention from matters more directly relevant to survival. There is also no need for beliefs to be true. According to naturalism, any belief about the world—as long as it contributes to survival—is as valid as any other belief. It does not matter whether what one calls true is actually true. However, such an outlook is devastating to an important element of rationality: that people can have knowledge that actually tells them something about the way the world is.

Second, not only does naturalism fail to give an adequate account of rationality; it similarly fails to explain morality. Morality makes sense in a naturalistic outlook to the extent that it fosters people's interests—particularly survival (including reproduction). However, much of morality works contrary to that. It involves self-sacrifice, compassion, forgiveness, and unconditional love in ways that put people at competitive disadvantage. In fact, the ultimately admirable sacrifice of giving up one's life for another is the epitome of *not* fostering one's survival. The same problem arises with moral obligations. Many of those—such as repaying a debt, rescuing someone in need, and even simply not stealing—at least sometimes do not further an individual's self-interest. Naturalism, then, cannot account for moral obligations; yet most people consistently recognize obligations and are subject to judgment and shame when they violate them.

In naturalism, whatever has evolved simply "is." There is no reason why it should be otherwise. In other words, there is no satisfactory basis for maintaining that anyone should be or do anything other than what already is—especially if "what is" increases the chances of their survival or reproduction. Accordingly, the evidence that suggests that rape throughout history has sometimes been motivated by the desire to reproduce (when no consensual mate is available) becomes a naturalistic justification for the practice. There is no basis for moral opposition to anything promoted during the evolutionary process.

Naturalism, then, cannot account well for rationality or morality. If those capacities are why people matter, then naturalism is an insufficient basis for human significance. However, as Rae notes, the attempt of some naturalists to establish human significance by trying to present naturalistic accounts of such capacities is itself a weak approach to human significance. People have rational and moral capacities to differing degrees. If such capacities are what give people significance, then some people have less significance than others.

Particularly at risk are those with the least capacity, such as people with severe cognitive disabilities.

Human significance—whether identified as human dignity or something else—is necessarily a casualty when one understands all living beings as nothing more than the product of the blind, random forces of evolution. Nothing has dignity or warrants special regard, because everything simply "is." We would like to think that people are meaning-creating, free beings. However, on the naturalistic outlook, we are ultimately meaningless—the predictable result of a vast array of interactions of matter with its environment. There is nothing and no one behind and beyond this world to invest anyone with significance. Naturalism, then, provides little basis for the widespread conviction that people matter.

Transhumanism

Unlike naturalism, transhumanism attempts to find its hope not in nature per se but in biotechnology's attempt to overcome natural limitations. As Patrick Smith describes in chapter 6, transhumanism envisions humanity breaking free of basic limitations such as bodily suffering and a limited life span through advances in biotechnology. Biotechnology can supposedly enable people not just to improve themselves as humans but to become better than human—to become "posthuman." Intellectual, physical, and emotional capacities would so exceed those of present human beings as to render them something beyond merely human.

People do need to grow and improve; but as Smith argues, when being human itself becomes something to escape rather than something to value, serious problems arise. As with the other four non-Christian outlooks, so too transhumanism not only directly undermines human significance but also suffers from more general problems that warrant summarizing here.

Some of the general difficulties with transhumanism are more problematic for some supporters of transhumanism than for others. For example, a commitment to overcoming the weaknesses of the human body leads some to aspire to do away with the body entirely. The ultimate goal is for people to be able to upload their consciousness to a machine so that they can continue to exist forever without being subject to increasing bodily frailty. This aspiration overlooks the fact that the primary source of human suffering is not merely the physical body. Instead it is our selfishness—some would call it our sinful nature—which would continue to plague us and cause us to suffer in an eternal, digitalized existence.

Another problem for some transhumanists is the inability to identify any standards of right or wrong to govern a posthuman future. Influenced by contemporary postmodern individualism, in which there are no objective values binding on all people, such transhumanists give ethical relativism even greater sway. In a postmodern era, not only will individuals differ among themselves, but posthuman people will also be so different from present-day people that people today would be presumptuous to impose ethical standards on them. The result is the promotion today of a future without a moral compass.

Partly in recognition of this problem, some transhumanists acknowledge that there will need to be an elite authority in a posthuman world. Its purpose will be to prevent individuals, groups, and societies from living in a way antagonistic to the overall reduction of suffering that drives transhumanism. Already there is increasing pressure on people to participate in prenatal testing to identify certain potential genetic diseases. In a posthuman world, one role of an elite government would likely be to deal with those deemed irresponsible in their unwillingness to participate in technological monitoring and sacrificing for the good of society. The danger to individual freedom here is substantial.

Not surprisingly then, some transhumanists do not welcome a posthuman future but warn against what they worry is its inevitability. The mind-set driving transhumanism, they say, poses extreme dangers to the human race for reasons far beyond the concerns noted above. One additional concern involves the hubris of striving not just to be better but even to deny one's very existence in order to be something different. Such an aspiration fosters debilitating discontent with all forms of current existence. Another concern involves justice between humans and posthumans. Some of the most vexing challenges throughout the world already concern disparities between different groups of people. Since posthumans are by definition radically enhanced beyond what current people are capable of, the disparities and injustices involved will be different not only in degree but in kind. The danger of posthumans oppressing humans and of humans violently rising up against posthumans is predictably great.

As Smith notes, perhaps the biggest problem with transhumanism in general concerns its eugenic orientation. At its heart eugenics involves favoring people with some traits over people with others. It fosters dissatisfaction with what is inferior in order to promote what is superior. Whereas in the past eugenic efforts have focused on removing or at least reducing certain traits in the human population, today transhumanism aspires to replace humans with a superior species of posthumans. The risks of augmenting past forms of eugenic discrimination, coercion, and even greater harm directed against those deemed inferior are substantial. These risks are only increased by the vague understanding of what radical changes to humanity are in view. The door is wide open for different groups to champion with eugenic feror whatever technological enhancements favor themselves.

Implicit in many of these general weaknesses of transhumanism are serious threats that it poses to human significance. Most basically, transhumanists' focus on posthumans and on particular human capacities undermines human dignity. In transhumanism, the goal is to replace humans with a superior species of posthumans. In other words, humanity does not have any inherent dignity that warrants respect and protection. Human dignity—the basis on which even the weakest of human beings should be valued and sustained—is replaced by an outlook that sees all of humanity as weak and to be replaced for that very reason. Transhumanism sacrifices the notion of equal regard for all human beings by denying that there is anything about human beings per se that protects them from being expendable and replaceable.

Smith concedes that the language of dignity is not absent from transhumanist writings; however, it refers not to the dignity of all humans but only to that of certain humans. In transhumanism, not all humans have dignity—or at least they do not have it to the same degree. Rather, those who have admirable traits or capacities have dignity to the degree that they have those traits or capacities. The goal is to achieve a far greater dignity grounded in far greater (posthuman) capacities. Such an understanding of dignity as variable, however, is profoundly destructive of human significance. Circumstances such as accidents, illnesses, and economic setbacks can always have a detrimental effect on one's capacities at least for a time. The inherent dignity of being human is what warrants attempts to restore the variable dignity that can be diminished by circumstances. An outlook such as transhumanism that denies the dignity of being human per se loses the basis for restoring circumstantial dignity when it is assaulted.

From the undermining of human dignity flow several other problems. Human rights, including the basic respect and protections that all human beings should have, depend on the recognition that all people have dignity. Without that foundation, human rights and human solidarity are in jeopardy. Spending time and resources to help people in need becomes a distraction from the real goal, which is to remove those needs by replacing needy people with a superior, posthuman species. The sense of a shared human condition motivating care for others disappears in the process. One of the great ironies here is that in the quest for greater fulfillment through biotechnological transformation, people may well end up less satisfied in the end. As transhumanism nurtures people's repulsion at limitations and needs that are unavoidably a part of being human, they may become less able to experience the joys that come from appreciating the wonders of life precisely in the face of limitation and need. For a basis of *human* significance, then, we will need to look elsewhere than transhumanism.

A Christian Outlook

How different is a biblically grounded Christian outlook from the five non-Christian outlooks we have examined! Part 3 has presented a positive case for a biblical-Christian outlook as a ground for human significance. What remains here is to summarize how such an outlook contrasts with the five other outlooks under consideration.

In contrast to *utilitarianism*, a Christian outlook provides a powerful basis for respecting and protecting individuals. It does that by insisting that both ends and means matter—that not only society (and its good) but also each individual that constitutes society (and its good) matter. The apostle Paul was a great champion of pursuing the good of all (Gal. 6:10). However, he was scandalized at the thought that anyone would interpret that to mean "Let us do evil so that good may come" (Rom. 3:8). Everything we do and every person who is affected matters to God. As Proverbs so well encapsulates the idea: "Better is a little with righteousness" than much gain with injustice (Prov. 16:8).

Life is not merely about how much can be achieved. After all, God could achieve everything in an instant. Rather, people created in God's image have significance because they are connected to God and because everything they think, say, and do matters to God; they are to be a reflection of God's good character. Not only *what* they accomplish matters but also *how* they get there. They cannot oppress and destroy people along the way, even to achieve a great good.

Nevertheless, people are prone to do so, because in their self-centeredness and pride they all too easily overlook the differences between themselves and God. As noted above, utilitarianism considers an action to be right if it produces better overall consequences than any possible alternative action would. People must include consequences throughout the world and indefinitely into the future in their calculations. No wonder someone has quipped that God may be a utilitarian but humans cannot be: no one but God has the omniscience necessary to run the required calculations. No one but God is responsible for the well-being of the entire world every time they act.

People often find that hard to accept. The Bible suggests that from the very beginning, people such as Adam and Eve have been grasping for the knowledge that they think will make them "like God," able to know "good and evil" (Gen. 2:17; 3:22). If something looks good and beneficial, people offer their own utilitarian justifications for their actions (Gen. 3:6), even if those actions contradict what God has directed. A Christian outlook says that only God truly knows everything that is at stake in any situation—whether an action will end up as beneficial or as deadly. True wisdom begins with respecting God (Prov. 1:7). That is the best protection for people. That provides the safeguard for human significance—the significance of all—that utilitarianism is unable to offer.

The difference between a Christian and a utilitarian outlook here is not merely theoretical. In contrast with the utilitarian atrocities mentioned above, the Christian insight that every person is in God's image has been a source of great liberation for women, people with disabilities, and oppressed and enslaved people throughout the world (see chap. 7). The exodus as well as Christ's ministry has validated the great significance of all sorts of people, including those widely demeaned because others consider them to be deficient in terms of race, class, gender, age, family, or vocation (see chap. 8).

Any outlook—a Christian outlook included—can be twisted and invalidly blamed for atrocities that it truly does not sanction. However, the difference between a Christian and utilitarian outlook is that whereas the latter explicitly maintains that it is the good of the whole rather than the good of the individual that necessarily matters, a Christian outlook rejects that claim explicitly. Both humanity as a whole and particular individuals matter, for both are in God's image according to Genesis 1.

As Jesus taught, to love people, including oneself, is important. However, such endeavors to benefit people merely fulfill God's "second commandment" to "love your neighbor as yourself." They are subject to the demands of the "first commandment," which is to love God (Matt. 22:37–39). The priority of loving God means that God's valuing of every person establishes limits on what others can do to them. God has communicated the standards of the moral law to people throughout history and has placed that law in everyone's heart (Rom. 2:14–15) in order to protect individuals, as well as to foster the well-being of society as a whole. God has gone to great lengths to communicate that people—individually and collectively—matter.

In contrast to *collectivism*, a Christian outlook provides a basis for human significance that goes beyond the standards of any one group. According to a Christian outlook, there is a God who is beyond all individuals, groups, and humanity as a whole who provides a vantage point from which to assess the legitimacy of everything that people want to do. Such accountability works in numerous ways. First, individuals and humanity as a whole are created in the image of God. That means, for example, that each person matters to God and is closely connected with God. One person (or a group) cannot kill another (Gen. 9:6) because in doing so one is affronting God at the same time. The affront is not only because the one who is killed is in God's image but also because the one who is doing the killing is in God's image (and therefore responsible to manifest God's care for every person). Moreover, not only are the fatal atrocities that collectivism can foster ruled out in a Christian outlook; even abusing or belittling people is unacceptable (James 3:9–10). The belittled and the belittler are both in the image of God. This identity is more basic and binding than the agenda of any group to which a person belongs.

At the same time, accountability involves much more than individuals as they are at present. Humanity as a whole is created in the image of God. That means groups as well as individuals are responsible for more than furthering their own agendas. They are accountable to God for the degree to which humanity as a whole reflects such corporate attributes of God as justice and love. Moreover, collectives must view and treat people in God's image not merely in terms of their present dignity, but also in terms of their destiny to be a reflection of God—to be God's glory. Such a perspective on people's identity and significance is vastly different than the collectivist perspective that all people can be used in any way necessary to further the collective's purposes. History demonstrates that even the most enslaved or oppressed people in society—including many women, ethnic minorities, and people with disabilities—have experienced something much better when a Christian outlook has prevailed.

Needless to say, people claiming to be Christians have been oppressive as well. However, one can claim to be a Christian without living according to a Christian outlook as defined biblically. Regardless of the outlook that one affirms, Christian or otherwise, a person can be influenced by the self-centeredness within or by ideas or pressures from without. Christians, like everyone else, need frequently to confirm that how they are living fits with their life outlook. A Christian outlook offers particularly potent protection for oppressed people. When their identity (and that of their oppressors) in God's image is properly recognized, there is a strong impetus toward liberation and protection.

The accountability missing in collectivism also takes other forms in a Christian outlook. For example, the life and ministry of Jesus Christ powerfully affirm human significance. In the life of Christ on earth, God willingly endured the humiliation of taking on lowly human form in the incarnation (Phil. 2:7–8). Whereas the tendency in collectivism is to view people from a distance—reducing their identity to the groups with whom they share particular characteristics—God draws near in Christ.

Christ's physical closeness is a confirmation and reminder that God is always close enough and cares enough to know the number of hairs on each person's head (Matt. 10:30; Luke 12:7). If the number of hairs on a person's head is meaningful enough for God to attend to, then there are a huge number of physical and nonphysical characteristics that help make each person unique. Seeing and treating people only in terms of a few of those that group them with others—their age, gender, ethnicity, health, wealth, and so on—is a dehumanizing assault on human significance. Ultimately, though, significance is not a function of any or all characteristics that people have. Their creation in God's image, and thus their dignity, is about the attributes God intends them to have, not about the degree to which they manifest them now.

In collectivism, people inside and outside the group are subject to various levels of sacrifice because the good of the group requires that. The group must prevail at all costs. The well-being of many is at risk as a result. In a Christian outlook, the sacrifice has already been made. But in a startling turn of events, it is the one sacrificed who prevails—putting the lie to the notion that human significance requires human strength. Christ is crucified. (Says his collectivist condemner in words reminiscent of John 11:50: It is better that one man, even if innocent, be sacrificed than that all of my people suffer.) However, Christ is then resurrected from the dead. In that triumph over the worst that this world can inflict on a person, God establishes Christ, not some human collective, as the source of human significance. Christ will be the judge to whom all individuals and collectives will be responsible. Therein lies true accountability.

What people will be accountable for is telling. In the judgment scene of Matthew 25:31–46, what counts is not how effectively one has helped one's group to prevail over others—eliminating everything (everyone) weak that hinders the cause. Rather it is how faithfully one has reflected God's valuing of all by caring for those who are weakest. Doing so is both a service to the creator and redeemer Christ and a reflection of Christ's own ministry. Christ did not get rid of those who were weakest. Rather, Matthew 12:20, quoting Isaiah 42:3, writes of Christ: "He will not break a bruised reed or quench a smoldering wick until he brings justice to victory." God's strength and human significance are most powerfully demonstrated through human weakness (cf. 2 Cor. 12:9). The one whose eye is on the sparrow has an eye on every person—because each person matters. This is a far cry from social Darwinism or oppressive national regimes (even those with worthy goals), which require human strength for human significance.

More benign forms of collectivism focus on strength in a different way. They attempt to take the place of God by replacing godly ends or means with their own. There is an overarching preoccupation with some achievement such as academic prowess or economic gain; and the search is on for the collective that can deliver it (via the structure of an "authoritative community," the tools of marketing demographics, etc.). Although it is unflattering to our individual and corporate egos, it is tremendously freeing to recognize that the secret to human flourishing lies in living in accordance with how God has made people to flourish. God has designed people to seek divine guidance (e.g., from God's written word) for direction regarding ends and means. People are to forswear ultimate allegiance to all merely human collectives in favor of identifying with a special kind of collective—one without a collectivist outlook. This collective has an allegiance beyond itself. It is the church, understood as the body of Christ (Rom. 12:5) or the eternal family of God (2 Cor. 6:18). God's desire that none would refuse to accept the offer to join this eternal fellowship (1 Tim. 2:4; 2 Pet. 3:9) underscores the importance of every human being.

In contrast to *individualism*, a Christian outlook provides an unshakable, objective foundation for human significance and meaning. It does so, most importantly, by insisting that there is a God beyond all individuals who makes all the difference. People are not alone in the universe, ultimately subject only to their own perspectives and agendas. There is an objective reality in which all people are significant regardless of who does or does not think that certain people matter. That reality ultimately includes an eternal future marked by *shalom*, in which peace and justice will ensure value and blessing for each individual.

People have a greater purpose outside of themselves that is as big as God and as long-lasting as eternity. As the prophet Jeremiah put it, people's lives are not their own; it is not for them to direct their steps (Jer. 10:23). Rather, Christ is Lord over all creation, including people. From before creation Christ, as the image of God, has been the standard of humanity; people have never been their own standards. Christ has gone to great lengths to demonstrate his willingness to help people be their best, for their flourishing as well as for God's glory. Christ humbled himself to take on humanity's form and laid down his life to pay the price for humanity's self-centeredness so that reconciliation with God could occur. Those reconciled recognize that they are not their own; they were bought at a price (1 Cor. 6:19–20). Even when unreconciled and separated from God, people are blessed by God's watchful care for them, because they are created in God's image. They have a special connection with God and are intended by God to be a reflection of God in the world. People matter because God matters, not because individuals matter somehow without reference to God.

Whether or not they realize it, individuals are no more independent from God than they are from humanity. In God "we live and move and have our being" (Acts 17:28). People are not limited to what they can be in themselves, because the Spirit of God can transform them into the likeness of God. Among other things, the model of God not as an individual but as three-in-one—the Trinity—suggests that both relationship and individuality matter. Being in the image of God is a hallmark of humanity as a whole, not just of individuals. By ultimately limiting human significance to individuals alone, individualism pales in comparison with a Christian outlook in its ability to give individuals significance.

Individualism has no way to protect individuals against the worst humiliation and harm if other individuals choose to pursue that, since individuals are free to pursue whatever they deem best. A Christian outlook also celebrates and facilitates freedom, but it defines it differently. Freedom is not doing whatever one desires at the moment, since people's enslavement to self-centeredness renders them at times unable to choose what would truly be fulfilling to them. Their creator knows what is most fulfilling. Only through a commitment to following God's will rather than one's own can a person experience true freedom to become all that they can be. Such an exercise of freedom will not result in doing evil. It protects people from themselves in a way that individualism is incapable of doing. It protects others as well by consistently valuing other individuals—and communities—not only when doing so is personally beneficial.[3]

Although a Christian outlook does not support individualism—reducing what matters to individuals alone—it is a champion of individuality. God is gathering people into a body of godly people who will be glorified and will glorify God. Yet each member of the body is important. The head cannot say to the feet, "'I have no need of you.' On the contrary, the members of the body that seem to be weaker are indispensable" (1 Cor. 12:21–22). In a Christian outlook, the connection of people with the body of Christ offers a far greater assurance that every person matters than does the changing, self-interested perspective of each individual.

3. For this biblical understanding, see such biblical passages as 1 Pet. 2:16: "Live as free people, yet do not use your freedom as a pretext for evil"; cf. John 8:31–36; Gal. 5:13. See also Anthony A. Hoekema, "The Question of Freedom," in *Created in God's Image* (Grand Rapids: Eerdmans, 1986), 227–43; and Gilbert Meilaender, *The Freedom of a Christian: Grace, Vocation, and the Meaning of Our Humanity* (Grand Rapids: Brazos, 2006).

In contrast to *naturalism*, at the heart of a Christian understanding of the world is the recognition that God is "the Alpha and the Omega . . . who is and who was and who is to come" (Rev. 1:8). There is more to the world than meets the eye ("things visible and invisible," Col. 1:16). From before the beginning of everything else that exists, God had a plan for creation and has carried it out through Christ, the Word of God ("All things came into being through him," John 1:3). Everything has meaning and significance beyond its state at the present moment, because it purposely, not randomly, came into existence, is being sustained on purpose (Heb. 1:3), and has a future purpose as well (Rev. 22:5). In such a world, rationality, consciousness, and morality make much more sense than in the world of naturalism.

Such capacities are meaningful for a Christian not simply because they are meaningful per se but because they also reflect aspects of who God is, to God's glory. These capacities can continue to develop regardless of whether the environment is hospitable or not (as naturalism would require). The Holy Spirit is able to develop capacities in people according to God's eternal purposes even under the most difficult of circumstances. Humanity's creation in the image of God does not mean that people have certain capacities now. Rather, it signals that God intends for individuals to develop such capacities as they are able, and intends for humanity as a whole to exhibit other capacities such as loving care for those with the least capacities. Human significance resides not in people actually having capacities but in God's glorious intentions for humanity, which will be fulfilled in eternity.

Whereas in the outlook of Darwinian naturalism "the survival of the fittest" is an understandable slogan, God demonstrates throughout history that the survival of the weakest is what demonstrates most powerfully that God exists and is at work. What you see is *not* what you get—at least it is not all that you get. With its faith in selection, naturalism thinks that existence "chooses" the strongest to succeed. However, "God chose what is weak in the world to shame the strong; God chose . . . things that are not, to reduce to nothing things that are, so that no one might boast" (1 Cor. 1:27–29). Naturalism boasts that it knows everything that exists, when all that it knows are the things that it thinks "are" according to self-generated criteria that leave out all of reality that is not empirically verifiable.

A Christian outlook is particularly better suited than naturalism to account for the existence and importance of morality. If morality is nothing more than something people invoke to gain a competitive advantage, then there is little reason for others to pay any attention to it—much less be constrained by it. But if morality is rooted in the character and purposes of God, and God reveals those to people through covenants, laws, and other forms of revelation, then there is a reason to pay attention. In fact, since history has direction and God's assurance that God and the people of God will prevail, there is a powerful reason for people to do whatever God says they will be accountable for. Christ has demonstrated through resurrection and ascension—and will confirm by returning—that there is far more to the earthly and heavenly story than naturalism tells.

Naturalism, then, falls far short of a Christian outlook in accounting for such human capacities as rationality and morality. If human significance depends on having such capacities, as naturalism suggests, then naturalism fails to provide an adequate account of why people matter on its own terms. However, grounding human significance in people's capacities can never do justice to the conviction that people matter. Some people have limited capacities and lack certain capacities altogether. People with serious mental disabilities are cases in point as are people with significant moral failings or ethnic or gender identities that society disrespects. Naturalism provides no compelling reasons to provide better circumstances for people than those that have befallen them. In fact, "better" is really a misnomer in this outlook, since there is no external standard that beckons circumstances to be anything other than they are.

In sharp contrast, a Christian outlook recognizes that Christ, as God's image, provides a standard and model for human character and action. People and the world are other than they should be and eventually can be. This predicament is due to sin, not merely due to amoral natural processes. By creating and maintaining all people in the divine image, God establishes a connection with them that cannot be broken and an intention for them that cannot be shaken. God intends for them to be a reflection of various divine attributes, including some attributes that will not become evident until after death and transformation, including a spiritual body (1 Cor. 15:42–44).

Human dignity resides in this special connection with God and intended reflection of God, not in the degree to which such reflection occurs. Thus all people, regardless of current capacities, warrant the respect and protection due to all other human beings. Part 3 has documented many examples of what that has looked like in practice in Old Testament times, in the New Testament church, and in the many centuries since. Naturalism is unable to affirm such human dignity, for there is no dignity in human beings per se. Only because people are more than the product of naturalistic processes and competition—only because God is real and has created them and cares for them eternally—do people matter.

Finally, a Christian outlook offers a powerful alternative to *transhumanism*. Whereas transhumanist aspirations are rooted in the inadequacy of remaining human—a direct assault on human significance—key Christian convictions ensure that people matter today. People are in God's image already. They have a special connection with God, and God intends for them to be a reflection of glorious divine attributes. Accordingly, people have a dignity that does not vary with their circumstances or the particular capacities that they have.

People should not be treated in certain ways, and they should have access to certain resources necessary to their survival. In other words, they have moral rights in the sense that God has rights over them as the one who created them, has sovereignty over them, and knows best how they will flourish. For example, as created in the image of God, innocent people must not be killed (Gen. 9:6) or even verbally abused (James 3:9). Moreover, as the recipients of God's compassionate care, mandated by the Old Testament prophets and modeled by Jesus and the early church, people are to have access to what they truly need in order to live.

The impetus here is not to get rid of weakness by getting rid of the weak or to get rid of suffering by getting rid of the sufferer. Rather, Jesus and his disciples demonstrate in their lives and words that human ability is not the point of life. What matters is God's ability, and that ability is best displayed in the midst of human vulnerability and limitation rather than in a transhumanist, posthuman world. A transhumanist mind-set is eugenic in nature, willing to sacrifice not only deficient individuals but humanity as a whole due to its deficiencies. In a Christian outlook, the strongest one of all—God—makes the sacrifice in the death of Christ on the cross. The aim is not the replacement of humanity; it is the redemption, resurrection, and restoration of humanity. A greater affirmation that people matter the world has never known. The very people most at risk from a transhumanist eugenic mind-set—those impoverished, disabled, enslaved, or oppressed—receive special affirmation in a Christian outlook, as history has amply illustrated.

Perhaps the greatest similarity between a transhumanist and a Christian outlook is the vision of the future that each espouses. Both look forward to a time of great and even unending happiness and health. However, there is a fundamental difference in how each outlook expects to get there. Transhumanism depends on human scientific power to achieve a future that is ill defined. Accordingly, any ethical safeguards developed today would likely be ill fitted to a race of posthumans whose capacities are far beyond those of humans today in unknowable ways.

In evidence here is the hubris of Adam and Eve in the garden of Eden, who try to usurp godlikeness by doing things their way (eating the forbidden fruit, Gen. 3:5, 22) rather than God's way (living in the image and likeness of God, Gen. 1:26). Transhumanists who aspire to discard the bodies that they see as the source of their limitation commit a similar error. They overlook the fact that the selfishness that is the true source of their suffering will accompany their consciousness into an eternal, digitalized existence. Much better is the Christian alternative, in which a merciful God prevents Adam, Eve, and everyone since from living eternally in their sinful state (Gen. 3:22–24). God required people to die because they had decided to pursue godlikeness in their own way rather than God's and had become forever yoked to self-centeredness. So today the best way to a glorious eternal life is through death and resurrection rather than through biotechnology.

In a Christian outlook, people are not left wondering if their best efforts will really lead to an amazing existence or if enhancing some capabilities will ultimately harm human bodies or damage human community. People are created in the image of God, which means that God intends for them ultimately to become the image of God in Christ—to be so close to God that they actually reflect many of God's attributes. That will include a resurrected and glorified body following the model of Christ's own resurrected body (1 Cor. 15:42–49), a body that no longer suffered and that had amazing abilities such as appearing and disappearing (Luke 24:31; John 20:26). Created in God's image, humanity has a destiny that is assuredly awe-inspiring, modeled on that of Christ, who is the perfect image of God. Although we do not know all of the particulars, we know that people will be amazing as Christ is amazing (1 John 3:2). Becoming Christlike will be far more fulfilling than being technologically enhanced.

God Makes All the Difference

In light of everything discussed in this book, several concluding observations are warranted. Whereas nearly everyone agrees *that* people matter, there are many different views of *why* people matter. These views are shaped by the way of thinking or life outlook that guides how each person sees the world and lives in it. A Christian outlook is only one such outlook. Utilitarianism, collectivism, individualism, naturalism, and transhumanism are among the most influential alternatives. Because these non-Christian outlooks actually undermine the idea that people matter, reflecting on how that occurs can help non-Christians see how their life outlook is at odds with what even they know to be true. Dissatisfaction with one's own life and life outlook is an important first step in being open to consider an alternative. A Christian outlook's ability to give a compelling account of why people matter commends it as a great alternative to consider.

Adopting a Christian outlook, since that involves acknowledging the lordship of Christ, is wonderful in its own right. Moreover, as this book has demonstrated, it is also the best hope for fostering agreement on ethical issues. The reason is that a person's position on an ethical issue is not determined by the conviction that people matter. Rather, how one reasons or intuits from that conviction to a conclusion about the ethical issue is the key. One's life outlook is what guides that journey.

Talking about a person's "way of thinking" or "life outlook" may sound academic and removed from everyday life. However, which outlook one adopts makes a huge difference, as this book has repeatedly demonstrated. Some of the greatest oppression and destruction that individuals, families, communities, and societies have experienced have been due to the prominence of one of the five non-Christian outlooks discussed in this book. People calling themselves Christians have also done bad things in history—and continue to do so. However, that occurs when people who profess to be Christians are knowingly or unknowingly guided by a non-Christian outlook rather than allowing a genuinely Christian outlook to guide their actions. Christians must be as careful as anyone not to allow any of the non-Christian outlooks considered here to shape their thinking.

Non-Christians need to recognize that to adopt a Christian outlook is not to abandon a "reasonable" and "objective" outlook in favor of one based solely on unreasoned "faith." As each of the chapters in this book has explained, all outlooks have certain "faith" commitments. Every outlook assumes certain things about the way that people and the world are without being able to prove them to everyone's satisfaction. The challenge, then, is not to adopt a "rational" or "secular" outlook rather than a "religious" or "faith-based" one; those categories are not particularly relevant here. Rather, the task is to adopt an outlook that best conforms to what we know to be true about life. The fact that people matter is one such widely shared core conviction. A Christian outlook can explain and support that conviction whereas the other five outlooks considered in this book cannot.

A Christian outlook has a huge advantage over those other outlooks: it has its basis in God, revealed concretely in Jesus Christ. Only when human significance depends not on how great people are (on people's capacities) but on how great God is (on God's capacities) can human significance truly be substantial and secure. Only when human significance is "alien"—rooted not in ourselves but in something or someone outside of ourselves—is human dignity inalienable, unlosable, unshakable. In the end, then, God is why people matter.

Subject Index

afterlife 19
aging 115, 131
Angier, Natalie 50n20
artificial intelligence 113, 114, 117
Augustine, St. 36–37
autonomy 3–5, 7–8, 10, 29, 66–69, 72, 79, 85,
     90, 126, 148, 196

Bacon, Francis 111, 113
     Baconian project 113
Barth, Karl 152n66, 179, 182
Bauckham, Richard 122–23
Beecher, Henry 24
Beker, J. Christiaan 182n43
beneficence 71, 74
Billing, Einar 30
bin Laden, Osama 53–54
bioethics 4, 6, 8, 24, 25, 96
biotechnology 5, 13, 110, 112–13, 115–17, 120,
     127, 128, 130–31, 190, 201, 213
Blizinsky, Katherine 43, 58
body
     of Christ 39–40, 53, 84, 183, 208–9
     physical 22, 39–40, 71, 92, 113–15, 118,
          130–31, 157, 180, 182, 201, 213
     resurrected 131, 213
     spiritual 152, 211
     See also embodiment
Bono 43n5
Borg, Marcus J. 176n31
Bostrom, Nick 112, 116
Brennan, William 7

Brueggemann, Walter 169
Bush, George W. 10
Buss, Sarah 72, 79–80

Camus, Albert 74
Carr, Anne 139
Casas, Bartolomé de las 137
Channing, William Ellery 138
Cheshire, William 121
Chesterton, G. K. 79, 84
Chiao, Joan Y. 43, 58
Chua, Amy 43, 55–57, 63
Churchland, Paul 93, 101
cloning 5
collectivism 11–13, 19n7, 39, 41, 43–44, 55, 59–
     62, 69–70, 74, 189–92, 194–96, 205–8, 213
Condorcet, Marquis de 111
Cone, James 165–66
consciousness 28, 89–92, 98, 100–102, 108, 121,
     199, 210
     evolution of 47
     uploading 13, 115, 201, 213
creation theology 14, 122, 162
Crosby, John 37
Crossan, John Dominic 176n31

Darwin, Charles 45, 96–97, 123. See also social
     Darwinism
Dawkins, Richard 96
Deane-Drummond, Celia 126, 128
death 24, 33–34, 48, 54, 110, 114, 131, 144,
     152n67, 170, 181–182, 211, 213

death penalty 6–7
de Grey, Aubrey 114–15
  on negligible senescence 114
Dennett, Daniel 49–50
Descartes, René 69, 111, 113
design
  of God for humans 14, 80–81, 208
  of the world 13, 89, 91, 93–94, 96, 199
destiny
  human 81, 146n47, 153, 157, 159, 179, 183,
    206, 213
  of Israel 164
  of the world 28
Dickens, Charles 30, 79
disability 127, 136, 149, 154, 157, 201, 205–6,
  211
diversity 157–58
Dixon, Ben 97
donation
  gamete 26
  organ 5, 24
Douglass, Frederick 138
Dower, John 40
duty 19n7, 28, 31, 45, 67, 106, 126, 167
Dworkin, Ronald 96–97, 119

egalitarianism 162, 171
elitism, technocratic 115–16
embodiment 22, 26, 115, 120, 131, 180, 181n42,
  182
embryonic stem cell treatment 5
Enlightenment 44, 49, 113–17
environment 121–22, 124
equality 34, 116, 119, 154, 163, 167–68
equal regard 120, 127–28
eugenics 125–28, 202
eusociality 50
euthanasia 4, 33–35
  pediatric 33
evolution 13, 19, 44, 46–52, 58, 89–93, 95–98,
  101–3, 105, 116–17, 130, 199–201
Ewing, A. C. 102
existentialism 70

Finnis, John 28
forgiveness 105, 174, 200
Foster, Charles 8
freedom 7, 19n7, 27–28, 30–32, 45, 94–95,
  118–19, 125–26, 131, 138, 148, 165, 202,
  209, 209n51
Freeman, Morgan 110
Fukuyama, Francis 10, 44, 120, 124

future 13–14, 33, 45, 48, 75, 83, 93, 109–11,
  113–17, 120, 125–27, 130–31, 162, 173, 199,
  202, 204, 208, 210, 212

Galton, Francis 125–26
Garnet, Henry 138
Garrison, William 138
Gaylin, Willard 7
gender bias 59
glory 83, 122, 140, 143, 145, 146n47, 148, 206,
  208, 210
God
  attributes of 143, 145, 206
  care for humanity 14, 28, 30, 40, 51, 83, 94,
    153–54, 161–65, 169, 173, 178, 206, 212
  human dependency upon 80, 209
  and human significance 13–14, 17, 19, 22, 26,
    38, 43, 59, 62, 83, 85, 107, 122, 153–55, 159,
    161–63, 180, 182, 204, 209, 214
  intention for humanity 14, 26–27, 81, 143,
    150, 152, 155–58, 210, 213
  as lawgiver 166–69, 205
  rights over humanity 155, 212
  See also image of God; Trinity
Gold, Julie 53
Gould, Stephen Jay 46–47
grace 22, 41, 51, 62, 111, 154, 169
Graham, Elaine 110
Gray, John 110
Gutiérrez, Gustavo 165

Haidt, Jonathan 43–44, 53–55, 63
Harman, Elizabeth 67
health care 5, 176
hedonism 18, 20
Hegel, G. W. F. 45–46, 48n18
Helms, Jesse, Jr. 43n5
history 21–22, 36–37, 40–41, 44–48, 51, 62, 69,
  74, 93–94, 102–3, 110, 140, 147, 153, 163,
  165–66, 179, 200, 205–6, 210–12, 214
holiness 175
  of the law 167
  Levitical Holiness Code 172
hope 45, 47–48, 55, 60, 110, 127, 139, 158, 165,
  201
hospitality 176
Hughes, James 113, 115–16
human
  attributes 123, 144–45, 149–150, 154–55, 157,
    159
  dignity 3–10, 17, 19–20, 22–29, 31–36, 38,
    44, 85, 93–100, 111, 118–25, 127–28, 131,

135, 138, 146n47, 153–55, 157–59, 161–63, 164n5, 165–67, 169, 173, 175, 177, 179–82, 185, 201, 203, 206–7, 211–12, 214
finitude 29, 109, 111, 117, 129, 131
flourishing 48, 50, 111, 123, 126, 131, 172, 180, 196, 208
fulfillment 129, 203
limitations 70, 110–11, 113, 117, 120, 125, 129–30, 152, 154, 201, 203
nature 11, 20, 29, 89, 97–99, 110, 115, 156n77, 179, 197, 201
significance 3–4, 6–7, 10–11, 13–14, 19–20, 23, 41, 51, 66, 73, 77–78, 80, 90–91, 93–101, 107–8, 111, 147, 150, 152–55, 193, 195–96, 198–201, 203–12, 214
solidarity 120, 124, 127–28, 156–57, 203
subjects research 24, 43, 119, 193
suffering 112, 163, 180
Hume, David 54
Huxley, Aldous 27, 193

image of God, the 13, 81–83, 92, 94–95, 98, 124, 131, 135–59, 162–63, 171, 180n39, 204–13
in Christ 124, 131, 158, 213
creation in / according to 140, 144–47, 150, 152–53
eikon 142–43, 150
imago dei 138, 162
as intended reflection 13, 81, 141–43, 150–53, 155, 157–59, 204, 206, 209, 211–12
likeness-image concept 152
as reflection of divine attributes 141–43, 149, 153, 155, 206
renewal of 146, 148, 153, 157, 159
as special connection 13–14, 141–43, 146, 150–52, 155–59, 208–9, 211–12
transformation into 143, 145–46, 148, 153
tselem 141–42, 150
undamaged 144, 146–48, 152, 158
immortality 109, 114
individualism 11–13, 17, 38, 41, 44–45, 66–85, 91, 189–92, 195–99, 202, 208–9, 213
infanticide 136, 164
Israel 14, 37, 47, 62, 66, 142, 162, 164, 166–73

Jennings, Bruce 7
Jesus Christ
ascension of 14, 162, 182–83, 211
cross of 14, 157, 162, 174, 180–82, 212
death of 54, 107, 144, 179, 181–82, 184, 212
incarnation of 14, 131, 162, 173, 179–80, 206
resurrection of 14, 54, 107, 131, 162, 179, 182, 211–13

teaching and example of 173–79
See also body: of Christ; image of God: in Christ
John Paul II 182n44
Jonas, Hans 24–25, 110
justice 23, 67, 95, 139, 155–56, 164–66, 168–69, 171–72, 175, 177, 202, 206–8

Kaiser, Walter 167
Kant, Immanuel 19n7, 44–46, 67, 69n10
Keener, Craig 138, 183n46
Kennedy, Anthony 7, 65
Keynes, John Maynard 18
Kierkegaard, Søren 45–46, 48n18
Kiernan, Peter 56
King, Martin Luther, Jr. 136–37, 150, 168
Kitayama, Shinobu 43, 57–58
Kurzweil, Ray 114–15, 117
Kuyper, Abraham 80
Kyung, Chung Hyun 139

law of accelerating returns 114
Lebacqz, Karen 169
LeMay, Curtis 60, 62
Lewis, C. S. 21, 23, 32, 60–62, 65–66, 75, 80, 83–84, 104
liberation theology 165–66
life
meaning of 32, 67–69, 71, 76, 78–79, 82, 85, 93–96, 105, 123, 125, 128, 130, 158, 198, 201, 208, 210
radical extension of 109, 115
sacredness of 96, 154–55
likeness
demuth 150
of God 136–37, 139, 145–46, 149–52, 163, 209, 212
homoiosis 150
See also image of God
Lincoln, Abraham 137
Lindemann, Hilde 98–99
Locke, John 35, 69
Lord's Supper 39, 48, 52–53, 55, 61
Lossky, Vladimir 180n39
love 105, 123, 200
of God 107, 164–66, 169, 174–81
for God and neighbor 70–71, 184, 205
as group cohesion 53–54, 194
and justice 156, 158, 206
and trust 28, 30, 32
Luther, Martin 84

Mackie, J. L. 107
Maritain, Jacques 95
Markus, Hazel Rose 43, 57–58
Martin, Civilla D. 39
Marx, Karl 45
Mavrodes, George 107
McInerny, Ralph 17–18
McKanan, Dan 138
McKenny, Gerald P. 113
McNamara, Robert Strange 44, 59–63
medically assisted reproduction 125
Mehlman, Maxwell J. 130
mercy 169, 175, 179
Messer, Neil 124
Metz, Thaddeus 67–69, 76
Midler, Bette 53
Mill, John Stewart 26
Moltmann, Jürgen 44, 47–49
Moore, A. W. 130
Moore, Zoe Bennett 139
morality 19, 53, 68–69, 83, 89–94, 96, 98, 100,
    104–5, 107–8, 167, 199–200, 210–11
  moral capacity 100
  moral judgments 106–7
  moral law 70, 167–68, 205
  moral principles 107
  moral realism 60, 81, 104
  moral reasoning 19, 28, 100
  moral status of persons 67, 82, 121–22
Moreland, J. P. 101–2, 105
Morris, Errol 44, 59–62
Mouw, Richard 137
Muilenburg, James 164
murder 147, 151, 156, 164, 170

Nagel, Thomas 20n9, 74, 89–90, 100–102, 106
  on "harmless emergence" 101
naturalism 11–13, 69–70, 74, 89–97, 100–102,
    104–8, 189–90, 199–201, 210–11, 213
  evolutionary 89, 105
  and Platonism 91
natural kinds 123–24
natural selection 46–47, 53, 106
New Jerusalem 170
Niebuhr, H. Richard 154
Niebuhr, Reinhold 21
Nussbaum, Martha C. 128–30
Obama, Barack 10
objectivism 76–77, 81
  objective truth 12, 66, 68, 73, 107, 196
obligations 105, 107, 200
Oduyoye, Mercy Amba 139

O'Mathúna, Dónal 118, 120
oppression 137, 139, 149, 155, 157, 159, 165–
    66, 171, 174, 214

personhood 57, 98–99, 144
physicalism 93
physician-assisted suicide 4
Pinker, Stephen 99, 119
Pittman, Bob 42–43, 55
Plantinga, Alvin 77–78, 82, 90–91, 102–103
Pleins, J. David 167
posthuman. *See* transhumanism
poverty 6, 120, 136, 157, 177
  preferential option for the poor 165
punishment 6, 23–24, 164n5

Rachels, James 91, 96–97, 100
racism 96, 125, 157, 159
Ramachandra, Vinoth 131
rationality 89–91, 97–98, 100–104, 106, 108,
    123, 199–200, 210–11
reductionism 149, 191
Reinders, Hans 154, 157n80
relativism 68, 73, 77, 116, 202
reproductive technology 25–26, 125–27
Robinson, Marilynne 33
Rorty, Richard 98
Rowe, Nicholas 156
Rubenfeld, Jed 56
Rumsfeld, Donald 62
Ruse, Michael 91, 105
Ruston, Roger 137, 155n76

Sartre, Jean-Paul 68, 70
Schneewind, J. B. 30–32
scientism 92
Searle, John 95–96
self-interest 66, 72, 105, 107, 209
self-transcendence 26
shalom (just wholeness) 14, 162, 169–74, 208
Sidgwick, Henry 18–19, 19n7, 20, 22–23,
    28–29, 32
sin 130, 143–44, 146–48, 154, 158, 161, 166n11,
    179, 182, 211
Singer, Peter 90, 96
Singularity 114–15, 117
Slade, Kara 52–53
Smith, Gerrit 138
social Darwinism 41, 43–44, 47–49, 207
Socrates 37–38
soul 22, 43, 92
Soulen, R. Kendall 126–27
speciesism 90, 96, 121

Spitz, Vivien 193n49
subjectivism 68, 75–77, 81, 85, 91, 104
Sulmasy, Daniel P. 123
Sutton, Agneta 122
Swinburne, Richard 106

Taylor, Charles 129
Taylor, Paul W. 118, 121
Taylor, Richard 69
Teel, Karen 138
Teilhard de Chardin, Pierre 47
Thurman, Howard 173n25, 177n34
torture 6, 82, 181
transcendence 21, 26, 78, 111, 130
transhumanism 11, 13, 69–70, 74, 91, 109–13, 115, 117–18, 125–28, 130–31, 189–90, 201–4, 211–13
Trinity 36–37, 82n31, 209

ultimate reality 12, 92, 94
unity 154, 162–63, 171–72
universalism 116
Usry, Glenn 138
utilitarianism 11–13, 17–18, 20, 29, 32, 69, 74, 189–94, 196, 204–5, 213

values 104–5, 107
Verduin, Leonard 157
victimization 166, 181
violence 138, 169–70, 173–75
Vitoria, Francisco de 137
vocation 30, 71, 205

Walzer, Michael 165
Warren, Mary Anne 67
Waters, Brent 112, 117, 130–31
Weber, Max 83
Weems, Renita 138
Welch, Jack 10
Weld, Theodore Dwight 138
Whipper, William 138
Willard, Dallas 65–66, 78–79, 83
Williams, Christian 42
Wilson, E. O. 43, 50–55, 63, 91, 93, 95, 100
Wolterstorff, Nicholas 90, 98

Young, Simon 117
Yudkowsky, Eliezer 117

Zaru, Jean 139

Scripture Index

Old Testament

Genesis

1 140, 146, 149, 205
1–2 162, 163
1:26 145, 148, 150, 152, 159, 212
1:27 145, 148, 150
2 162
2:17 205
3 146
3:5 212
3:6 205
3:22 212
3:22–24 213
5 146, 149
5:1 145, 150, 152
8–9 178
8:21–22 178
9 146, 147, 149
9:6 145, 147–51, 156, 206, 212

Exodus

1:22 164
2:23–25 164
14:30 164
19:6 84
20:2 169
20:16 168
20:20 166n11
23:6–8 168

Leviticus

19:15 168
25 172

Numbers

5:6–7 161
25:12 170

Deuteronomy

1:17 168
15:15 164

Judges

21:25 66

Psalms

82:3–4 165

Proverbs

1:7 205
3:5 79
16:8 204

Isaiah

9:7 170
25:7–8 170
31:1 170
32:15–20 171

35:5–6 172
42:3 207
45:8 171
53:5 181
56:1 172
56:3–6 171
56:4 171
56:5 171
56:7 171, 172
57:18 172, 172n24
59:14 172
60–61 171
60:5–7 171
60:11 170
60:18 170
60:20 172
61:1 171
61:1–2 172
61:3 172
61:4 171
61:6 84
62:5 172
62:9 171
65 170
65:21–22 171
65:25 170
66:12 171

Jeremiah

10:23 208
16:14–15 171

17:9 79, 197
30:18–22 171
30:19 172
31:5 171
31:12 171
33 170
33:6 170
33:15 170

Ezekiel

34:11–13 171
34:14–15 171
34:16 171–72
34:25 170
34:29 171
36–37 170
36:10 171
36:27–28 173
37 62

Daniel

3 141–42
3:6 141
3:21 141

Hosea

1:7 170

Joel

2:23–24 171

Amos

5:26 142
9:13–14 171
9:14–15 171

Micah

4:1 172
4:3 170
5:4–5 170
5:10 170
7:2–3 170

Zephaniah

3:9 172
3:11–13 173

Zechariah

9:9–10 170
9:17 171
10:7 172

New Testament

Matthew

4:17 178
4:23–24 176
5:1–12 177
5:21–22 147
5:23–24 174
5:38–40 174
5:39 174
5:41 174
5:43–48 174, 178
6:14–15 174
6:19–24 177
6:26 122, 178
7:7–11 178
8:5–13 176
8:16–17 176
9:9–13 177
9:10–13 176
10:29 39
10:30 207
12:1–15 175
12:11 122
12:11–12 122
12:20 207
15:1–20 175
15:21–28 175
18:1–9 176
18:10 178
18:22 174
19:13–14 176
19:16–24 177
22:37–39 205
23 175
25 180
25:31–46 176, 178, 207
25:35–36 180
25:40 180
26:51–52 174
26:53 174

Mark

1:14–15 178
7:1–23 175

9:33–40 176
9:37 176

Luke

4:18 177
5:29–32 176
7:1–10 176
7:11–17 177
9:54–55 174
10 158
10:25–37 177
10:29 158
10:36 158
11:13 178
12:7 207
12:13–21 177
13:10–17 175
13:15 122
13:34–35 174
14:5 122
15 174
15:3–7 178
15:11–32 176
16:19–31 177
17:3–4 174
18:1–18 178
18:9–14 177
19:2–9 176
19:41–44 174
20:46–47 177
21:1–4 177
21:5–6 174
23:27–31 174
23:34 174
24:31 213

John

1:1 179
1:3 210
1:14 179
3:16 178, 181
4 175, 177
8:31–36 209n51
10:30 142
10:38 142
11:50 207
12:45 142
14:9 142
20:15 175
20:26 213

Acts

2:17–18 184
6:1 183
7:43 142
8 183
10–11 183
17:26 163
17:28 80, 209

Romans

1:19 81
2:14–15 205
3:8 204
5:10 184
8:29 143–44, 147, 153, 159
12:5 208

1 Corinthians

1:19–25 143
1:27–29 210
6:19–20 208
7:21 184n47
11:7 150
12 53, 84
12:21–22 209
13:12 81
15:25–26 152n67, 182
15:42–44 211
15:42–49 213
15:44–47 152n67
15:49 152n67

2 Corinthians

3:7 143
3:9 143

3:10 143
3:18 143, 146, 148, 153
4:4 140, 143, 145, 146
4:6 143
5:16 184
5:18 184
6:18 208
12:9 207

Galatians

3 183
3:28 183
5:13 209n51
6:10 204

Ephesians

2:14 183
2:15 183
4:17 143
4:18 143
4:20 143

Philippians

2:1–11 179
2:7–8 206

Colossians

1 146
1:15 81, 140, 142, 145–46
1:16 210
1:17 80
3:10 145–46, 148, 153
3:10–11 144
3:22 183n47
4:1 184n47

1 Timothy

2:4 208

Hebrews

1 143
1:3 140, 210
2:8–9 143

James

3:9 145, 147–52, 156, 212
3:9–10 206

1 Peter

2:5 84
2:9 84
2:16 209n51
2:21 184
2:21–25 184

2 Peter

3:9 153, 208

1 John

3:2 213

Revelation

1:6 84
1:8 210
5:10 84
22:5 210